P. N. FURBANK

Italo Svevo

THE MAN AND THE WRITER

LONDON
SECKER & WARBURG

First published in England 1966 by
Martin Secker & Warburg Limited
14 Carlisle Street, Soho Square, W.1

FOR PATRICIA

Printed in Great Britain by
The Camelot Press Ltd., London and Southampton

CONTENTS

PREFACE

Not only does he murder literary form, but he kills form altogether as form, and does so in the epoch when form is the only God recognised. Precisely because he is fully aware of a new content, for him content is everything and form nothing. Or to put it more exactly, form is itself the thing in its effectual truth, that is to say in its intellectual and material existence. What matters to him is not whether a thing is reasonable, or moral or beautiful, but whether it is so. . . . The basis of life, and therefore of knowledge, is *nosce te ipsum*, knowledge of the world in its reality.

So wrote the great nineteenth-century Italian critic Francesco de Sanctis about Machiavelli, in a passage much admired and taken to heart by Italo Svevo. And there is a growing feeling among Italian critics that what Machiavelli did for Italian prose, Svevo did for Italian fiction. A writer who was out of the main stream of literary society, a Jew writing in a city of the Austro-Hungarian empire, a business man who spent his best years not in writing but in the manufacture of ship's paint, he succeeded, almost unnoticed, in introducing the modern novel into Italian literature, and was first seen to have done so not by Italians but by an Irish writer (James Joyce) and by critics in Paris. It is an odd and fascinating piece of literary history, and for a long time Italian critics have written as much about the 'Svevo case' as about his work itself.

For the non-Italian reader the 'Svevo case' is not important and he would not be wrong to read Svevo, as he might read Musil or Kafka, simply as a 'mid-European' writer. And if he has to read him in translation, he can comfort himself with the thought that at least one Italian critic has complained that the original reads like a bad translation. Svevo was certainly someone to whom what matters is 'not whether a thing is reasonable, or moral or beautiful, but whether it is *so*'; and to read him, whether in the original or not, is to make the acquaintance of a writer of quite extraordinary originality. There are ideas in Svevo's novels which, like certain things in Kafka, once you have met with them, keep scratching at your mind for ever. The seminal joke in *The Confessions of Zeno*, the one about giving up smoking, is somehow inexhaustible, there is no end to the contexts where you find it applying. I think of Kafka in connection with Svevo, not because they were alike in their work, but because they were both isolated writers, placed in a rather similar social and racial situation, who made extraordinary discoveries in a narrow field of writing, and who lived the sort of life which is mainly interesting for what light it throws on their work. As to Svevo's stature, I would in fact put him on a level with Kafka, and should not be surprised if before long he were as widely read.

The present book is in two parts, first a short biography of Svevo, then a discussion of his principal writings. Since he was almost totally unknown outside Trieste till the very end of his career, his life is rather badly documented, and for many aspects of it I have had to rely mainly on his widow's memoir. It is a charming book, but it leaves a number of questions unanswered, and I can't pretend to have answered them all myself. Perhaps one day—and it is a job for an Italian writer, not an English one—someone will fill in the gaps.

Note:

The following abbreviations have been used in the text:

Vita—Livia Veneziani Svevo, *Vita di mio marito (stesura di Lina Galli) con altri inediti di Italo Svevo*, nuova edizione a cura di Anita Pittoni, Trieste, Edizioni dello Zibaldone, 1958.

Saggi—Italo Svevo, *Saggi e pagine sparse*, a cura e con prefazione di Umbro Apollonio, Milan, Mondadori, 1954.

Corto viaggio—*Corto viaggio sentimentale* e altri racconti inediti di Italo Svevo, a cura e con prefazione di Umbro Apollonio, Milan, Mondadori, 1957.

Except where otherwise mentioned, the original language of quotations may be assumed to correspond to the nationality of the speaker or writer concerned and the translation to be my own. At the first mention of any writing by Svevo I have provided an English translation of the title in parenthesis—in italics if it is the title of an actual published translation, otherwise in inverted commas.

ACKNOWLEDGMENTS

My thanks are especially due to Signora Letizia Fonda Savio, Svevo's daughter, for her great kindness in giving me access to her father's unpublished papers and her patient and generous help at every stage of my researches. I also owe a particular debt to Signora Anita Pittoni for most valuable discussions of Svevo's Triestine background and to the late Roberto Bazlen and to Mr. C. A. S. Ducker and his mother Mrs. K. N. Poole for their anecdotes and recollections of Svevo. I should also like to thank the following, among others, for their help: Mr. Nicola Bravin and his son Peter Bravin, Mme. Marie-Anne Commène, Professor Bruno Maier, Mme. Suzanne Paul-Henri Michel, Dr. Sauro Pesante, Professor Giuseppe Prezzolini, Herr Bürgmeister Konrad Schlegelmilch, Mr. Oliver Stallybrass, Mrs. Federica Schmitz Svevo, Dr. Edoardo Weiss, Mr. Leonard Woolf.

My thanks are due also to Faber & Faber Ltd. and the Viking Press, Inc., for permission to use my own translations of four letters from James Joyce to Italo Svevo or Valéry Larbaud, which are or will be included in *Letters of James Joyce* (volume 1 edited by Stuart Gilbert, volumes 2 and 3 edited by Richard Ellmann); to the Hogarth Press and Basic Books, Inc., for the extracts from Sigmund Freud's *Complete Psychological Works*; to Oxford University Press Inc., New York, for four extracts from *James Joyce* by Richard Ellmann; and to the Society of Authors for permission to quote from a letter written by James Joyce to Svevo's wife.

Finally, my thanks are due to the Radio Times Hulton Picture Library for the two views of Trieste.

PLATES

PART ONE

The Man

1

Early Years

The name 'Italo Svevo' is a pseudonym, formed on the model of some mediaeval royal sobriquet, meaning 'Italus the Swabian', i.e. the Italian-Swabian. Svevo chose it at the time of publishing his first novel, having used one or two other pen-names previously in newspaper articles, and it expresses his feeling of being a hybrid, an Italian by language, an Austrian by citizenship and a German by ancestry and education. His real name was Ettore Schmitz, and he was the sixth of the eight surviving children (Natalia, Paola, Noemi, Ortensia, Adolfo, Ettore, Elio and Ottavio) of Francesco Schmitz, a Triestine glassware merchant.

His father Francesco was a Jew of German–Italian parentage who had been born in Trieste but had spent most of his childhood in Vienna. It was a poor family, and Francesco had become a successful business man through his own efforts and after various wanderings and struggles. His own father, Svevo's paternal grandfather, had come to Trieste from Kopcen in Hungary (though the family originated in the Rhineland) and had married an Italian from Treviso. It is not clear what he did; Svevo, writing near the end of his own life, referred to him rather vaguely as an 'Imperial functionary'. Certainly in Francesco's own childhood the family was living in considerable penury, and Francesco, at the age of thirteen, was sent out, with two florins in his pocket, to earn his living peddling trinkets and matches in cafés. After some years of wandering, and once, near Padua, nearly dying of starvation and cold, he got a job on the railways in Hungary, and in 1848 he became involved in the Hungarian revolution. He was expelled to Venetia by the Austrian authorities as a result, and imprisoned as a suspected deserter, but managed to escape conviction by virtue of his Triestine citizenship, the Triestines at this time being exempted from the *levée en masse*. That, at least, was his account of this period of his life as he gave it to Svevo's brother Elio; but in 1910 one of Francesco's sisters, Svevo's Aunt Marietta, by this time old and rather crazy, gave Svevo a slightly different account, according to which he had hidden for some time in a filthy cellar in Udine to avoid his call-up but was finally caught. 'Then they made him a soldier,' says Svevo, quoting Aunt Marietta, 'but he, like the crafty Jew he was, managed to become a *vivandier* and to send home quantities of *napoléons*. . . . So in a sense, pillaging the Austrians as he did', remarked Svevo, 'you might say he fought for Italy'.

After his release by the Austrian authorities, Francesco went to work in Dalmatia, but in 1849, when he was still only twenty, his father died, and he had to return to Trieste to look after his orphaned brother and sisters. In Trieste he found work with a glass-merchant, and he managed to support the whole family on his tiny earnings, finding the time to take lessons in book-keeping in the evening, for which he gave German lessons in exchange. Eventually, after several years of intense effort and hardship, he got a job in the largest firm of glassware merchants in Trieste, and soon afterwards he married Allegra Moravia, a Triestine Jewess three years younger than himself. He still had a brother and sister (Svevo's Uncle 'Vito' and Aunt 'Peppina') on his hands, and in 1854 Allegra bore him a child, Natalia, soon followed by two more daughters. There was still very little money in the household during the first few years of the marriage, so much so that in 1857 when Noemi was born, they couldn't afford a midwife. By 1861, the year of Svevo's birth, however, he had managed to raise enough capital to set up in business on his own account.

The 1860s were the happiest years of Francesco's life. He felt he had all the rewards of a self-made man. He had a flourishing business, he adored his growing family—saying every time a new child was born that it was another million on his income—and he was in a position to play the benefactor to a whole string of poor relations. He was a narrow, generous, self-reliant man, physically very much of the German-Jewish type, with a long hook-nose and powerful chin, an imposing, bushy-moustached, slightly irascible presence. In the home he was an autocrat, but a benevolent one, with a nervous trick of laughing when he was worried or embarrassed. (Allegra was said to have been so put off by this habit when she first knew him that she was on the point of accepting another suitor, when her father appeared to her in a dream and begged her to marry him.) He was very modest in his social ambitions, but made a religion of responsibility and business integrity and had an intense faith in his own convictions, a point hit off by Svevo in a semi-autobiographical fragment *L'Avvenire dei ricordi* ('The future of our memories')

> Once he had given his opinion he stuck to it with the same obsitnacy with which, single-handed, he has built up his business. If suspicions arose about someone he had trusted, he would find all the arguments in the world to defend and justify him. And when at last even he couldn't ignore the harm he was being done by him, he would put the blame on human nature in general—as much as to say that, even then, the man he had decided to love and trust was better than the rest of mankind. (*Saggi*, p. 205)

He was determined that his sons should not grow up idle gentlemen but become good business men like himself, and he loved boasting about his early struggles. It was a habit of his to postpone important decisions about his children's careers till the 20th March, the anniversary of the day he was sent out with his pedlar's tray to earn his living. His children, at least in their early years, seemed to have admired him, and as their mother was as mild and indulgent as he was stern, the home atmosphere was distinctly happy.

The Schmitzes were practising Jews, of a not very strict kind. They did not observe the Jewish rules about diet, but they seem to have observed the Sabbath and the main festivals. Indeed they must have been fairly highly regarded in the Jewish community, since in 1880 Francesco was elected *Hatan Bereshit*, or 'Bridegroom of Genesis' (i.e. the person called up in the synagogue on the last day of the Festival of Tabernacles to begin the new cycle of readings from the Pentateuch), an honour of some importance. On the other hand one of Allegra's brothers-in-law, Abraham Ancona, was too strict a Jew (and too much of a snob) to have anything to do with the Schmitzes—at least until he lost all his money, upon which he and his family joined the list of Francesco's dependants.

The atmosphere in Trieste, a polyglot and commercial city *par excellence*, was very favourable to Jewish life. From the days of Maria Teresa the Jewish community there had tended to receive special privileges.* The gates of the ghetto were torn down in 1785, and during the next century Jewish families, such as the Morpurgos and the Parentes, became very prominent in the city's life and sometimes held the highest civic offices. The Triestine Jews had a reputation for loyalty to the Empire, though after the Italian victories over Austria in 1859, and the subsequent emancipation of the Italian Jews, this declined.

Francesco's own national loyalties were rather mixed, as in a different way Svevo's own were to be. Belonging to what was, linguistically and historically, an Italian town, he felt himself to be an Italian, and became a supporter of the irredentist movement, which aimed to rescue Istria from the Austrians and unite it to the new Italian kingdom. At the same time he remained a germanophile, and one of his son

* The Jewish population, which was almost entirely restricted to the city, as distinct from the province, of Trieste, was smaller than that in the other great cities of the Empire (4% in 1910, as compared with 8·6% in Vienna, 8·1% in Prague, 21% in Cracow and 27·8% in Lvov).

Elio's earliest recollections was of an argument between his father and his uncle at the time of the Franco-Prussian war. Uncle Vito took the side of Napoleon III, Italy's ally in the days of the Risorgimento, and thought the French would soon be in Berlin. Francesco took the Prussian side, and firmly predicted the fall of Paris.

When Svevo was born, the family was living in the Via dell'Acquedotto (now Viale 20 Settembre) a handsome street in the well-to-do quarter (the 'new town') of Trieste. The younger children, sometimes six of them together, slept in one vast room, and as their mother was usually either pregnant or recovering from a pregnancy, they were looked after by their Aunt Peppina and the maid 'Cati', who washed and dressed them and taught them to read and say their prayers. Nothing very characteristic has come down to us about their mother. A photograph of her in middle age shows her as motherly and heavy-chinned, a little in the Roman emperor style, wearing ringlets and an old-fashioned frilled blouse. She was a mild, simple, intensely maternal woman, and the children all seem to have adored her. When Elio, at the age of 12, was spending his first miserable night at a German boarding-school, his one thought was when, if ever, would he have the chance to sleep with his head on his mother's arm again.

In due course Adolfo and Ettore were sent to the public elementary school for Jews, which was run at that time by the Vice-Rabbi, S. R. Melli. The school, which was attended by about a hundred Jewish children of both sexes, was historically of some importance, being one of the first schools for Jews of the type prescribed by the Emperor Joseph II in his Edict of Tolerance of 1782, i.e. providing teaching in the normal branches of liberal education, including arithmetic, Italian and German, in addition to strictly rabbinical instruction. Elio join ed them after a year or two, and in 1872 they all moved on to a private commercial school run by Emanuele Edeles. They didn't think much of this new school, though they appear to have been star pupils, and according to Elio they spent most of their time reading novels. However, in 1873, hearing Ettore stumbling ridiculously over a German word one day at table, Francesco decided his sons must go somewhere where they would learn German properly. He always said that a good business man (and he took it for granted that this is what they would become) ought to have at least a smattering of four languages and to know at least two perfectly—above all German. German was the key to a business career, he used to say, just as German education was the best in the world. ('. . . learn to write German well', he wrote to his youngest son Ottavio, years later, when Ottavio was beginning life as a bank clerk in Vienna; 'keep yourself clean and tidy, stick to the straight path and pronounce your r's well, and you will be a made man.') Moreover, he said, it was time for the boys to get away from home; they would never grow up to be self-reliant if they were always under their parents' eyes. He began advertising for a school for them—a place where they would get a really solid commercial education without pampering and luxury—and in due course he heard of one in Germany which seemed to fit this description, a commercial academy called the Brüssel'sche Handels- und Erziehungsinstitut (Brüssel Trade and Education Institute) at the village of Segnitz-am-Main, near Würzburg.

It was decided that Adolfo, Ettore (who was now eleven and a half) and Elio were all to go to Segnitz, but Elio made himself ill at the prospect of leaving home, and when the day came for the parents to set out for Germany with the boys, he had to be left behind. Svevo has left what appears to be an account of the journey in *L'Avvenire dei ricordi*. On the train from Innsbruck the father tells Armando (corresponding to Adolfo) that he is making him responsible for his younger brother, and Roberto (corresponding to Ettore) falls into a violent rage—up to now it's always been he who has run Armando. In Würzburg there is a quarrel with the hotelkeeper, who won't accept Bank of Trieste notes, and the father goes off in a fury to have them changed, leaving the family as hostages. Their mother, who doesn't understand German, is frightened and weeps, but Roberto feels perfectly serene—money is something he has always taken for granted, it has never occurred to him that anything depended on it. Their father comes back with the cash at last, cursing the Germans for thieves and ignorant provincials; it is the first time Roberto has ever heard him say a word against them. They reach Segnitz at last, and when it is time for the parents to leave, the headmaster concerts a little conspiracy to make the parting easier. He takes the boys for a walk, promising them that it is a short cut to a spot where they can give a last wave to their parents' train, and in fact merely leads them in a circle back to school again. Discovering the trick, Armando cries but accepts the *fait accompli*, whereas Roberto rushes furiously in to revisit the spot they said their last goodbyes in.

The Brüssel Institute was a well-known and expensive school for the sons of Jewish business men. There had been a colony of these in Segnitz, mostly in the wine trade, since the eighteenth century; owing to the restrictions on the right of Bavarian Jews to settle in towns, such colonies frequently established themselves in small villages. The school had been founded in 1838 by a cantor and Hebrew-teacher called Julius Brüssel. At the time the Schmitz boys went there it numbered about 170 boys, from various parts of Europe and America, and was no longer exclusively Jewish, there being thirty or so boys from Catholic homes and also one or two non-Jewish teachers on the staff. It was mainly a boarding school, the boys being housed in a complex of large converted private houses on the banks of the Main.* The headmaster was a Jew from Hesse called Samuel Spier. Francesco had apparently met him while he was soliciting for pupils in

* There are interesting details of the school in an unpublished pamphlet by G. Walter, *Von den Juden in Segnitz im 18 u. 19.Jahrhundert und dem Brüsselschen Handels- und Erziehungsinstitut*, [Segnitz, 1964]

Trieste and had made up his mind he was a man of genius, an impression which Spier seems to have been eager to foster. There was thought to be some mystery about his background; he was said to have had a revolutionary past and to have been a member of the Frankfurt parliament in 1848, and there was a story at the school that he was in some kind of enforced exile at Segnitz. He was a tall man with (according to Elio's later account) a 'thinker's brow'. Wherever he went he took a book with him, and he settled down to read it at spare moments, wrapping his frock-coat round himself impressively. The boys called him 'Slalomes' or 'Halomspeter' ('Peter the Dreamer'), and he was famous for his meanness.

The two Schmitz boys generally stayed at Segnitz term and holidays alike, and it was two years before Elio saw them again, when they all met on holiday at Cilli in Slovenia. They were very full of themselves and talked fluent German, and Elio decided he had better resign himself to joining them. Next term, in floods of tears and more dead than alive, he was bundled into the train for Germany, with his two brothers and the headmaster himself for company. Poor Elio's one thought, once he was on the train, was to get back to Trieste and never leave it again, and the longer the journey lasted and the more boys that were picked up on the way, the worse he felt. Nobody could understand a word of his German, and Ettore and Adolfo kept alarming him by their warnings. They pointed out a gigantic and extremely stupid youth, the son of a Bohemian millionaire, whom they said it would be fatal for him to offend. He looked at the monster in panic, though his brothers assured him no one should bully him while they were there to protect him.

At Vienna they waited four days for more boys to turn up, and Spier, who had been particularly asked to look after Elio, read his newspapers and went on his errands, totally ignoring his existence. Knowing Spier's reputation, Elio was surprised at the luxurious style of their hotel rooms, till he learned that Spier had shares in the hotel. At midnight at

Budweis, near the Bavarian frontier, the other boys all got out and drank a farewell cup of coffee—after that it would be nothing but chicory, they told him. His heart sank even further when they finally got to Segnitz and he was taken into the dining-hall; the din was unspeakable, and he decided that German boys must be quite different from Italian ones, they seemed positively not to mind being parted from their parents and homes. He went to bed in a study which seemed to have been designed for midgets (the wash-basin held rather less than a litre of water) and lay there wondering if he would ever be happy again.

Elio never got used to Segnitz and had to be taken away after a year or so, but Adolfo and Ettore got on very well—though, according to Elio, Spier once tried to get them to write home asking to be allowed to stay in Segnitz over the holidays, Spier being frightened that if they once got home they wouldn't come back again. Ettore was a social success at the school; he figured in philosophical disputations and formed his own literary debating society, and in general learned more about literature than he did about commerce. He read Schiller, Jean Paul and Turgeniev, and spent sleepless nights over *Hamlet*, though Dr. Spier confiscated his Shakespeare before he could get on to *King Lear*. He paid very little attention to Italian literature, and when Elio once tried to persuade him to look at the Italian classics he laughed in his face, exclaiming 'Schiller is the greatest genius in the world'.

Svevo's schooldays at Segnitz lasted till he was seventeen, and he returned to Trieste thoroughly dreading the idea of a business career and secretly convinced he was destined to be a writer. He didn't dare tell his father this in so many words, but he asked for further time to consider his future, and Francesco allowed him to enrol at the Istituto Superiore Commerciale Revoltella* (Revoltella Commercial Institute)

* Founded from funds left by Baron Pasquale Revoltella (1795-1869), a Triestine financier of Venetian origin who made a fortune out of the Austro-Prussian war.

which was the nearest thing to a university Trieste had to offer.* At the back of his mind there was the idea that he might one day persuade his father to send him to Florence to perfect his Italian, and meanwhile he dabbled in various courses, including law and medicine; he said it was a curious thing that he always found himself changing to a new faculty just about examination time.

The Schmitzes were still a very united family at this period, and Elio later looked back sentimentally to these years as the time when they were all still happy.† Elio had become an intense admirer of Ettore, and on this basis they had become devoted friends. In October 1879, on the occasion of their parents' going to Italy on a business trip, the three older brothers (Ottavio being still only a child) produced a family newspaper called *L'Adotajejojade di Trieste* (a sort of anagram of 'Adolfo', 'Ettore' and 'Elio'). 'There is widespread discontent', begins the leading article, 'at the news that in the absence of their illustrious majesties, the kingdom is to be placed under the rule of the Archduchess Natalia' (i.e. their elder sister). The police notices report the arrest of three brothers taken in the act of breaking into a baker's shop; in reply to questioning the accused claimed to have been systematically starved during the absence of papa and mamma, and the police doctor confirms symptoms of acute insanity induced by prolonged abstinence. In the personal columns, the house of Schmitz & Co. advertises for a traveller with a thorough knowledge of the glassware business, combined with extensive experience in the cheap jewellery, candle and matchbox trade, and a young man (i.e. Elio) height 29 feet 6 inches seeks employment as a lamp-standard. There is also an announcement concerning a lost dog:

* The Austrians, for political reasons, would never allow Trieste to have a university proper.

† He was thinking of the immediate family circle, as his sister Noemi had already died in childbirth in 1878 and Paola was unhappily married.

LOST

A dog (mongrel) which answers to the name of

ETTORE

As this dog is very lazy and loves sleeping in the sun, he should be easily found in the vicinity of the Acqueduct. The esteemed finder, if he will bring him to No. 10 via dell'Acquedotto first floor will receive a suitable

REWARD

If found sleeping, please do not wake.

There was a rage for the theatre just then among the young in Trieste, and both Ettore and Elio pretended to fall in love with the famous Gemma Cuniberti,* an eight-year-old theatrical prodigy who gave a season at the *Filodrammatica* theatre early in 1880. Indeed Elio really did more or less fall in love with her, and collected all her press notices, convincing himself that her parents were exploiting her and that she would die young. Ettore wrote her two ardent letters, which he signed 'Herod', and he even wrote a play for her, as several well-known writers had done. He offered it to her father, and when Signor Cuniberti didn't turn up for their appointment, he lay in wait for Gemma at the railway station to declare his homage. (He later played a similar game with Duse, sending her a copy of *Romeo and Juliet* with the compliments of 'G. Shakespeare' and telling her that he reserved only those rights of authorship which the law granted the author during his lifetime.) He actually toyed with the idea of acting himself, and had an audition with the great Salvini,† who turned him down on the score of his defective r's, (a family weakness). Indeed as a writer, all his early enthusiasm was for the stage, and when his friend Silvio Benco first knew him in 1890 he

* Gemma Cuniberti (1872-1940) came from a well-known family of Piedmontese actors and made her début in Milan at the age of six. She retired from the stage at the age of ten and later became a successful playwright.

† Tommaso Salvini (1829-1915), an Italian actor of world-wide reputation.

was still proclaiming the drama as 'the form of forms, the only one in which life communicates itself directly and without disguise'.

Elio was convinced Ettore was going to be a great writer and he began a diary at about this time, partly to keep trace of his brother's literary career. 'Even Napoleon didn't have a chronicler who admired him as I admired Ettore' he wrote later. However, his efforts to be Ettore's literary conscience didn't bear much fruit. Ettore produced a number of first scenes and first acts of plays but never succeeded in finishing anything.

From the tenth of this month [February 1880] Ettore has been working on a play in 'versi martelliani':* *Ariosto Governatore*. So far he has written twenty stanzas. But he is very lazy about everything and I don't know when he will ever have actually finished a work. So far he has never done so. This time however, I have made him sign an agreement to finish *Ariosto Governatore* by the 14th of March, otherwise for the next three months he is to pay me 10 soldi for every cigarette he smokes.

Ettore begged for an extension when it reached the 13th; moreover he had a splendid new idea for a play—it was to be called *First Love*—it would be a pity to spoil it by hurry:

So I gave him five promissory notes [wrote Elio] at twenty days each, beginning the 14th March, i.e. tomorrow. This will give him twenty days for each act. . . .
18 July 1880. Ettore has begun a new play. The last one is not to be completed. 'Le Roi est mort; vive le Roi!' But I don't suppose he will finish this one either.

No doubt one of the reasons why Svevo at first chose to write for the stage was that he was nervous about his grasp of literary Italian. It was a question very much in the minds of all Italian writers, and Svevo later made the remark that Italians never wrote without a dictionary in their hands. But

* Alexandrines, named after Pier Jacopo Martello (1665-1727), who revived them.

in his own case, that of someone brought up to speak the Triestine dialect and educated in Germany, the problem was particularly acute, and indeed it had a crucial effect on his whole writing career. When he eventually formed his own narrative style, it was an intensely anti-literary one, poles apart from the graceful belle-lettrist Tuscan then in vogue; it was a kind of business man's Italian, sprinkled with Triestine words and constructions, one which the Italian critics found impossibly ugly. But of course his whole cultural situation was rather equivocal. At school, as I have said, he more or less ignored Italian literature, and though politically speaking he became a declared italophile, in other respects he often felt more German than Italian, and more 'European' than either, and his pseudonym 'Italo Svevo' expresses his feeling of not fully belonging to any one national culture.

The difficulties facing him, of course, were those which to some extent faced any Triestine writer. What was exceptional was his way of turning them to his own advantage. He became, almost as much as his friend Joyce, though for different reasons, the novelist of a particular city. And as the city is not one of the world-famous ones, I ought now to say a little about it.

In the 1880s, when Svevo was learning to be a writer, Trieste was a town of some 150,000 inhabitants, of very mixed national origin.

Historically, it was a small Italian port-town of the Austrian Empire, with a solidly Slav (mainly Slovene) hinterland; but as the result of nineteenth-century immigration it had acquired considerable Greek, German and Jewish communities and a large Slav working population. In 1850 the Emperor Franz Joseph granted it its own Municipal Council, so that it became responsible for its own internal administration, under the supervision of the Austrian governor and police. The official language was Italian (the maritime language of state of this part of the Mediterranean), and the city was still predominantly an Italian one, though the racial composition is difficult to estimate precisely, as many Slavs put themselves down as 'Italian' on census returns as a mark of class distinction.

The city is divided into the 'old town', a cluster of narrow streets and crowded tenements flanking the castle hill, and the 'new town' on the other side of the *Corso*, handsomely laid out with broad streets and *palazzi* in the late eighteenth century. In Svevo's youth all sorts of Slav and Levantine costumes were to be seen on the streets, the same costumes as made the *Schiavoni* in Venice a favourite tourist spectacle, and it used to be said that the East began at Trieste. It had been a free port since 1719, but the modern port of Trieste was really the creation of the German financier Baron Bruck, the founder of the Austrian-Lloyd shipping line (and later Austrian Minister of Finance and propagandist for an 'empire of 70 million Germans'). When Austria lost the north Italian provinces in 1859, Trieste became her chief outlet on the Mediterranean and began to rival Hamburg as an entrepôt between south-east Europe and the East. It got the railway in 1857, and the port became for many years virtually a monopoly of the Franco-Austrian *Südbahn* railway company ('an *imperium in imperio*, a financial despotism in a constitutional land' as Sir Richard Burton called it, making Trieste 'a mere canal' for the purposes of the transit trade).

The whole city was notorious for its single-minded obsession with business. 'The streets are crowded with well-dressed, well-conditioned men', wrote an English visitor* in 1849, 'the rotundity of whose proportions indicates a dark den of wares in town and a neat snug box and hanging gardens in the environs'. There was no hereditary aristocracy or *rentier* class in Trieste, and the Austrian officials, though often of aristocratic family, were not very well paid and couldn't compete socially with the richer Greek and Jewish

* A. A. Paton, *The Highlands and Islands of the Adriatic*, 1849, p. 214.

merchants. When Sir Richard Burton the explorer was there as British Consul (1872-90) he and his wife regarded 'the enlightened and hospitable Hebrews' as their best friends. 'It is the Jews who lead society here, the charities and the fashion; they are the life of the town', wrote Lady Burton.* The Italians formed the professional class, and the artisans and lower civil servants, including the police, were mostly Slav.

Travellers always commented on the Triestine passion for business, sometimes rather disagreeably. Stendhal, who became consul there in 1831, was full of groans: 'je vis au milieu de paysans qui ne connaissent qu'une religion, celle de l'argent' ('I am living among peasants who only recognise one religion, that of money'). Charles Lever, the Irish novelist, disliked it equally when he went there as British Consul. He thought it was 'one of the dreariest, dullest, and vulgarest dens, without even that resource one had in the Austria of yore—of a gentlemanlike class in the higher beaurocracy [sic] and the soldiers in command—all was canting and communistic. . . .'† A French visitor in the 1870s, Charles Yriarte, asks, slightly affectedly, how you can live a civilised existence in a town where at 8 p.m., when dinner is over, everyone, from the financier to his clerk, looks at his watch and makes for the Exchange to see what ships have been reported. He finds it a cheerful, rather provincial town.

By day the town is active and humming with work and business. . . . At 8 o'clock in the evening, in the Corso, one has the illusion of being in a great city—a spacious street, not very elegant indeed, but brilliantly lit and lined with richly-furnished shops. The whole city is to be found gathered there; but by half past nine the place is deserted, everyone is at supper, and those who have no meal to go home to resort to the *birrerie* or beer-houses, which are so numerous and vast as to outdo even those of Vienna and Pesth.

---

* Isabel Burton, *Life of Sir Richard Burton*, 1893, vol. 1, p. 535.
† W. J. Fitzpatrick, *Life of Charles Lever*, new ed., 1884, p. 342.

The frugal elegancies of the teacup, the *bon mot* under the lamp-light, are unknown here; substantial suppers and something a bit lively in the way of entertainment are what is demanded. (*Le bord de l'Adriatique et le Monténégro*, 1878, p. 81)

The city also acquired a reputation for irreligion and suicide. Lady Burton thought the two phenomena were connected and put them down to the 'utter throwing off of religion'. She claimed to have seen 'thousands accompanying a *felo de se* to the grave, with verses and laurel leaves and a band of music, as if he had done something gallant and brave. Indeed, one was considered very narrow-minded for not joining in his eulogy. They say that forty years ago Trieste was a charming place to live in; but that with increase of trade, luxury and money flowed in and faith flowed out.'

The place was notoriously riven by factions and famous for its riots and street-disturbances. The Italian-nationalists hated the Austrians and the austrophiles, the Slavs resented the Italians, the Christian Socialists came to blows with the Social Democrats, and the Austrian government always did its best to play off one group against another. '. . . the *exaltés* and the *Italianissimi* hate their rulers like poison' wrote Burton in 1876.

In this they are joined by the mass of the wealthy and influential Israelites, who divide the commerce with the Greeks. The former subscribe handsomely to every Italian charity or movement, and periodically and anonymously memorialise the King of Italy. The lower class take a delight in throwing large squibs, here called by courtesy 'torpedoes', amongst the unpatriotic petticoats who dare to throng the Austrian balls. The immediate suburbs, country, and villages are Slav and even in the city some can barely speak Italian. This people detests all its fellow-citizens with an instinctive odium of race, and with a dim consciousness that it has been ousted from its own. (Isabel Burton, *Life of Sir Richard Burton*, 1893, vol. 2, p. 500)

'When we went there', says Lady Burton, 'an Austrian would hardly give his hand to an Italian in a dance. An Italian would

TRIESTE AT THE TURN OF THE CENTURY
(*Above*) the quayside and (*below*) the Bourse (right) and the Tergesteo (left). The Union Bank, where Svevo worked as a young man, was on the second floor of the Tergesteo building.

(*Above left*) FRANCESCO SCHMITZ, Svevo's father (1829-92)

(*Above right*) ALLEGRA SCHMITZ, née MORAVIA, Svevo's mother (1833-95)

(*Centre*) SVEVO AS A SCHOOLBOY

not sing in the concert where an Austrian sang. If an Austrian gave a ball, the Italian threw a bomb into it; and the Imperial family were always received with a chorus of bombs—bombs on the railway, bombs in the gardens, bombs in the sausages; in fact it was not at such times pleasant.'*

The Italian-nationalist movement was already a force in Trieste by the mid-century and A. A. Paton reports a famous dinner in honour of Cobden in 1847, when a young pro-Italian Liberal made a speech in favour of free trade, progress and an all-Italian commercial union.

Upon this I saw the Germans frowning and looking serious; and before the speech was finished, up rose Herr von Bruck, and shouted aloud, 'We are Triestines; we are cosmopolites; we know nothing of Italian and German, and have nothing to do with Italian and German nationalities. (*Op. cit.*, p. 221)

Italian claims to Istria and the Trentino were already in the air and the Austrian censorship banned the words 'patria', 'Italia' and 'libertà' at the theatre. Many young Triestines were smuggled across the border to fight with the Italians in the war of 1859, and in 1866 (as again in 1915) the irredentists in Trieste anxiously watched the quays for the expected Italian fleet. The Italian nationalists frequently had a majority in the Municipal Council and from time to time, after some act of defiance of Austria, the Council was dissolved and new elections held. Various irredentist organisations, such as the *Lega Nazionale*, which promoted Italian-speaking schools, and the *Società di Ginnastica*, were formed, and, when dissolved, were sometimes re-founded under another name. The record of the *Società Ginnastica* (Gymnastic Club) illustrated the process: founded as the *Società Triestina di Ginnastica* in 1863, dissolved by the Austrians in 1864, reconstituted as the *Associazione Triestina di Ginnastica* in 1868, dissolved in 1882; reconstituted as the *Unione Ginnastica*, as the *Società Ginnastica*, as the *Associazione Ginnastica*, as the *Società*

* *Op. cit.*, vol. 2, p. 18.

Ginnastica Triestina; dissolved for the sixth time in 1915, and finally revived, with its political aims granted, in 1919.

The movement had two newspapers, *L'Independente* (founded 1877) and *Il Piccolo* (founded in 1881). They were once described as the Don Quixote and Sancho Panza of irredentism. The *Independente* was undisguisedly propagandist (it made it a rule never to include news of the Austro-Hungarian empire on the front page), and was constantly having whole issues seized or its editorial staff arrested; it claimed to be the most sequestrated journal in the Empire. The *Piccolo*, with a much larger circulation (about 100,000 in the period just before the 1914-18 war, as compared with the 1,000 or so of the *Independente*) was more cautious and specialised in political innuendo and irony.

The Slavs developed their own nationalist movement in the 1870s, the chief organs being a political society called *Edinost*, which ran its own newspaper, and later, in the 1890s, the 'St. Cyril and St. Methodius', an association for promoting Slav-speaking schools, in rivalry with the irredentist *Lega Nazionale*. The Slavs and the italophiles frequently came to blows and the Italians claimed that the authorities encouraged the Slavs to use violence. With the great influx of Slav artisans in the period 1890-1900 the Slav nationalist movement became a serious rival to the irredentists, though the Italians were still inclined to look down on Slavs as culturally inferior. Lady Burton remarks that Italian visitors to the parish church at Opcina, a Slav village in the hills above Trieste, showed their sense of superiority by refusing to kneel. Slav banks were despised in Italian business circles, and it was said that for a non-Slav to deal with one signified a last desperate throw before bankruptcy.

From the point of view of cultural life Trieste in the 1880s was distinctly provincial and second-rate. There were literary *salons* of a sort, particularly in the circles of the irredentists, but they didn't rise much above the level of Annetta's pretentious 'Wednesday club' in Svevo's *Una vita.* There was, according to Svevo's play *L'Avventura di Maria*, only one, eminently bribable, music critic in Trieste, and the audience's main passion was for Hungarian dances and showy cadenzas. There were several flourishing theatres, but audiences expected to be able to talk during performances and thought it an uncomfortable German custom to turn down the houselights. An old-established club called the Gabinetto di Minerva met weekly for the exchange of learned papers, and there were also a local *Circolo Musicale* and *Circolo Artistico*, both of which Svevo frequented at various times, but there was not much in all this to stimulate a creative talent. And, of course, a Triestine writer, writing in Italian in an Austrian city, was out of the main stream of Italian culture and could hardly expect much attention from the Italian press. On the whole, therefore, such original writers and artists as Trieste produced did their best to escape to Florence or Paris. The prospects for a young man like Svevo, with ill-defined aspirations to be a writer, were not very rosy.

2
Family Misfortunes

In 1880 catastrophe overtook the Schmitz family. Sometime during the year the father Francesco's business affairs took a bad turn and the shock seems to have set off a general degeneration in him. He became prematurely senile (he was then only about fifty) and from the old pattern of strong-mindedness and principle he turned into a querulous, shuffling, Harpagon-like figure, perpetually complaining about money and making the household a misery with his gloom and rages. For the next few years Elio's diary keeps returning to the theme. '. . . at home everything depends on papa's mood,' he writes, 'and naturally he does his level best to be in a bad one.' He has days when he won't eat or talk. He loses interest in his children's education, which had been a passion with him. He even seems to be turning against their mother, who keeps making every effort she can think of to comfort him and keep the household going.

His money troubles, in fact, went back some years and were partly the result of his own sense of principle and passion for helping his relations. Of the 100,000 florins* capital he possessed in 1876, some had gone on the children's education, and a considerable amount on dowries and trousseaux for his married daughters, but a good deal also went in paying a brother-in-law's debts. Then there was the affair of Uncle Vito's legacy. When Vito died, his wife Sofia

* About £10,000 in English money at the same period.

was pregnant and he left 25,000 florins to go to her on the child's behalf if the latter survived for twenty-four hours or more, otherwise (apparently) to revert to the Schmitz business, in which he was a partner. In fact the baby did not survive long enough for Sofia to inherit, but Francesco, who was trustee, generously persuaded the doctor to sign a certificate saying that it had done so, and offered to pay the inheritance by instalments. Sofia greedily demanded immediate payment of the whole sum, however, and he had no choice but to pay up.

After the bad year of 1880 he attempted, not very successfully, to deal in other goods as well as glassware, and towards the end of 1881 he tried his hand as a manufacturer, taking a lease on a small glassworks at Log (a town in the Julian Alps, fifty miles or so from Trieste). The failure of this venture, which cost him another 15,000 florins, was the final blow, and from then on he struggled on in a hopelessly hand-to-mouth way, sometimes resorting to money-lenders, which in his own eyes was the last disgrace, and sinking deeper into melancholia and money-mania. Elio came to the conclusion he had never really understood modern business methods (and Adolfo and Sam, Noemi's widowed husband, who had come into the family business, weren't much better). He seemed to have no idea of drawing up a proper balance-sheet or making a serious analysis of his resources and long-term prospects; all he thought of was raising the next hundred florins to get him through the month. At one point he managed to persuade Adolfo that it was his duty to save the family business by marrying a rich wife. Nothing could have been more unlike the old Francesco than this wild scheme, but in fact Adolfo was rather taken with it, and so was the rest of the family. The only thing they hadn't thought of, remarked Elio bitterly, was finding the rich woman. Sometimes the children would go into the father's affairs with him and prove that he was imagining them much worse than they really were. He would say helplessly that he knew they were right—'I'm not my own master'.

As a result of the collapse of the Schmitz family fortunes jobs had to be found at once for the sons. Ettore left the Revoltella, and in September 1880 his father advertised in the 'Appointments required' column of the *Cittadino* for a position for him. A firm of merchants called Mettel gave him an interview, but nothing came of it, owing to his being a Jew. He was relieved, and for a moment he had the blissful idea that he might be left to his own devices, apart from the few hours' reading required towards his 'volunteer-examination' (the examination which all students took to allow them to substitute one year's volunteer military service for the usual three years' compulsory service).* Then, however, Natalia's fiancé 'Pepi' Vivante announced that his brother Fortunato, who was a director of the Trieste branch of the Viennese *Unionbank*, could offer Ettore a post, and on the 27th September he began the life of a bank-clerk. Elio, who was still at school in Trieste at the I.R. Accademia, was found a job with a firm of merchants called Finotti and Macerata, whilst Adolfo began to travel on behalf of the family firm.

We have Svevo's word for it that the description of Alfonso Nitti's life as a bank-clerk in *Una vita* (*A Life*) is autobiographical. And no other writer has caught so well the quality of a life like this for a young man of frustrated literary ambitions—the mixture of deadening routine and endless circling day-dreams, his oscillation between trying to find satisfaction in the job (in his day-dreams he becomes the saviour of his firm by some inspired act of business acumen) and ignoring it as a stupid and insignificant necessity (his day-dreams turning to literary fame and sexual triumphs). What is most poignant about Alfonso's experience, as it was no doubt for Svevo, is the desire to be recognised. He is torn between despising what he is doing and being unable to bear the thought that no one is going to witness it. He must know what his superiors think of him, and he spends hours specu-

* Compulsory universal military service was introduced in the Austro-Hungarian empire in 1868.

lating on what exactly a casual word or some unexpected expression on their face means. Was the Director's face red with *anger* when he met him in the corridor? Perhaps it is always red like that, only he has never noticed it. His nightmare is that no one will ever even recognise his existence, and that he will start doubting it himself.

There are other recollections of Svevo himself in Alfonso. Like Alfonso he spent two hours or so every evening in the public library, and no doubt his picture of Alfonso during these sessions, dreaming of literary greatness and drawing up synopses of unwritten philosophical masterpieces, is partly self-caricature. In fact it was also the period when he was reading Flaubert, Zola and Daudet and was beginning to look at the Italian classics. And most important of all, it was the time when he was discovering Schopenhauer, who became a major influence on him.

He had not given up the idea of being a writer and indeed began to have a little success, publishing one or two articles and reviews in the literary columns of *L'Independente*. (His first published work, which appeared in December 1880, was an article on Shylock, written after a local performance of *The Merchant of Venice*.) Otherwise, he went on for several years dabbling in playwriting, though rarely getting anything finished. In May 1881 he announced his conversion to Zola and the school of Naturalism.

From time to time he made gloomy stock-takings of his own progress, such as the following of the 24th February 1881:

HISTORY OF MY WORKS

1. *Ariosto the Governor*. More thought about than written. I believed I had worked out all the details so well that this first effort was going to be a masterpiece. How I let my wishes deceive me! I didn't even finish the first scene, because that was where I realised the abstruseness of the idea and the wretchedness of the style.

2. *Discords of the Heart*. One scene of this has survived, and it

makes me blush. Conventional phraseology, clumsy development, prose that would like to be poetry and isn't even prose. The *dénouement* (at least the idea of the *dénouement*) seems to me logical but impossible. I ought to have dedicated it to the Chinese —it was like their favourite *Hoci-lai-ki.** The title is tragic; the play looked like being comic.
3. *Regeneration.* I wrote two acts of this, I regret to say. It was the sort of thing that might have done as a one-act play, and I wanted to stretch it out into four.

The hero-worshipping Elio began to be critical, and they lost their tempers with each other.

2 June 1881. Today I had a little quarrel with Ettore. . . . He is studying, certainly, but he's not writing anything serious, and as I see it he won't get where he wants to without some success that will make papa feel like encouraging him or will give him confidence in himself. . . . I used to say to myself that at least he was losing nothing by studying; I still thought so till the other day, when Ettore told me that he had to neglect his work at the office to be able to study. I told him what I thought then, and for the rest of the day he didn't speak to me; but yesterday, when I asked him what he had done overnight, he replied it was nothing to do with me, and that, seeing how encouraging I was being, he was never going to read me anything more. So that was that. However yester-evening he read me a poem.

The family disaster of 1880 and its consequences certainly played a crucial part in Svevo's development. The sudden collapse of his sense of security and the dismal spectacle of his father's degeneration are the kind of experience which, you feel, might have led to a lifetime of neurotic day-dreaming and maladjustment. And in *Una vita*, his first novel, with its final suicide which comes, as he once said, 'brusquely and coldly, like the term of a syllogism', he imagines what at the worst his own life might have become. Indeed day-dreaming and senility became the dominant themes of all his writing, and it seems likely that the paradoxical conception of

* The well-known *Circle of Chalk* by Hsing-tao Li.

senility which runs through his work, and his casting of himself while still a young man for the role of the 'senile' hero, had some connection with his father's premature degeneration —in the way noted by Freud:

Hostile impulses against parents (a wish that they should die) are also an integral constituent of neuroses. They are repressed at times when compassion for the parent is active—at times of their illness or death. On such occasions it is a manifestation of mourning to . . . punish oneself in a hysterical fashion (through the medium of the idea of retribution) with the same states of illness that they have had. (*Complete Psychological Works*, 1953—, vol. 14, p. 240)

In fact, though, for all his self-doubting, there was a toughness and intelligence in Svevo which saved him from a fate like Alfonso's. Elio didn't share these, and for him the family tragedy turned out to be fatal. For two or three years he had jobs as an errand-boy or copying clerk with one or other of his father's business acquaintances, or with his father himself. They didn't even think it necessary to pay him, so that it was a year or more before he actually earned anything, and he complained continually in his diary: 'To have to obey someone who, as in my case, is inferior to us in education, in feeling, in everything except money—is degrading.' What spare time he had he devoted to the violin and he told his father he wanted to study composition. Francesco was quite encouraging at first, and engaged a master for him, but he only regarded it as a hobby; and Elio gradually realised that he would never have the courage to defy his father, as Ettore might have done, and try to make a career of music. He quarrelled with his father and spoke of leaving home, but without much conviction. By the age of twenty he had become a confirmed nostalgic and day-dreamer, perpetually harking back to their old happy family evenings of the 1870s or going to pluck laurel-leaves from the tombs of Noemi and Uncle Vito. He clung desperately to the idea of himself as the 'good', the virtuous Elio, and warned himself earnestly that were he once to commit an unworthy action he would have lost the right to indulge in delicious memories. But as time passed he began to think of himself as a disillusioned man. 'I no longer have faith as I used to in this, that and the other thing. I see all too clearly that many things I used to think were done for altruistic reasons are really done for money. I am still a modest person, but I shall change. Up to now my modesty has only brought me harm.'

In 1883 he developed symptoms of Bright's disease and his diary becomes more and more despairing and nostalgic, as he is sent away for one fruitless cure after another. He began to lose interest even in Ettore and his writing, and the atmosphere at home became steadily more depressing. His father got it into his head that Elio's illness was an injury to himself. 'He *enjoys* his nephritis and I have to *suffer* the expense of it' he quotes his father as saying, and comments: 'this has become his favourite obsession; it sums up his general idea of the importance of money as against health, i.e. *his* money as against other people's health.' The only member of the household who still remained entirely unselfish, he wrote, was his mother, who believed devoutly in each new cure as it came along—the iron, the sulphur, the goat's milk and the hot baths.

During one of his cures he met a Signorina U—— from Trieste and fell in love with her. She was training to be a concert pianist and he used to go and play duets with her, though his friends told him she was a light woman. He was half convinced they must be right—'I can find an excuse for the visits to the actor, but I can't forgive the evenings with the pianist. . . .' he wrote; but he went on visiting her; only the trouble was he could never tell if she was glad to see him or not. Sometimes she didn't come down from her room and he had to make conversation with her mother. He put it down to her 'frivolity'. (In all this there are touches of Alfonso's bungled affair with Annetta in *Una vita*.)

By the autumn of 1885 he was visibly dying and as a last

desperate measure he was sent to spend the winter with an uncle in Egypt. He found that his mother had put his diary in his travelling chest, and he added a few more pages to it in Cairo, before bidding it a solemn farewell:

Goodbye hopes! Goodbye illusions! Everything is gone now; there is almost nothing left for me to lose. If they rob me of certain illusions about my country's future and the love of my family, and the thin thread of hope in the future that I imagine even the suicide has a minute before killing himself, everything will have been taken from me. . . . And now you, who were my companion for many years, perhaps goodbye—or perhaps *au revoir*.

He came home to Trieste soon afterwards, and within a few months he was dead.

3

Writing and Marriage

In 1887, shocked and left lonely by his brother's death, Svevo turned seriously to fiction and, drawing on his own and to some extent on Elio's experience, he began the massive, Zolaesque case-history of maladjustment which was to become *Una vita*. It was originally to have been called *Un inetto* ('The Inept One') but he later changed the name after the Milanese publishing firm of Treves had refused the book, saying they could never publish a novel with such a title. The writing took Svevo several years, and in December 1889 he refers to it gloomily in another of his stocktakings:

Today I am 28. My dissatisfaction with myself and with other people couldn't be more complete. I note this impression down, in case some time in the future I am able to look back and either call myself a fool for writing in this way (things being even worse by then) or cheer myself up, finding I am not as bad as I was. The money question gets worse and worse; I'm not happy about my health, about my work, or about the people round me. And as I'm not contented with my work, it's perfectly reasonable that no one else should be either. But with all the enormous ambition I once had, not to have found anyone, *anyone at all*, to take an interest in what I'm thinking or doing; to spend my time having to take an interest in other people's doings as the only way of getting a little attention for my own. Two years ago exactly I began that novel which was to have been God knows what; and in fact it's a disgusting mess and will choke me in the end. My real strength always lay in hoping, and the worst of it is, I'm even losing my talent for that.

The whole period was rather a depressing one for Svevo—though also a busy one, for some time during the 1880s, in addition to writing for *L'Independente*, he had begun to do part-time editorial work for it, searching the foreign press for items bearing on the irredentist question. As always, the paper was in trouble with the authorities, and in 1889 the whole regular editorial staff was put in jail, upon which Svevo and some other young sympathisers (among them Silvio Benco, later a well-known journalist and novelist) volunteered to keep the paper going. He used to get up early to do the work before the bank opened at 9. Benco has described him at this period: he was the one mature man in the group (he was nearly 30) and impressed the rest of them with his air of worldly experience, though he chattered a great deal and made a constant stream of jokes (his *Witze* they came to be known as) at his own expense. They knew he wrote, but they didn't take him seriously as a writer, putting him on the level of one's friends' aunts who paint in watercolours. It was generally agreed among them that he wrote a barbarous style, an awkward contorted Italian full of solecisms and rather Germanic in flavour—they put it down to his having gone to school in Germany.

He was known as the inseparable friend of the painter Umberto Veruda. Veruda was some eight years younger than himself but already a successful artist. He was temperamentally very different from Svevo, a dedicated bohemian in the manner of the period, a great swaggerer and flouter of the bourgeois, dressing in loud checks and extravagant cravats, and fond of insulting his native city—'that indecent spot which by the purest coincidence was and is my fatherland'. (Though in fact he was a dutiful son and was already supporting his parents out of his earnings.) He had studied at Munich where he came under the influence of Max Liebermann, and later in Paris, under Bouguereau. Liebermann at this time was still in his pre-Impressionist period, and Bouguereau, of the soulful Madonnas so much loved by our grandmothers, was the arch-enemy for the Impressionists. None the less Veruda caught a mild flavour of Impressionism, and when he held his first exhibition in Trieste, on his return there in 1888, the show caused quite a stir. It soon earned him a clientèle as a portrait-painter and in the following year he won a scholarship to Rome. He later won a very minor European reputation, and there are works by him in public galleries in Venice, Rome and Vienna, as well as several portraits of the Duke of Marlborough's family at Blenheim. His anecdotal paintings look very dated now, though the portraits show some talent.

Svevo got to know him shortly after his return to Trieste, and they soon became very intimate. Veruda seems to have had a liberating effect on Svevo. He later quoted Silvio Benco's remark about himself, that he got from the painter the gift of learning to laugh at life instead of dying under it. Benco gives a picture of them at that period:

They were always to be seen together, passing remarks on women in the streets, or frequenting fashionable drawing-rooms (which they were both fond of); Svevo always very correct and bourgeois, with a look of a clerk *à la mode*, his twinkling eyes set flat in his huge, yellowish, Buddhist philosopher's head; Veruda immensely tall and spectacular, wearing fantastic clothes with imperturbable gravity. ('Italo Svevo', in *Pegaso*, Florence, January 1929)

Veruda preached art and friendship and refused to hunt after rich clients, choosing what friends he had from among his few fellow bohemians in philistine Trieste. He made a cult of cynicism about women, regarding them as a threat to art, and refused to admit the word 'love' to this vocabulary, though at one period he declared he was going to marry for money. When he read about a fashionable wedding in the newspapers he would calculate how much he had lost by it—a million, two million, three million at a single blow. 'No one lost millions as cheerfully as Veruda', said Svevo. The feat of his life he was proudest of was to have slapped his mistress's face in public.

The sculptor Balli in *Senilità* (*As a Man Grows Older*) is partly based on Veruda, though as Svevo himself pointed out Veruda was a much younger and more unstable man than Balli (he was also a success as an artist, which Balli was not). There was certainly something of Balli's relationship to Emilio in Veruda's to Svevo:

He had always exercised a sort of paternal authority over him, which Emilio accepted only too gladly; for although his lot was rather drab and perfectly ordinary, and though his life was entirely devoid of unforeseen happenings, he did not feel safe without a few hints as to its conduct*. . . . Their friendship bore witness to Balli's influence at every point. It became, like all the rare friendships of the sculptor, more intimate than Emilio, from motives of prudence, might perhaps have desired. Their intellectual relations were confined to the representative arts, and here they were in complete agreement, because Balli's absorbing idea reigned therein supreme, namely, the necessity of discovering afresh for ourselves the simplicity or naïveté of which the so-called classicists had robbed the arts. Agreement was easy: Balli taught and the other had nothing to do but learn. Never a word passed between them of Emilio's complicated literary theories, because Balli loathed everything that he could not understand, and Emilio was influenced by him even to the point of walking, speaking and gesticulating like him. (*As a Man Grows Older*, trans. Beryl de Zoete, standard ed., pp. 12-13)

A photograph of the two together taken in 1892 strikes one as characteristic: Veruda has one arm round Svevo and is gesturing eloquently with the other, while Svevo quietly smokes. (See plate facing p. 50)

When Veruda was in Trieste, the two friends saw each other two or three times a day. Veruda would come to collect Svevo at the bank, amusing himself by sketching as he waited, and they would spend their evenings in cafés, or at Veruda's

* Thus Beryl de Zoete's translation. I would prefer to translate: 'needed props in order to feel secure'. The notion of 'props' is important in Emilio's thinking.

studio or elsewhere. When Veruda painted a portrait of Svevo and his sister Ortensia in 1893 he dedicated it to 'Ettore Schmitz, more brother than friend'. The friendship only cooled a little after Svevo's marriage in 1896, which Veruda took badly, guessing it would come between them, which to a considerable extent it did.

In 1890 Svevo began his year of military service—presumably on the 1st December, the date on which the training year normally began. For the first six months it merely meant his reporting to barracks for lectures and physical training in the early morning (7.30 to 9) and afternoon (2.30 to 6), while for the rest of the day he lived his normal existence. From the 1st June onwards, however, he began full-time service with his regiment, the 22nd Infantry Regiment, and lived in barracks or in camp. He was stationed near Trieste for most of the period, and rose to the rank of corporal, but nothing much is known about his experiences, except that, as might have been expected at this period of Austrian history, he came up against some anti-semitism. He used to be proud of a retort he made to one of his officers, an overbearing Austrian baron: the Austrian, having to climb up a bank in front of Svevo, during an exercise, said 'See you don't bite me in the behind'. To which Svevo answered 'Don't you know Jews don't eat pork?'. A friend of Svevo's, Giani Stuparich, who, years later, used to invite his friends to drink wine in his garden, remembered Svevo once jumping up on to a garden seat and going through the drill movements he had learned as 'a conscript of Franz Joseph'.

In October of the same year he made his first appearance in print as a writer of fiction, when *L'Independente* serialised a long short story, written under the pseudonym of 'E. Samigli', called 'L'Assassinio di via Belpoggio'. It was a sort of *Crime and Punishment* in little, the story of a robbery and murder done on an impulse by a young petit-bourgeois with a grudge against society. It is not unimpressive as a study in paranoiac psychology, though Svevo didn't think much of it later and never returned to this Dostoevskian manner.*

His novel, *Una vita*, had been finished a year or two before, and towards the end of 1892 he had it published at his own expense by the small Triestine firm of Ettore Vram. (It was postdated 1893.) His father had died in the spring of the same year, and this perhaps had something to do with his decision to publish. It received one or two kind reviews in the local press (together with some sharp remarks about his faulty Italian), but it was almost completely ignored by the Italian literary world. The only Italian paper to review it was the *Corriere della Sera* of Milan, whose reviewer, Domenico Oliva, reproved Svevo for borrowing the title of Maupassant's *Une vie*† but said that for all its faults it revealed a 'clear-eyed observer' and that it wasn't a novel 'from a first comer'. The most extensive critique it received (but this was much later) was in a letter from Paul Heyse. Heyse, who had been one of the leading figures in the literary circle formed by Maximilian II in Munich, was well known as an italophile (which was no doubt why Svevo sent him the book), but all the same he was the last man to have liked a novel so impregnated with Zola and Flaubert, being bitterly engaged in a rearguard action against the current trends and indeed being the arch-enemy of Naturalism and 'scientific materialism' in art. His letter was what might have been expected.

Munich, 19 June 1897.

. . . this novel falls into the same mistake as almost all the Italian novels I have read in the last ten years. I find such a profusion of words in it that it could easily be reduced by half without injuring anything essential, eliminating superfluous details and endless repetitions; and further, you haven't yet realised the necessity for subordinating the secondary figures so as to bring the principal ones into relief. You are tireless in describing the most insignificant

---

* Though the story 'Il Malocchio', about a young man with the evil eye, published in *Corto viaggio*, has affinities with the earlier story.

† Svevo later said he hadn't heard of Maupassant's novel at the time.

procedures of life at the bank. The secondary figures are developed with as much loving care as the leading ones, as if what you were aiming at was a scientific exercise *à la* Zola.

And what is more to the point, the hero of your novel is so weak, so insignificant, that occupying oneself so persistently with him and his *milieu*, analysing his minutest feelings, his thoughts, his soul, seem not really worth the trouble. If, despite that, I read your book to the end it is because, notwithstanding these defects, which may be attributed to a false artistic theory on the part of modern naturalism, I found in it a serious research after truth and a consistent devotion to psychological problems. If you were to choose a theme which would allow you to apply these gifts to a happier and more significant subject-matter, and would keep a severer control over your narrative, you would certainly win a place among the best novelists of the day.

The letter wasn't unperceptive from Heyse's own standpoint, though of course he missed the very thing which made the novel so original as far as Italian fiction was concerned, i.e. precisely the choice of a 'weak' and 'insignificant' bourgeois hero. However, by the time he received the letter, Svevo had already written a new novel, dealing with an equally 'insignificant' hero, so he was in no danger of being influenced by Heyse's advice. Meanwhile the first edition of *Una vita* gradually sold out, with the aid of numerous presentation copies. Vram advised against a further printing, and the book was soon quietly forgotten.

Svevo's mother died three years later, in October 1895. The date of her death took on a symbolic significance for him. He had always been fascinated by the calendar (and appears to have celebrated his own birthday once a month), and he was in the habit of searching it for a propitious day, one presenting a particularly happy numerical combination of dates, on which to give up smoking for ever. This was a lifelong preoccupation for him, as it was for the hero of *La coscienza di Zeno*. From now on, the day, the hour and the minute of his mother's death became a cult for him, a daily opportunity for beginning the new life. In a diary which he kept during his engagement there is an entry which keeps recurring, sometimes after a reference to smoking, sometimes unexplained: 'ore 4-7 m. pom.' ('seven minutes past four in the afternoon').

Svevo in 1895 thought of himself as a confirmed bachelor, a life-weary *enfant du siècle* without the will for anything beyond short-lived and mercenary liaisons. Some time in the 1890s he had had the long and serio-comic affair with a working-class girl which lies behind his second novel *Senilità*; she was called Giuseppina Zergol, and later became a circus equestrienne. Benco relates how he met Svevo, a year or two after his affair with her, at a performance of *Carmen*. In the interval before the third act (the one in which Carmen breaks faith with Don José) Svevo said to him 'Now I am going to suffer', and began to tell him the story of his affair with Giuseppina and the wild career of jealousy it led him—how he stood whole nights, in the snow and icy *bora*,* watching the door of a house where he thought she might be with another man, cursing himself all the time for his slavery to this 'worthless' creature. *Senilità* was actually conceived during the affair and Giuseppina was the first to read it, as he wrote some of the earlier chapters for her instruction. (This idea of a lover justifying a liaison on 'educational' grounds became a favourite comic theme with him in his later writing.)

One of the effects of his mother's death was to put it into into his mind that he might get married. At his mother's death-bed he had been touched by a little gesture which had been made to him by a cousin of his, Livia Veneziani. Noticing him in great distress at the sight of his mother's agonies, she had brought him a glass of marsala. The action somehow stuck in his mind and, according to him, put it into his head to fall in love with her. Livia was thirteen years

* Trieste is famous for its *bora*, a peculiarly nasty Alpine wind. There are several varieties of *bora*: the *borino*, the white *bora* and the dreaded black *bora*, which practically paralyses the city and has been known to blow horses and trains into the sea.

younger than himself, and he had known her from her childhood, her maternal grandfather, Giuseppe Moravia, having been an uncle of Svevo's (his mother's brother). Her father, Gioachino Veneziani, was a Jewish-Italian industrialist who manufactured submarine paint (the 'Moravia anti-fouling composition'). The firm was a thriving one, with connections in Austria, Italy, France and England, and the family lived in fairly lavish style in a large house out at Servola, a suburb of Trieste, next to the parent factory. Her parents had left Trieste for Marseilles for some years to get away from Livia's dictatorial Austrian grandmother, Fanny Moravia, but they had returned there when she was eleven and she had then been sent to convent school. She had met Svevo again at his father's deathbed in 1892 and soon became intimate with the Schmitz family, coming twice a week to the house in the Corsa Stadion* to teach French to Svevo's nephew. Svevo and she had developed a mildly flirtatious friendship. They once made a bargain that if he gave up smoking for three months she should give him a kiss. He at once began to cheat, with his sisters' connivance, but on settlement day he took his kiss. Next day he sent her an expensively-bound copy of Manzoni with an inscription: 'For cousin Livia: a testimony to her goodness of heart in wanting, though failing, to help me in my struggle with vice; but also a testimony to a piece of cunning of my own, of the two the nobler action. Trieste, 13-1-1895.'

Within a month of his mother's death, and no doubt partly out of an unconscious wish to replace her, Svevo made a formal proposal for Livia through her parents. Her mother, Olga, refused to hear of it, having grander plans for Livia, and forbade him to speak about it to Livia herself. However she found out, accepted him, and argued her parents into submission. They got engaged in December.

During his engagement Svevo kept a diary, intended for

* The Schmitz family had moved from the via dell' Acquedotto to the nearby Corsa Stadion (no. 18). The house is now via Battisti 22.

Livia's eyes (it was written in a keepsake album, decorated with sentimental quotations from the German poets, which Livia had been given by a schoolfriend). It is odd to compare this document with *Senilità*. In the novel he follows out the wild distractions and neurotic paradoxes of the hero's affair with his working-class mistress with superlative lucidity and a wonderful, detached comic irony. With his engagement to Livia, he is back in the vortex like his hero Emilio, half enjoying the spectacle of his own paradoxes but half genuinely tortured and driven. Indeed, the diary did what it was intended to. He laid himself out in it like a patient with his analyst. Part of the time he is the analyst himself, part of the time the patient projecting a mother-son relationship on to Livia, acting the child who is deliberately naughty so that he can be punished. He is determined to try everything out on her. He begins gaily:

> . . . When I gave you that first kiss, I did it quite coolly, like someone signing a contract. When I gave you the second, I did it with an enormous desire to analyse you and myself, but in fact I could analyse nothing, I could understand nothing; some timidity still inhibited me. With the third kiss, and all the later ones, I felt at last I was holding in my arms the sweet girl I had been looking for, the desire of what remained of my youth. (*Vita*, p. 40)

He starts exploring his perversities. He only enjoys her when he is making her unhappy: 'There is no more intimate relationship than between the person who suffers and the person who causes suffering'. He wants to hurt her. He wants to be like her (calm, natural, loving, healthy). He wants to be her. He wants to eat her. 'My wife is a bon-bon', he writes in a sort of prose-poem, 'and I am hoping that by eating it my bad teeth will be made better. . . . All the parts that my teeth and my old stomach cannot consume will be left unharvested, created in vain, tormenting me, who have to stand guard over them.' Equally, he wants to alter her, though the discovery scandalises him:

It was a leading feature of my own character up to now to let all others around me behave and develop according to their own nature. Any interference on my part would have seemed a crime to me. I wanted to observe such manifestations like a connoisseur; if possible, actually to encourage them, so that the words or actions of the person, whoever he was, should achieve their own perfection; I even managed to put up with annoyance if I could leave others their liberty. My own closest friends called it tolerance; in fact it was something else, an imperative feeling of duty. So where you are concerned, I ought to feel the same duty, or so it seems to me; I oughtn't to want to alter your character to impose mine on it. I shouldn't try to stop it from developing in whatever way it likes. . . . But it's no good my saying so. I spend my whole time deciding to tell you I don't like you like that, I want you like this. I feel quite humiliated by it; through you I'm losing the quality I most prized myself for. (*Diario per la fidanzata*, 1962, pp. 85-6)

They begin to have quarrels. He makes a joke to her, the point of which is that the only thing to which he is not entirely indifferent is cigarettes. She is upset, and he defends his old Schopenhauerian attitude.

My indifference towards life is still there: even when I'm by your side enjoying myself, there is something inside me that isn't sharing my enjoyment and that says to me: 'Watch out, it's not as you think it is, it's all a comedy, the curtain will come down in the end. Besides, indifference towards life is the essence of my intellectual life. Whatever's worth-while in my own talk comes from irony, and I'm afraid lest the very day you managed to make me believe in life (but you never will) I should find myself diminished by doing so. I'd almost beg you—almost—to leave me as I am. I have a great fear of happiness making me stupid. (*Diario per la fidanzata*, 1962, p. 49)

Then, in spite of his cherished 'indifference', he gets wildly jealous when a man catches her eye in the café and she returns his glance. His prospective mother-in-law, Olga, says something to upset him, and he starts imagining the family look down on him socially. He makes a scene with Livia, sulkily demanding permission to go and find a mistress; she refuses, and he thanks her for doing so. He is smoking like a Turk and renouncing cigarettes more often than ever. He can't sleep, and his 'frogs' (his name for his neurotic doubts and fears) give him no rest. And all the same he is enjoying himself a good deal. 'During these days', he writes, 'I passed from one extreme to another. The extreme of rancour and misery in that moment when I sat there in the carriage full of despair, and the extreme of sweet and serene tranquillity at the moment I was writing you that diatribe.' By the time of the last entries in the diary in the following March, he has set the pattern of their relationship, and of the regular cycle of his own feelings towards her, for ever.

Meanwhile Livia was superbly mild, forgiving and unruffled, as she was almost always to be. And Svevo, for most of the time, threw himself gaily into his new role. He would arrive at Servola on his bicycle, bringing bottles of iced coffee, ready to spend the afternoon playing nursery games such as puss-in-the-corner with Livia and her sisters. He read Goethe's *Italian Elegies* with her. He also took to weight-lifting, for his health—'my one prop from the physical point of view'. The Venezianis' objections to him were overcome, and only one serious problem remained, apart from the ones Svevo kept inventing: Livia was a practising Catholic, whilst Svevo was a non-practising and freethinking Jew and thoroughly disliked the idea of a church wedding. They argued about the problem for months and Livia eventually unhappily resigned herself to a civil marriage. They were married in July 1896, and Olga arranged a slap-up reception.

4

The Business Man

Livia was Olga's favourite daughter, and under her persuasion it was decided that Svevo and Livia should set up house in the Villa Veneziani, where they and a cook occupied three rooms on the second floor. (They moved downstairs five years later to make a common household with the parents-in-law.)

The house at Servola had originally belonged to Olga's mother and had been enlarged and done up in opulent *nouveau riche* style by Gioachino. On the ground floor there was a spacious dining-room, complete with stained glass windows and Russian stag's-horn chandeliers, leading into a large music-room, in eighteenth-century Venetian style with plasterwork to Gioachino's own designs; this was used for receptions. Beyond it lay the verandah (more stained glass, and Murano-crystal chandeliers) and the terrace, overlooking spacious gardens and a bowling-green. The upper floors, after various extensions, were large enough to house several families with their own servants. It was the only house of its kind in this area of factories and dockyards, and the factory was only a few steps away, so that it was always under the eye of Gioachino or Olga. There was a great deal of coming and going of nieces and cousins, and a regular Sunday afternoon reception, sometimes with a hundred or more guests.

Gioachino Veneziani, the founder of the Veneziani enterprise, was a tall, calm, imposing-looking figure, with bushy black eyebrows and flowing Garibaldiesque white beard and moustaches. In his youth he had been a kind of natural genius, with a gift for all sorts of handicrafts and a natural flair for chemistry. When he was still a young man, and working for his father-in-law Giuseppe Moravia, who ran a chemicals firm, he had invented the 'Moravia anti-fouling composition', an anti-vegetative and anti-corrosive paint for the keels of ships, and this became the basis of his fortune. He set up his own factory to manufacture it, and by the 1890s he was supplying navies and private customers all over the world (the navies of Italy, Austria, Britain, the U.S.A., Russia, Japan, Turkey, Greece and the Argentine all used his products). He was a man of grandiose ideas and was known in the family as 'The Masterbuilder' because of his passion for ruinous building schemes. He also dabbled in country life and in farming, and when he went to Russia for the wedding of his daughter Fausta he insisted on bringing back a string of horses. In his heyday he had been an energetic and ebullient character, but when he was forty-five or so he had a serious illness, after which he gradually grew indolent, with a tendency to moroseness. The real force in the firm and the household from this time on was his wife Olga, a little, wiry, bustling woman of intense nervous energy. Her mother, an Austrian Catholic, had been very severe with her as a child—so much so that once, at the age of five, she packed up all her dolls and left home in protest—and she had grown up immensely masterful and self-reliant, not to say domineering. She had her hand in everything; she ran her own children and their families and she ran the workmen in the factory. In later years she had a telephone-exchange in her bedroom, connecting her with all the various families in the house. Orders streamed forth from it night and day: 'It was pure Orwell,' a friend of Svevo's said later. Olga was known as the best business man in Trieste. Nicola Bravin, who was foreman of the Veneziani factory in England for many years, described her to the present writer as 'a woman in a million', and said that for years after her death he never passed a week without dreaming of her. (The dreams stopped, for some reason, when he began receiving his pension.) Svevo often dreamed about her too: for instance in January 1901 he had a dream of her exhibiting the whole family in a menagerie. He was nervous of her, as many people were, and treated her with elaborate courtesy, grumbling a good deal about her to Livia behind her back. It was plain she intended to run him too, and for a time he made himself miserable trying to resist the process. In the end he more or less resigned himself to it, and got on very well with her, though he always reserved a special note of rueful alarm and irony for referring to 'the dragon'. She herself always said she liked him but found him a 'difficult' man.

As for Livia, she was obviously the source, in many particulars, of all the wife-figures in Svevo's novels and stories. She was a handsome woman when she married him, fair-skinned, green-eyed, with the magnificent blonde hair which Joyce later celebrated: blonde in her appearance, blonde in her sentiments too, Svevo said, though she had a rather deep and harsh voice out of character with all this blondeness. She was mild, loving, literal, religious in a convent-educated way, responsive to Svevo's feelings and quite impervious to his ideas. On the whole she was perfectly happy to let him go his own way, and, like the favourite child of wealthy parents, rather good at going hers. When she wanted to go to a spa, there was a fuss, since he would be jealous and, at least in the early days, would be worried about the cost; but somehow she always went. When he objected to her buying expensive things for the house, she took his objections seriously, after which he began to see much reason in her point of view.

On the first anniversary of their marriage, Livia by now being pregnant, they had themselves photographed (Livia's condition being concealed for the occasion by a photographer's balustrade) and Svevo wrote a commentary on the photograph, entitled 'Family Chronicle'. It was meant for her eyes, but hits off one aspect of her accurately.

. . . The woman, obviously blonde, who has the honour to be photographed at my side, was called Livia Fausta Veneziani and now, since a year ago precisely, she is my wife. I am bound to say I am astonished that she should be. She takes everything seriously; Maria the cook, her husband, life itself. . . . Even after a year of marriage she still does so. Her husband—why, of course, the father of her children. And the same with all the rest of her relations. Her mother is 'she to whom we owe our life', her father ditto, and then in him there is also mamma's lord and master and the head of the household. She may not realise it, but in this respect I don't think she has yet reached the French Revolution, and a *lettre de cachet*, signed with proper paternal authority, would be no surprise to her. After all, it's the king! An honour, really, to be locked up by the king! . . . Thus the world is a beautiful ideal construction where everyone has his role and must respect the role of others. As a sociologist my wife is no evolutionist; for her it's all quite simple; people change, but the roles remain the same. And there is no 'social contract' either: the roles were created with their occupiers already in possession.

After all this, it can be seen how seriously my wife takes life itself. She fills her roles one after the other with perfect punctiliousness. I am sure that even as a baby she must have had a certain dignity. For of course the function of a baby was to be sick, to scream in the night and to have illnesses. Duties came later; and as far as I know there never was a time when my wife didn't know her house-clothes from her outdoor clothes or know that she shouldn't even stand at the garden door in her indoor clothes or waste a moment in taking off her outdoor ones when she got home.

I think that that serious life of hers must have been neatly divided into periods, each with its appropriate joys and sorrows; so that whenever she sees someone younger than her, she remembers what she was like at that period. It gives her an extraordinary sense of justice. Even she once experienced the pleasure of disobeying, of breaking things to see what they're like inside, of dancing and yelling and rampaging. . . .

'When I was like that' she is always saying, without regret. There's another thing I can't understand, her having no regret for the past. I can only think she is so fair to the present she can put it side by side with the past as if there were no difference between them. You might think this was indifference, and in fact it's the most absolute and inexplicable *joie de vivre*. (*Vita*, pp. 51-3)

Livia was intensely devoted to Svevo and he, whether or not he was always faithful to her, was quite as devoted to Livia. She was 'la mia bionda, l'unica mia grande, grande speranza di vera, solida felicità' (the cadence is not really translatable—'my blonde, my sole and great, great hope of true, solid happiness'). She was the fixed point his life came to revolve round; and he never stopped being jealous of her, and imagining what it would be like to lose her. One of the favourite forms of his jealousy, almost as soon as he was engaged to her, was picturing her behaviour at and after his own death. This fantasy already occurs in the *Diario per la fidanzata* ('Diary for my Bethrothed'). He has been to pay his last respects to the corpse of a dead friend, and it has made him think about his own death. He sees himself on his death-bed, hearing Livia weeping in the next room, and guesses that her tears are shed more for life and the future than for his own death. She is *thinking*, not suffering, intensely.

He always insisted that she must marry again after he was dead, and in a little comic sketch called *Livia* he pictured the whole scene of her remarriage. He has been dead for six months, and Olga and Livia agree it is time she accepted her new suitor—a tall, handsome man with magnificent teeth and the most un-*fin-de-siécle* moustaches. She tells him she has always been attracted to him—or if not *quite* at first, then only because she was already engaged. To her surprise he obviously believes her—Ettore wouldn't have done. Olga leaves the room, and the suitor gives her a kiss (Ettore's ghost groans protestingly from the door-hinges). 'Your past belongs to you,' says the suitor, stroking his moustaches imposingly; 'but I want to be told about it, if you please.' She tells him about K.; he says nothing. She tells him about M., and he laughs. Finally she begins to tell him about Ettore himself, and at once he interrupts her. 'I'm not worried about *him*' he says (the door screeches piteously). 'Your mother has already told me you only took him out of pity.' She stares at him, but doesn't protest, reflecting that it's all for the best. So poor Ettore has to die twice over.

During their engagement Svevo hopefully gave her Schopenhauer, Marx and Bebel to read, but she never opened them. (She did sometimes read French novels, though the Abbé Prévost's *Manon Lescaut* shocked her. 'And he a clergyman!') The volume by Bebel (*Woman and Socialism*) was meant to expound Svevo's own views about marriage as a 'free Socialist union'. Nothing could have been further from Livia's ideas, and for Svevo himself it was only half serious, and half simply a remembered role, like his famous 'indifference'. (In another mood he took the opposite standpoint and praised the 'dear, good bourgeoisie' which made her indissolubly his.) There was an exchange of letters between them on the subject in 1900, in which he tried to excuse his petty day-to-day jealousies by the formal offer of her freedom should her happiness one day demand it. She firmly refused the offer. And their letters are so characteristic that I will quote them in full.

Trieste, 17 June 1900.

My dear, my kind, my sweet fair one,

I have just got up after a long, refreshing sleep. I dreamed that you were dead and had been laid on my bed in your coffin. You have no idea how happy I felt this morning seeing the sunlight and knowing that you were still alive after all, even if at Salsomaggiore. The dream must have been over in a moment, a fraction of a second. The coffin was dark and you were all shining inside it. The only occupants of the room were you, dead and motionless, with your eyes shut and your mouth obstinately set; your mother, who was running to and fro (even in a dream she couldn't keep still), bringing flowers to strew your corpse; and myself, studying your face, which bore a look of reproof, as if I hadn't brought enough joy into the life that had been entrusted to me. Your mother was bustling about as she does in the office. She kept arranging your great floods of golden hair round your stiff body. I thought: 'Why does she bother?' But in fact she was enjoying you quite as much as if you were still alive. I woke up overjoyed at being able to hope I could be the one to die first. I am still full of the sweet feeling it gave me and want to share it with you. I'm all alone in the house and shall give up the whole afternoon to my letter. I wouldn't go out, though it was Sunday, so that I could write it. I think I must have dreamed about your death several times before (you know how the idea of death is always in my mind), but never as vividly as this. I am glad of the dream now, as I am of anything which reminds me of the joy of possessing you. Possessing you fully and legally. But fairly, rightly, I wonder? No, it's plain I never should have married you. Today of all days, when I feel so close to you, I realise that the remains of youth which I have to offer you weren't meant for such intensities. The first few days you were away I had my old dream of what I would do when you got back, how I would take you, lie beside you, exhaust every force and passion on you. Now, today, I would like you near me just to take you by the hand and let you sleep, willing you to sleep deeply, to be refreshed, to get better once and for all. I agree with Tolstoy (even he only arrived at this opinion in old age) that the easiest relationship is the one between brother and sister. Admit it—I would be an excellent brother. You don't know what sacrifices I would make to save you unhappiness. How could you, seeing that when the jealous husband takes over I breathe fire and slaughter? So your husband is your enemy, the husband who fails to give you what is due to you and contrives to do you out of the mildest enjoyment you might get from your own beauty. All in all, I am a poor neurotic delinquent, and it makes me unhappier sometimes than you can imagine. When you are home again I want to see if I can't have more control of myself. I have no hopes, and neither have you, that I can do so on the matter of jealousy . . . only that's the very point where I most want to. But it's no good. It's exactly those little pleasures I have been talking about that I'm always going to rob you of. But instead, I make you this formal promise. I deny you those little pleasures of vanity which the mother of Titina [nickname of their daughter Letizia] can cheerfully renounce, but I promise you formally that if ever life offers you a great opportunity of happiness, one of those a young woman might give up peace, virtue, conscience and life itself for, I shall know how, granted that I have your full confession (you know I tolerate everything except lies) to put you in the way of having it. Having made this declaration, which ought to make you feel freer, my conscience is easier. What it amounts to is, I deny you the right to trifle with your life and mine, but I don't forbid you to turn your back on them altogether if something should make it worth while. Indeed, I will hear your confession like a father and we will discuss the situation to see how it can be made to cause you the least possible suffering. Not a single stupid word of rebuke. You wouldn't want me to kiss you any longer, and I wouldn't try to.

Only like this, it seems to me, can our marriage be a free Socialist union. You are to stay with me just as long as you feel you should. Pay no attention to my silly petty jealousies; they will always be over silly petty things. I promise you by all that's dear to me you won't have to put up with a single harsh word if you make me a confession about something involving not your vanity but your happiness. I know this is sincere and comes from my deepest convictions. Only on those terms is it right to own a woman as young as yourself.

Meanwhile I kiss and embrace you with the old love, both the pure and the impure. I don't think I shall have to ask the same liberty from you. Yours as long as you want me,

Ettore*

Salso, 19 June 1900, 2 p.m.

My beloved,

Your letter of Sunday morning breathes the deepest and sweetest love and makes me very proud and very happy; but it also expresses a harsh philosophy.

No doubt you have all the qualities to make you a good brother, but you are also a very good husband. Believe me, my dearest, I have not suffered half as much from your jealousy as I have been given pleasure, exquisite pleasure, by your kindness and goodness to me. I am grateful to you from the depths of my heart and I bless you a thousand times over, thanking God for you.

I utterly refuse the freedom you so generously offer me. I am bound to you by very strong and very sweet links which nothing

* *Lettere alla moglie*, Trieste, 1963, pp. 244-7.

will ever break now; I gave myself to you out of love, and I will never withdraw the gift. I thank you for all that you have given me and that you think of as so little—that ardent love which your very jealousy proves to me, that brotherly tenderness, that intense and sweet friendship which links us and will never perish and on which I mean to lean for the rest of my life. Don't think which of us will die first; let us hope we can die together, so as not to feel the agony of parting.

My beauty (if it exists), and my youth, are for you alone; enjoy them to the full, in perfect confidence. It is not merely Letizia's mother, it is your wife, my dearest, who cheerfully renounces her little pleasures of vanity. If I am beautiful, I want to be so for you, for you alone. I want to spare *you* every kind of worry and pain too. In a word, I love you, and I refuse the freedom that you give me.

Believe me, all the sweet emotion you felt in writing to me found an echo in my own heart and made me feel closer to you than ever.

Au revoir, my beloved husband, my dear brother, my sweetest friend, I kiss you—full of the tenderest feeling—with my whole heart, and I wish I could give you a thousand times as much happiness as I am able to.

Yours for ever,
the faithful Livia*

In September 1897 Livia gave birth to a daughter, whom they named Letizia, in imitation of Svevo's mother's name Allegra. As a result of the birth Livia fell seriously ill and with the thought of an early death in her mind she became more and more disturbed at her sin in having married a Jew. Finally, Svevo, on an impulse (or, according to another account,† at the suggestion of their family doctor) said to her: 'You accept the idea of having a Jewish husband? Well then, I'll make you a present in return. I'll get baptised!' Livia began to recover almost at once. 'My poor wife, still suffering from fever, received the news with such joy', Svevo told Marie-Anne Commène, that 'I have never troubled to decide

* *Vita*, pp. 61-2. Livia, as always, wrote in French, the language of her schooldays.

† Marie-Anne Commène, 'Italo Svevo', in *Europe*, Sept. 1960, p. 114.

SVEVO WITH THE PAINTER VERUDA, 1892

SVEVO AT THE EPOCH OF *UNA VITA*
A photograph taken by Veruda

whether it was the Jewish God or the Christian who performed the miracle.' He went along to a priest and began his religious instruction, but finding it impossible to learn the catechism he gave the priest an ultimatum: 'Either I get baptised without learning from memory, or I don't get baptised.' The priest baptised him on his own terms, and when Livia was sufficiently recovered she and Svevo had a church wedding.*

In the following May, when Livia was well enough to travel, she was sent to a spa at Salsomaggiore, near Parma; it was the first time she and Svevo had been parted, and it was the occasion of a quarrel, one which stirred up all the doubts and fears Svevo had rehearsed during their engagement. He wrote to her nearly every day of the month that she was away, and the letters go through the whole spiral of jealousy, fury, self-doubt, despair, and laughter at himself.

The quarrel began before she set off for Salsomaggiore. He had remarked during the day that, of course, a wife going to a spa alone would want to live in the quietest possible manner; and in the evening he watched her pack. He got a nasty surprise. Livia was putting in all her jewellery and smartest clothes and had obviously been looking forward to the trip. He made a scene, but then backed down, remembering her state of health. However the whole thing broke out afresh and more violently a few days later when he suggested that he should come and join her in Salso, and she replied 'Olga ne serait pas satisfaite de nous voir jeter l'argent' ('Olga would not approve of our throwing money away'). It was a fatal remark, for it reminded him that Olga had helped pay for the trip, and that in fact he had had to be a bit disingenuous to get her to do so (he made Livia tell her mother that the doctor was in favour of her going, not mentioning that they had already decided to take his advice). He immediately saw himself in other people's power, a poor man humiliated by his

* Information from Svevo's daughter.

wife's rich family, an elderly husband (he was thirty-seven) unable to look after his young and desirable wife. He told her that if he had ever thought of coming to Salso, he would never do so now. He wanted to give Olga back her 300 lire. He pictured Livia surrounded by would-be seducers. He heard his brother-in-law Pepi Vivante saying that the doctor had ordered his wife to Carlsbad, which of course meant that he (Pepi) must go too, giving up a trip of his own elsewhere—and he drew the parallel. Bursting with his chagrin, he told Gioachino the whole story, and Gioachino took his side, though he obviously thought the whole thing rather a joke.

As always, his feelings fluctuated wildly. One day he had gone to lunch with his sister Paola at their old home, feeling cheerful and hungry.

Someone made a harmless little joke, and I joined in; but a moment later I felt as if I were being throttled. I stopped eating and threw myself down on the sofa, completely exhausted, as if from struggling with things and people too big for me. (*Lettere alla moglie*, Trieste, 1963, p. 60)

As he was walking the street, one day, guiltily reading his latest letter from Livia, in which she told him she had received his own quarrelsome one, he was jostled by a young man. He ran after him, and though the young man turned out to be an elderly grizzled Englishman, he challenged him to a duel. However, he couldn't find a second who spoke English, and anyway he discovered that duels were beyond his means—'Imagine, the minimum you can have a duel for in Trieste, taking one thing with another, is 200 florins'.

Livia's absence, in fact, had left him thoroughly disoriented:

And to think there was a time when I got on quite well without you. I am suffocating with desire—with *angry* desire; I keep thinking with absolute rage of those little yellow boots which you would never put on, or at least not when with me, so that you could have them *nagelneu* when you went to Salso. (*Ibid.*, p. 35)

As a revenge, he announced to her, he had even considered going out and finding a woman:

You should know—I can tell you now—that though it may not have appeared so from my letters, I was already nursing a grudge against you before you left. Well then! Seeing that I couldn't put my bitterness into my letters, it struck me it would be an excellent revenge, a real outlet for so much unhappiness and bile, to work off my desires (which had already been accumulating) on another woman. I did nothing about it when the time came, but merely out of disgust, and for no other reason. I had the desire, I had the motive (I told myself that the proper revenge for what I regarded as your crimes would be a crime on my part), and all the same I did nothing . . . I even knew where to find a desirable woman, at least one whom others think so, and still I did nothing. (*Ibid.*, p. 69)

So she need never worry about his fidelity again. As soon as she has come home he will be able to relapse once and for all into senility, the only proper way of life for him. 'If I didn't try to be unfaithful to you this time, I never shall. I envy you; for so long as you only love me, you will never have to experience jealousy.' This was too much for Livia. For once, she lost her temper and sent him a furious reply:

Salso, 29 May, 1898.

. . . I have received your letter of the 27th and it would have been better for me if I had never done so. I will come to the point at once. I am not of the jealous type, you say! But as I told you the other day, if I find you have been unfaithful to me, beware! I will never be yours again for the rest of my life. Here was I, thinking only of being back home and in your arms, suffering like a dog at living here without you; and to punish me for my sins and revenge yourself for a crime I haven't committed you are ready to break your plighted faith; you have got as far as desiring another woman, a woman you know, a woman you find attractive. It's too much. I tell you; you want to drive me to extremes. Well, try it then. . . .

She doesn't know where to have him at all, she says. His whole behaviour during her stay in Salso has been so extraordinary. She had still secretly been hoping, after all their discussion, that he would come to Salso after all. She had imagined how she would suddenly see him as she came down to the restaurant, and would fall on his neck with a cry of joy. Well, he has made her cry all right, but not with joy, and she prays to God for help.

The immediate, and baseless, quarrel with Livia was in fact merely the focus for various worries and uncertainties. For one thing, he was worried about money. He was just about able to support Livia on his salary from the bank, together with what he could earn by giving classes in commercial correspondence at the Revoltella Institute; but things weren't easy, and he had been having some unsuccessful flutters on the stock exchange. In February 1898 he was making jokes about his imminent ruin. 'Everyone bullies me, everyone tramples on me', he wrote in one of his non-smoking covenants, 'and meanwhile I go on making a fool of myself. I lose money on the Exchange; I smoke—in short, I am ruining myself in health, in pocket, as a husband, as a father, as an illiterate clerk. So it is time to put an end to this. I now, at the height of desperation swear that today, 4 p.m., 27 February 1898, I finally give up smoking. If I am to be ruined, at least I want it not to be my own fault.' In March he drew up another covenant:

In three years I have lost about 1,000 florins on the Exchange. So I suppose it is time to stop speculating; but how can I, if it means writing all that off as lost forever? I have therefore decided to act in the following manner: smoking costs me at least 40 florins a year. Giving up smoking would thus produce a saving of F. 200
Wine, over five years, would come to another F. 200
Coffee, over five years, would come to F. 100

F. 500

So as not to do things by halves, I hereby promise, in order to recoup the whole sum lost in this shameful way, to do without tobacco, coffee and wine for the next ten years! Adopting this plan, I can forget about chasing after those wretched lost shillings and pence. 7 March 1898——7 March 1908

Four p.m.

Signed: The valiant Ettore Schmitz

Apart from his stock exchange losses, he was having from time to time to give financial help to Adolfo, who was carrying on the family business, and he began to consider the idea of leaving the bank and setting up in business on his own account, with Adolfo as a partner. It was not easy to see where they would get the capital, unless from a moneylender, and friends were not very encouraging about the scheme, partly because it seemed reasonable to suppose Svevo's father-in-law might soon be offering him a job, and partly, he suspected, because they didn't have much faith in his talents as a business man. He himself had doubts about them, and was inclined to bluster accordingly: 'I am amazed that you think I would be taking any risk in leaving the bank', he wrote to Livia in May. '. . . If I can have my liberty, I hope never to have to depend on anyone else again. My decision is irrevocable. Only the absolute impossibility of putting it into practice could make me think of being dependent on the *signor cavaliere** any longer.'

In the middle of these plans, a friend of Svevo's called Halperson, who had got him to act as guarantor for a loan, absconded to America, leaving Svevo to face the creditor. This was a serious blow to Svevo (it took him a year or more to pay off all that was owing) and some time in May or early June, when the situation was still fluid, he was writing in some distress to Livia:

I tell you, if the Halperson affair really turns out to be true, which I still can't quite believe, it will paralyse all my plans, all my faith in human character. You realise that even if I pay, which won't be at all easy, I am still going to be a public laughing-stock? How am

* Fortunato Vivante, see p. 24.

I going to get back the faith in my own ability which I shall need if I'm to be independent?

Behind the financial troubles, however, there was a further cause of bitterness for Svevo in his present situation, for he couldn't help feeling he was being dragged further and further away from the only career he had ever really wanted, that of a writer. 'You know I never used to be envious of people's money or to want it myself', he wrote to Livia,

but lately, after certain events that I needn't remind you of, I have changed a good deal on this point. I am having to stand by and watch the end of all my aesthetic dreams, and when I think about it, it seems a bad business to me. If I ever live to be old, I think I may have to pay for doing injury to my inner being in this way—for betraying the ambition that for thirty-eight years I thought was mine by right. *Schwamm darüber*. Let's leave it at that. (*Lettere alla moglie*, Trieste, 1963, pp. 63-4)

The quarrel rumbled on throughout the correspondence. Livia's replies were almost always calm and loving. 'The love I am bringing you is still unchanged, and I am yours for ever', she wrote on the eve of her return home. 'Separation, which makes others grow fonder, will not do for us—especially not for you, who are so jealous. Let us hope this has been the last in our lifetime.' One thing Svevo was definite about. Livia was never going to go away alone again. Next year at the same time, however, she was back at Salsomaggiore, and the quarrel revived, though less violently. Livia's doctor at Salso diagnosed her as suffering from 'a secret chagrin', but she denied it and put her bad health down to the earthquake.*

In November of 1897 Svevo published his sole piece of political writing, a curious and rather brilliant little apologue called *La tribù* (*The Tribe*), imagining the arrival of capitalism among a tribe of nomads. (As it is rather hard to come

* Trieste has frequent mild earthquakes, the fag-end of those at Zagreb.

by, I have translated it as an Appendix.) It appeared in Milan, in the periodical *Critica Sociale*, having presumably been too Marxist in flavour for *L'Independente*, whose Socialism, in so far as it existed, was of the Mazzinian kind. Between June and September in the following year, however, *L'Independente* serialised Svevo's new novel *Senilità* (*As a Man Grows Older*), and it was published in book form (by Vram, like its predecessor) towards the end of the same year. It fell distinctly flatter even than *Una vita*, though according to Silvio Benco it was widely read in Trieste itself, so much so that circulating libraries had to buy extra copies. None of its three reviewers could see the point of the novel. The hero's character is not consistent, complains a reviewer in the Istrian journal *L'Idea Italiana*: Emilio, who ends up saying that he wanted to teach Angiolina virtue, began by teaching her vice. He wishes the author had chosen a better subject for his original style. Paul Heyse also wrote more repressively than before:

Munich, 26 November 1898

Signor Professore Ettore Schmitz,

I thank you, dear Sir, for your courtesy in sending me your second novel, which I read with the same interest as I did *Una vita*. I found the same skill in psychological analysis in it, the same acuteness of observation.

The only regret that I felt was that you should have wasted your talent on such a repulsive subject—you must feel this yourself—a young man wasting his insignificant life, quite without purpose, and then obstinately attaching himself—oscillating wretchedly between illusion and a sense of reality—to a strumpet, whom he then regrets losing for the rest of his life. The problem of a passion so strong as to overcome the profoundest disgust and to be at the same moment repellent and intoxicating, is certainly a subject for poetry. Turgenev has dealt with the theme most powerfully in his little story *Petrouchka*. But with the wearisome amount of detail in which you follow out the minutest workings of your hero's mind, our compassion for such a wretched weakling is soon overcome by our dislike of his morbid moral feebleness —all the more so in that the fate of his unhappy sister, who seeks a fatal relief for her frustrated need for love, gives an additional darkness to the novel. Is life so poor in love-problems among the sane and healthy that the poet has to search for his themes in pathological case-histories?

I should be happier seeing you in a purer ambience; not this suffocating atmosphere of decadence.

Sincerely your devoted

Paul Heyse

The disappointment, coming at that moment, was decisive. 'Write one must', he decided; 'what one needn't do is publish.' In the following May, Olga at last offered him a job in the family business (or rather firmly told him to take it), and he bowed to his fate, deciding to accept it with as good a grace as possible. He took the decision, a heroic one in his case, to give up writing altogether.

For some years he kept to his decision fairly strictly, writing nothing more substantial than odd fables and fragments of self-analysis—occasionally also a short play. At various periods he still kept a diary, and in one of them he noted down his renunciation:

December 1902. I am keeping this diary of my recent life without the least intention of publishing it. I, here and now and for ever, have eliminated that ridiculous and damnable thing called literature from my life. All I want to do in these pages is to get to know myself better. The disease of all such helpless persons as myself, of not being able to think without a pen in our hand (as if thought weren't equally needed at the moment of action), makes this exercise necessary. So once again, the pen, poor rigid instrument, will help me to plumb the obscure depths of my being. That done, I shall throw it away for ever, and shall learn to think even in the midst of action, running from an enemy or pursuing him, with my hand raised to hit or to ward off blows. (*Vita*, p. 66)

Once he thought about writing at all, he said, he became incapable of doing anything else. He did not give up writing, he said afterwards, merely out of pique at not achieving fame: 'I was afraid that it would prevent me from doing the work that had been imposed on me for my own good and for the good of my friends and colleagues. It was a question of honesty, for it was plain that if I wrote or read a single line, my work was ruined for a week.'

By 1900 he was already feeling nostalgic about his literary life, as something belonging to his past:

I went into town at 10.30 and passed the rest of the morning with Veruda, Luzzatto and Urbano Nonno from Venice. For once in a way, I talked about art again, or rather listened to them talking; it was like a cool drink on a scorching summer's day. All the same, how distant from them I felt.

As an antidote to literature he took up the violin and spent endless, not very fruitful, hours practising. He never played at all well, and after a time got worse rather than better. 'If you begin learning the violin before you are forty the bow becomes an extension of your arm, but with me it was always just something badly attached to it.'

At Trieste I was able to organise an amateur quartet—a cellist in the very top flight, a first violin who was a brilliant sight-reader, a viola who was profoundly musical. The second violin (myself) was the most hard-working and the least successful. There is a great affection between quartet-players; so much so that when I played out of tune, turning the whole quartet into a nest of screeching serpents, no one looked in my direction. I withdrew into myself and, like a serpent, looked for my tail to bite it. A beautiful thing, friendship! (*Saggi*, p. 187)

One gets the impression he deliberately allowed his playing to be tenth-rate, so that there should be no doubt in his mind that it was a second-best, a cure, not a substitute, for writing. It was like life itself: one was always learning, and never got any better. And like smoking, it provided an excellent pretext for day-dreaming.

There was another reason why I got such wretched results from all my efforts . . . My mind was elsewhere. Every day I covered miles of ground with my bow, but a bow is not like a motor-car, with which, when there's an accident, everyone notices. Every time I travelled the same road I crashed in the same place . . . I could scrape away and play wrong notes and never suffer a scratch. (*Ibid.*, pp. 185-6)

He once wrote a little parable for his fellow-players, explaining the psychology of a second violin, tacitly associating it with his own failure as a writer.

Remember, I beg you, that for various reasons the three instruments are always on a level: the viola and the cello because of their tone, and the first violin because the limelight is always on him; meanwhile the second violin works away to support the others and no-one is aware of him unless he makes unpleasant noises. He is like a man's collar and tie; nobody notices them unless they're untidy. There he is, working away peacefully in the dark like an owl or a mole. But during every quartet there comes a certain moment when the poor mole, for a bar or two, has to come into the limelight and lead the others. He is all alone. The whole performance is in his hands. The bright light dazzles and frightens him. Not surprisingly, just when the greatest effort is demanded of him, he fails miserably. (*Ibid.*, p. 188)

Apparently they were kinder to him after reading it.

The Veneziani firm had recently set up a branch factory in Italy, to enable them to supply the Italian navy. It was located at Murano, beside the Serenella lagoon, in what had originally been a monastery. The procedure, as later with the factory in England, was for one of the family to go there from time to time, as orders accumulated, to take on casual labour and to produce enough paint for the next few months' commitments. It had to be a member of the family, for the formula of the 'Moravia' composition was a closely guarded secret, and the family representative, whichever he was (Olga herself very often), had to go behind locked doors to mix the special ingredients and then lug the stuff out to the workmen in a pail. Svevo was initiated into the secret not long after he joined the firm, and by the end of 1900 he was knowledgeable enough to take charge of operations at

Murano, with the aid of a foreman. He became responsible in due course for all the day-to-day routine: hiring labour, procuring the raw materials (white lead, turpentine, verdigris, cresylic acid, stearin, arsenic, soluble naphtha, etc.), supervising the whole rather old-fashioned manufacturing process and making delivery arrangements. When a 'cooking' of the paint was in progress he had to be on the factory floor most of the day, keeping a watch on the thermometers above the paint-vats. ('I am short of workmen', he wrote to Livia in 1906, 'and have to stand over them as you stand over a *crème frite* to see that it doesn't burn.') He received a stream of written instructions from Olga and was rather at her beck and call, not knowing from day to day when he would be despatched to Murano or told to come home again. He was not consulted about policy decisions at first, and used to catch himself day-dreaming about inspired *coups* which would establish him once and for all as a successful industrialist. There was the time when he read a book on distilling turpentine, and immediately had the idea of their producing the raw materials themselves. When they set up their new factory in France they would, on his suggestion, site it in a turpentine-producing region, and by unobtrusive economies he would gradually buy up the local pine-forests. He would reclaim vast stretches of sea on the Normandy coast and give employment to a race of sturdy Normans. Letizia, the Southern beauty, would reign as queen of these horny-handed peasants he had brought life and prosperity to.

Svevo eventually became a relatively wealthy man and an important member of the Veneziani organisation, but he was never in any serious sense an independent industrialist or a 'millionaire', as he has sometimes been described. The firm itself, through very prosperous, was a comparatively small-scale family business then, run on old-fashioned lines, and he spent a good part of his own working life on the factory floor. Near the end of his life he wrote:

It amuses me when my critics, unable to give me the pleasure of proclaiming me a great writer, kindly describe me as a great financier or a great industrialist. I am neither the one nor the other. As for high finance, I never had anything to do with it. I was certainly useful to my firm as an industrialist, through constant hard work—it was the fruit of iron resolution and gratitude for the comparative comfort and independence which industry provided me with—but I was never in charge of affairs and was only occasionally entrusted, and then with mixed success, with dealings with third parties. I worked, organised, inspected, made reports. Twenty-five years ago I began my trips to England and, I will say, held my own with the Anglo-Saxons fairly well, but always, I have to admit, as a colleague of those who knew more about them, and about how to deal with them, than I did. (*Saggi*, pp. 175-6)

His duties soon began to take him away from Trieste a good deal. The factory building at Murano was extended to provide a house for him, and he spent long periods there, continuing to do so up to the time of the First World War. He was kept house for by a cousin of Olga's, Gilda Moravia, and her cook-and-friend Italia, who had given up a dress-shop to come and live with her. Livia also came sometimes to keep him company. Svevo's 'iron resolution' not to spare himself if he joined his parents-in-law's firm was certainly real, and he rather enjoyed being busy from morning to night at something practical, after the boring routine of the bank. However, between his periodical bursts of activity, life went on slowly for Svevo at Murano. He called it 'the house of sleep', and in the two fragments for which he used it as a setting (*Cimutti* and *In Serenella*) the place appears as a symbol of radiant idleness. The hero of *In Serenella*, Signor Giulio, is a Triestine business man, in partnership with his brothers, who has had an unfortunate experience on the stock-exchange, and has been sent to Murano by his brothers to be out of mischief. Friends warn him and his wife that they will be wretchedly bored, but in fact the gentle idleness suits them marvellously; it would be paradise, if it weren't for the thunderbolts that fall from time to time from the brothers in

Trieste, or the periodical invasion of one of the brothers' wives, 'a somewhat impatient and dictatorial lady' (evidently a recollection of Olga) who, when she came, made 'Serenella' (i.e. 'place of serenity') a misnomer. For the rest of the time the business of packing and despatching bales of cloth involves Signor Giulio in a great deal of pleasant standing-about, smoking and diplomacy with his workmen, without distracting him from his own private train of thoughts. He has plenty of time each day to give to his favourite imaginary project, the erection of a giant white marble *Pietà*, representing Woman comforting Man, in the middle of the mud-flats, where the tides would wash it daily. Whenever he notices a particularly striking tint on the lagoon he calls his wife to the window, and she in turn has to call her maid. The maid herself makes an important discovery: at certain states of the tide you can get an entirely different view of the mud-flats, and of the charming pattern of puddles in them, merely by climbing a yard in height. This becomes a major preoccupation with him. His devotion to the lagoon and its beauties becomes a byword locally; he stands for hours observing them, 'dreaming of action, riches, and monuments, and studying his balance'.

Since his marriage, Svevo had seen much less of Veruda. Veruda and Livia were rather jealous of each other. Livia thought he was arrogant—'Veruda is very impertinent and everyone is tired of his rudeness and the grand airs he gives himself. He has often hurt me too', she wrote in June 1900—whilst Veruda himself was scurrilous on the subject of Olga and couldn't understand why Svevo should want a job in business when he could be a writer. Svevo for his part began to get annoyed at Veruda's habit of breaking appointments and to mutter that he would really have to break off the friendship. Anyway, Veruda was away from Trieste most of the time, though every now and then he sent a picture-postcard, with a brief inscription scrawled in an enormous hand. From Vienna he wrote:

Dear Ettore,

This son-of-a-bitch hereby reports his presence and is greatly enraged because yesterday he found his chamberpot full without himself, the entitled party, having had the least use or enjoyment of it.

Ciao

However, in 1903 Veruda's mother died, and the event had tragic consequences for him. On her deathbed she had kept asking for water, but as the doctor had said she was not to drink, Veruda refused to bring her any, and in her delirium she cursed him as a cruel and ungrateful son. Soon after her death, her 'curse' began to obsess Veruda and it eventually sent him into a nervous breakdown. He stopped painting, began to have premonitions of his own death, and wandered off to Paris with his pockets full of identification papers in case he were found dead in the street. Svevo heard the news and begged him to come to the house at Murano. 'You will work', he wrote. 'You will regain your confidence in yourself, in art, in life.' Veruda agreed to come, and for a time the change seemed to do him good. He made friends with Livia and began painting again, leaving the Schmitzes after a week or two to work on his own in Burano. By this time, however, he was physically ill with an internal abscess, and after a further collapse he rushed home to Trieste to die. Svevo wept on hearing the news, the first time Livia had ever seen him do so.

Some time about the turn of the century an English admiral in Trieste, examining the keel of one of the Austrian Lloyd Company's ships, which had been painted with the 'Moravia' composition, and noticing its excellent condition, inquired why the firm didn't set up a branch in England. The Venezianis already had their agent there, but being aware that England had just embarked on a vast programme of naval expansion, they decided to follow up the hint, and as Svevo knew a little English it was decided that he should go out to discuss the matter on the spot. He was also to take the opportunity to negotiate orders with the Admiralty and to give instruction in the use of the paint at British naval establishments.

Though as a young man he had once made a memorable trip to Istanbul, with his brother-in-law Giuseppe Vivante, Svevo was a bad traveller. He liked things to stay put. 'My feeble organism needs calm. I can't even be intelligent without it,' he once said. 'Every change of place produces an acute, an enormous sadness in me . . . like liquid in a vessel going cloudy when you shake it.' Beginning to travel at forty, he said, he didn't notice things as he used to—partly because he was old, and partly because he had lost the love of self which made him think what he noticed important.

His first visit to England succeeded in making him thoroughly miserable. He had to wear his overcoat in June, he disliked the chilly English manner towards strangers, he found the coffee undrinkable (and they served it in pint mugs), and the barman in a public house demanded his money before you started to drink. Nobody could understand his English, and he misread the pronunciation code in his dictionary and had to start all over again. He was lonely and bored, though in the evenings he began writing a comedy, and the first time he began really enjoying a conversation—it was with the most adorable little English boy, whom he found perched on the back of his seat at the hotel, watching the smoke come out of his nostrils—an icy English voice called 'Come along, Philip'. The owner of the voice carefully managed not even to look at him.

He found himself at a disadvantage in various ways. His collars weren't smart enough or his shaving good enough—in England you can wear a shabby coat but your collars have to be absolutely beyond reproach, and you had better be drunk than ill shaven. The Chief of Navy Contracts raised his eyebrows when he discovered that Svevo, the representative of the well known Veneziani firm, was staying at a boarding-house, like his own clerk. He got into a frenzy trying to make himself understood by the workmen in the Plymouth dockyards; the louder he shouted at them in Italian, German and French, the more they laughed. When he tried out his English at the Admiralty he found everyone staring at his gestures in amazement. And worse followed. He stretched out his arms in mock despair at not understanding what they said and hit the 'Chief Constructor'. To add to things, he made a mistake over the contract; he spent a sleepless night over it, and Olga was furious. 'Here I am,' he wrote to Livia, 'costing a fortune in money . . . and I make mistakes.'

It was a serious deprivation to him to have no one to chatter with and make his *Witze* to—'my favourite occupation . . . complementing and replacing my older one of writing'—and he fretted at the English rules about introductions. The fiction was that before three in the afternoon he and Wickland, the Marconi agent, who was his fellow-diner at the boarding-house, didn't know each other. By three o'clock Wickland was always drunk and would begin teaching him English.

By then Mr. Wickland, who at mealtimes, like everyone else, only drinks water, has numerous pints of beer and glasses of brandy and whisky in his stomach; his eyes have half disappeared in his head and he begins calling me 'old man'. The charming thing about it is that at these times, being half aware of his own condition, he never talks to women, never even says 'good-day' to them or seems to notice them at all.—'It would be shocking.' I wish you could see him, so neat, so beautifully dressed, so clean-shaven. Drink doesn't make him noisy and foul-mouthed, it makes him humble, gentle and benevolent. He goes to bed very early, 'tired by business'. Today he actually spoke to me in the morning, but I would bet that, seeing that it is Sunday, he had a drink or two inside him already. (*Lettere alla moglie*, Trieste, 1963, pp. 154-5)

The rule about introductions, he found when he stayed at a hotel in Plymouth, didn't apply among 'Commercial-room customers', who had their own peculiar protocol.

All country hotels in England have two sections: one for the 'Coffee-room customers' and the other for the 'Commercial-room customers'. The former is the more expensive, and corresponds to our 'Table d'hôte'. The latter does not admit women and is used exclusively by commercial travellers. . . . To realise the peculiarity of the arrangement you must remember that in England you enter or leave a room where there are men or women you don't know without making any acknowledgement. On first entering the 'Commercial-room', on the other hand, you must say a loud 'Good morning gentlemen'—to which, even more oddly, everyone religiously responds. The 'Commercial-room' is cheaper than the other one because service is largely eliminated. . . . On one side, at the head of the table, sits the president (the one who has been in the house longest) and opposite him the Vice. There is no election or discussion: the President sees at a glance that this is his position and that it is his duty and privilege to occupy it. With the excellent manners with which people here do whatever it is their duty to, the President and Vice-President take their places. And now for the verbal protocol. The phrases are always exactly the same, but they speak them as if they had just invented them. Someone arriving late asks 'Mr. President, won't you mind my joining you?' The president replies 'Most decidedly, yes!' If the President has his mouth full, the other respectfully waits for him to reply before sitting down. Meanwhile the servant puts a dish in front of the President and another in front of the Vice for them to select from. Everyone is silent. The Vice begins by informing the President that he has in front of him such and such items of food which are at his disposal. The President, who usually has in front of him a whole side of roast beef, the major part of a bullock indeed, an object visible at some miles' range, likewise informs the Vice that he has such-and-such an article of food in front of him, of which one part is well-done and the other underdone. Vice and President then earnestly apply themselves to seeing everyone gets served. However, anyone can ask for something himself, using the following formula: 'Mr. President, I trouble you for some. . . .' Ordering wine is a serious business. You have to ask permission from the President to be allowed to see the wine-list. He, of course, says 'Most decidedly, yes'. But that's not the end of it. When you are raising a glass of wine or beer etc. to your lips you must say 'Mr. President, Vice, Gentlemen, at your health!', to which the reply is 'I thank you'. (This is rather surprising, because in general you don't drink to people's health in England, and if you do, people look at you in amazement and ask why you don't eat to their health too.) At the Commercial-room table the convention is that everyone knows the people beside him, and talks to them. But when the meal is over, the acquaintance is at an end; conversation stops, and everyone goes about his business with the chilliest of nods, indeed not even a nod when he meets them in the street or in the hotel corridor. (*Ibid.*, pp. 163-5)

From the point of view of business his trip went quite well. The British naval authorities had a high opinion of the Veneziani products and he was able to report strongly in favour of setting up a factory in England. Gioachino and Olga accepted his advice, as they did his view that there was no call for one in France. He also received large orders on the spot. 'Frigid, reserved and malevolent-eyed,' he wrote to Livia, 'the English have ordered 120 tons of paint for immediate delivery.' He was struck by how casual the English were about such dealings. Many years later, when his attitude to England had changed, Svevo told a friend how he once went to the Admiralty about a very important contract and was received by a nonchalant young man in a dingy little room not much bigger than a cupboard. It contained only one chair, so the young official gave it to him and sat on the table himself. In five minutes they had settled an affair which would have taken five years' discussion in France or Italy. As he returned along Whitehall he felt like someone walking on air, but faintly guilty too.

As far as his own comfort was concerned, however, Svevo couldn't wait for the trip to be over, and his letters were full of groans at the prospect of more journeys of the same kind. Eventually, though, after some six or seven weeks, Livia came out to keep him company, and the visit ended idyllically with a holiday in Ireland, where Svevo supervised the painting of Lord Muskerry's yacht.

Svevo paid a second visit to England in November 1903, and this time his job was to help Marco Bliznakoff, the husband of Livia's sister Nella, in the setting up of the new factory, for which they had found a site in Anchor and Hope Lane, Charlton. Marco, who was the son of a Bulgarian orthodox priest, was a trained engineer, and he entered the firm at about the same time as Svevo. He and Nella had a house in the grounds of the Villa Veneziani and Svevo had seen a fair amount of him during the last year—more than he would have chosen, since Marco kept making violent scenes with Nella, and Svevo had had to keep the peace between them. He didn't like Marco very much but thought he was probably harmless. 'On the whole he seems to be a good enough fellow', he wrote to Livia. 'Not very frightening if you know how to handle him.' 'It's a pity that there can never be a real friendship between me and him', he wrote later. 'I shall always do what's proper by him, but feeling rather that I'm acting *à la* Canestrini, who is so kind to his mad-house patients.' There are some touches in this of Zeno's attitude towards his rival Guido Speier in *La coscienza di Zeno*, and I suspect Marco was a part-model for Guido.

Marco had already been in London for some while, supervising the building of the factory, and with him was a boy called 'Nicoletto' (Nicola Bravin) from Murano. Svevo had heard Marco wasn't well, and he found him in a great state of nerves, not eating or sleeping, and full of melodramatic despair in the face of difficulties. He had ordered a new type of self-feeding boiler, hoping to raise the rate of production at Charlton as compared with that of Servola, and for some days nothing would go right with them. Then the wood of the barrels began to expand under heat and they leaked. Marco wept and was suicidal; and Svevo saw that his most important job would be getting Marco better, which he did rather skilfully. He made him laugh and managed to persuade him to eat again.

A house had been rented for them in Charlton Church

Lane, a rather ugly little semi-detached villa belonging to a Thames master-lighterman called Francis, who lived in the other half. No one had had time to furnish it or instal proper heating, and Marco and Svevo mostly camped out in the factory, where Nicoletto cooked them meals, only going home to Church Lane to sleep; Nicoletto himself slept in the factory. They all got up at six, worked solidly till seven at night, and were in bed again at nine, shivering under all the blankets and rugs they could find. One exceptionally bitter night, having found it impossible to sleep from shivering, they all got up, each privately convinced, until they compared notes, that he was seriously ill. 'The sun here is about half the size of ours', wrote Svevo to Livia. 'It has the appearance of someone with skin-disease. It has lost the knack of emitting rays and has gone red from shame.'

Svevo's feelings towards England weren't much warmer after this second visit, and he would have been glad to get out of further ones. At one point he hopefully suggested that Livia's younger sisters Fausta and Dora, then twenty and eighteen, should be sent out to England to find husbands—and then the latter could look after the Charlton factory. Considering the close-knit character of the Veneziani business this was not too wild an idea; but nothing came of it. And from now on till the 1914-18 war he had to spend a month or two every year in Charlton himself—he also came again several times after the war. Livia quite often came with him, and they settled down fairly comfortably, engaging a housekeeper called Meggie May, the daughter of a local roadsweeper. Svevo once described his joy at finding Meggie there after an agonising four days' journey, during which he hadn't slept an instant because of the heat, and all the way from Dover to Victoria an elderly English lady had been trying to convert him.

I rang the doorbell, and as no one answered I turned my back on it with a sigh and began to retrace the Calvary which even two steps now seemed to me. But then the door gave a creak. Are we entertaining burglars? I wondered, and put several more steps between myself and the door, with the prudence which Marco always attributes to my race. Then I turned and dropped my umbrella (the first Baumgartner London has seen) to rub my eyes: Meggie! Meggie! in flesh and bone, that is to say with all that bone and all that very little flesh. I wept for happiness: bed all waiting, milk all waiting, bread and butter all waiting. Munching and weeping with relief I hurled myself into bed and slept for twelve hours. . . . (Letter to Livia; Charlton, 5 September 1906)

He wrote afterwards that he came to England too late, the translation was imperfect. Writing to Livia in English in 1909, he told her:

. . . I had a dream this night (it was a night of about 10 hours). I dreamt to have been translated in English but wholly you know. I ate beef and was stiff and well educated by the intervention of the Holy Ghost, I think. By awakening I found myself re-translated in Italian but I feel it necessary to retain a little of the second nature I acquired during the dream. This is the last letter I write to you this time and it is English. You have already tried once what it signifies to be translated. You have been translated in French. I tried to re-translate you in Italian and if this translation did not give you a great pleasure it was really my fault. The only one of our little family who has not been translated is our little one. We hope that she will not be worse than we have been. . . . (Letter to Livia; Trieste [in fact Murano], 1909)

He came to like England and to be fascinated by it, but never got used to it. He continued to go about London, he said, in a state of astonishment, muttering 'Splendid!', 'Colossal!', 'Appalling!' It was a long while before he visited the West End at all, and when he did finally go to a matinée at the Coliseum and then made his way towards Piccadilly in search of his favourite 'Sultan' cigarettes, it was such a labour, and he had to ask the way of so many policemen, that he half decided never to try it again. He wrote a description, again in English, of a later expedition to the West End by horse-tram:

Charlton, 3 August 1908.

My dear own darling,

. . . On Saturday evening I went to the Colyseum. We coosed this theatre because it is quite closed to Charing Cross. No special or interesting things were performed there and before midnight we fell asleep in our beds at Carlton-Disjunction like I call it. On Sunday morning we were again busy in the factory with our engines. At three o'clock p.m. Nicoletto, his bride* and me went to Greenwich by the usual horse-Tramway still existing from Church-Lane. I wanted to go through the Tunnel on the other side of the river to take there the electric Tramway and go to Westminster, a drive you already know. When we left the Horse-Tramway, we found awaiting us an electric car going straightway to Charing Cross. Well, it was all I wanted. The drive is more pleasant than that through gloomy White Chapel and you stop on the Strand. It was the first time I had a drive through London. London externally has changed very much. I fear that some of her changed features will not agree with you. You liked especially to see such a big traffic well regulated; in such a noise and movement you felt your life sure protected by the police and by every driver himself. That is quite changed. The traffic—it appears to me—has been increased still. It was on a Sunday, the day of rest. What a rest dear me! You see one street filled with carriages and buses and one or two horses, poor beasts feeling quite lonely in the crowded street. The smell is terrible; they say it is healthier then the smell of horses but quite sure it is not very pleasant. What may not be very healthy is to be injured by a motor-car or a motor-bus. It seems that at every moment the drivers loose control of their engines and every day the coronee has to held an inquest on the body of some killed man. The Londoners—like always—grumble about such a state of things but they are so many, you know, that they think it is a better thing to improve the life of several millions of living persons than to save the life of a few hundreds. We took a Horse-Bus and went to Hide-Park to the Preachers-Corner where I have like alwais my little lesson of Cockney. Afterwards we took the Tube (three pennies tube) and went to Vienna-Coffee where Miss Nell and Nicoletto had a tea and I a cup of coffee. At

* Nicoletto married Miss Francis, their landlord's daughter.

Charing Cross we saw a motor-bus going to Lewisham and we took our seats at the topo of it. It is something like the crossing of the Channel when there are moderate breezes. I was almost sea-sick. When they stopo they are obliged like all buses to clear the middle part of the road and to approach the pavement always the lowest part of the street and you believe always to be smashed to the approaching houses. . . .

What amusements and social life they had were almost all local. Svevo became a fan of Charlton Athletic and he frequented the local cinema, where his deafening laugh made the rest of the audience giggle. He also formed a chamber trio with the Charlton postmistress, Miss Streeter, and her brother. On Sundays he had a standing invitation to dinner with the resident Veneziani agent and his rich wife, but on the whole he preferred the Streeters' company.

I don't think we in Italy have anything quite like them, people so poor, so cheerful and so enterprising. Miss Streeter's voice is poles apart from that silvery, null one of Mrs. T——; it sounds more like an Italian one. (Letter to Livia; Charlton, 2 April 1906)

He rather enjoyed his suburban English Sunday mornings, with a bottle of Worthington and *The Referee*, and during the week the factory generally kept him busy.

Oh God, oh God, who will release me from machines, so many machines? As you can imagine, I go to bed very early; but I wake up early too, with ventilators and mixers and the devil knows what spinning round in my head. The ventilators blow out what small spark of fire there is still left within me, the mixers stir up ugly stuff from my soul which I would rather forget, the condensers condense all the fine gases in my head.

After lunch I am going to Shepherd's Bush* for the gymnastic display, but my engines will insist on coming too. Like Desdemona, I was born for love. (Letter to Livia; Charlton, 18 July 1908)

---

* i.e. to the White City, where the Franco-British Exhibition was being held.

His impression of England was largely based on Charlton Church Lane, 'a neat street built on a slope, lined with little brown English houses'.

. . . the smaller houses are all shops: dairies, tobacconists, drapers and newspaper-shops. You can buy there practically anything that you want. The shop occupies three quarters of the house. Entering one of these houses you wonder how on earth a kitchen, two bedrooms, and a reception-room with the inevitable piano can be got into the space we would give an umbrella-stand. (*Saggi*, p. 194)

He liked studying the various tides of passengers to and from Charlton Station and remarked that the whole hierarchy of English society could be seen neatly stratified up the slope from the river to Blackheath. He thought a good deal about the English class system, noticing that property values were always unpredictable in London, as the middle and upper classes were in a constant state of migration before the spread of industry. An English friend told him that for every shilling a day he raised his workers' pay they would move a mile further from the factory. 'The concept of luxury in England is identical for the poor and the rich', he said in an article about England.

A detached house in a quiet district is what everyone wants: travel, expensive sports and the fresh air of the seaside . . . this, the most important island in the world, contains a huge sum of unhappiness; it is expressed in the phrase 'a higher standard of life', the goal of everyone's efforts. They can resign themselves to not getting it, indeed the most imperialistic people in the world is as familiar with sacrifice as the humblest, but it *is* a sacrifice.

For this reason, he thinks, they will never give up Free Trade —though while he was there the great Protectionist debate was raging and all the Woolwich libraries ever seemed to supply was books on political economy—he never saw a novel.

What most passionately interested the English, though, he decided—what they thought about when they were alone—was religion. There was a stream of commercial travellers to the factory, a fact which pleased Svevo as it gave him practice in English, and talking with them, the conversation always came round to religion.

I knew some who had been converted several times. They left the United Church to become nonconformists and Presbyterians. Some of them went further and invented something infallibly calculated to give them peace of mind, and which in fact destroyed not only their peace of mind but that of the whole neighbourhood or even the country—i.e. a Reform: a church without a church (nature's own church), preaching without a preacher, reform or abolition of the prayer-book, etc. And then on top of that they all had another activity, which satisfied the human craving for martyrdom. Southern England abounded in the 'conscientious objector'. They were constantly being prosecuted in Greenwich itself. And by now the English legislator has got in the habit of adding a clause to every bill exonerating the 'objector' from obeying the law. Does your conscience forbid you to be vaccinated? Then you needn't be vaccinated. Does it forbid you to call a doctor? Then, if you're a working man, you are exempted from paying insurance. . . . (*Saggi*, pp. 183-4)

Svevo prided himself, though not very seriously, on his knowledge of English politics and said that one of the parties should have sent him round as a canvasser, with a charming young English lady to do the kissing. 'The newspapers, with their smell of fresh printer's ink, were my teachers. I belonged to no particular party, so I read them all. But I also had flesh and blood teachers, living as I did with the face of perfidious Albion stuck close to mine; surly, discontented, eternally grumbling about the imperfections of the world.'

His other passion where English newspapers were concerned was the court reports. They were his favourite topic with his English friends, who used to collect for him cuttings about the latest murders and divorces. The Merstham tunnel mystery* kept him happy for weeks.

A feverish investigation began of the whole life of the poor girl and all her friends. I identified myself intensely with this chase, sometimes feeling like the detective, sometimes like the criminal. One day one clue would be found, the next day another, then we were back at the beginning again and starting on a new trail. One day I talked so passionately on the subject to an English acquaintance that he nearly reported me to the police. (*Ibid.*, p. 177)

He was also a supporter of the petition to reprieve John Lincoln (the son of the notorious I. T. Trebitsch-Lincoln†), who was convicted of murdering a brewer's traveller named Richards on Christmas Eve 1925 during an attempted burglary. Lincoln admitted his guilt, but made a memorable remark about his crime in a letter to his fiancée: 'Perhaps there are ways in which this is well. Supposing I had succeeded in getting the money unobserved. At some other time, maybe when we were married, I should have done the same thing again, then what misery I should have brought you.'—'Think of it,' said Svevo. 'First of all, for all its simplicity, it is the most ardent declaration of love I have ever heard. Then, a lesser man would have written "If I had had you at my side, I would never have done murder"; whereas Lincoln, an alcoholic, knew better than this, and—extraordinary in a man who murders instead of writing—he had the strength of mind to say it.'

* A famous unsolved mystery. On Sunday 24 September 1905, Mary Sophia Money, a young girl living alone in Clapham, told a friend that she was going out 'for a little walk'. That night her body was found in the Merstham tunnel, near Croydon, badly disfigured. The murderer, if any, was never identified. There is a remote possibility that it was her own brother Robert, who in 1912 committed multiple murder and suicide.

† A Hungarian Jew who became successively Presbyterian missionary in Canada, Anglican curate, Liberal M.P. for Darlington, convicted forger and suspected German spy, German monarchist conspirator, adviser to Chinese war lords and Buddhist monk.

With a touch of bitterness about his own literary past, Svevo wrote that the Anglo-Saxons had rejuvenated him or at least restored his serenity.

Those 500,000 other inhabitants of my district, of whom, as far as I know, not one was nursing dreams of literary fame, or if he was, was managing to conceal it, gave me back my peace of mind. I was living in a place where, if I admitted out loud the ideas I had once had about myself, I would have been put in an asylum. Among such neighbours resignation came easily. True, I got to know the star footballer of the district, and he introduced me to a national Rugby hero; but in their case there wasn't the same thirst for glory. One enters the football field primarily for the good of one's health and appetite. Glory is only an afterthought. Whereas with us writers the lust for glory is something morbid. A beaten footballer has still his self-respect; a failed writer is merely ridiculous. (*Ibid.*, p. 182)

And if the Anglo-Saxons, as he sometimes imagined, were doing as he was doing and losing themselves in business as the best refuge from the infection of literature, they certainly achieved their aim. Books did sometimes filter into people's homes in Charlton Church Lane—mostly cheap nonsense though not always so. But when it came to the theatre, where the English deliberately met together in public in the cause of art, literature vanished altogether, elbowed out by stupid farces, dowdy mock-Parisian revues, and magnificent, infantile spectacles. If he wanted to see an intelligent play he wouldn't find it in the West End; he would have to go to the Greenwich Town Hall to see the Lena Ashwell Players.*

* Between 1920 and 1929 the Lena Ashwell Players gave regular performances of Galsworthy, Shaw, Ibsen, Chekhov, etc., in the town halls and public baths of various London boroughs.

5

Svevo and James Joyce

Svevo, as we have seen, went on having difficulty with his English. In fact it became one of those perpetually unsolved problems, like his violin-playing, which gave a kind of pattern to his life. However in 1907 he looked round for a private tutor, and the teacher recommended to him was James Joyce, whose lessons were much in vogue among the well-to-do in Trieste at that time.

Joyce and Nora Barnacle had originally come to Trieste more or less by accident. Joyce had left Ireland in 1904 on the strength of a supposed job at the Berlitz School in Paris, but the job proved non-existent when he arrived there. However, the director of the school was sympathetic and got wind of a similar post for Joyce in Trieste. Joyce and Nora set out there without hesitation (and without money) only to find, when they arrived there in October, that this job was mythical too. Joyce survived for a week or two by borrowing, after which a place was found for him at the school in Pola, the Austrian naval base at the tip of the Istrian peninsula; but after a few months the Austrians, having discovered a spy ring in Pola, decided to expel all aliens from the town, and the school had to close. Joyce's luck held, and a position was now after all found for him in the school at Trieste, to which he returned in March 1905. Throughout all these distractions he had been coolly working at *Stephen Hero* and some of the stories which were later to form *Dubliners*.

At first Joyce didn't like Trieste at all, nor indeed the

whole Istrian peninsula—'a long boring place wedged into the Adriatic, peopled by ignorant Slavs who wear little caps and colossal breeches'. But he gradually became very attached to it, and all his early work, including a good deal of *Ulysses*, is closely bound up with it. In many ways it reminded him of Dublin. It was, despite its size, a provincial town, where the same people constantly met at the same cafés or at the theatre and opera-house. He felt the likeness between the nationalist movement there and in Ireland, and later wrote a number of articles on Irish Home Rule in the Triestine press. And the town was congenial to him in other ways too. It was intensely cosmopolitan and polyglot, like his own later writing. It was an essentially bourgeois and utilitarian city, notoriously freethinking, without an aristocracy (except of money) and without traditional attachments—a perfect place in which to practise silence, exile and cunning. It was the 'sea-coast of his Bohemia', as Harry Levin puts it, and he was later to picture the Liffey as flowing into the Canale Grande.

Joyce lived the bohemian life in Trieste more resourcefully than it can often have been lived. In his early days there the Joyce furniture never seemed to stay put for more than a month or two, or the Joyce household to be able to subsist without endless small loans or painfully-extracted advances. Sometimes the Berlitz School paid Joyce on a daily basis, and he developed an extraordinary talent for borrowing; he put his genius into it, and it was his material salvation.

The arrival of his brother Stanislaus late in 1905 brought a little more stability into the household but not very much. Stanislaus, who obtained a post at the Berlitz School too, became the Joyces' financial conscience, but also often had to support them entirely for weeks at a time. They took him for granted, and exploited him shamelessly, and he in turn threatened and hectored, and sometimes used his fists on Joyce. James would spend his evenings drinking in working men's cafés in the Old Town and Stanislaus would come in search of him and drag him home, often by physical force. Once he found him unconsicous in the gutter and had to carry him back.

In the summer of 1906 the affairs of the Berlitz School were in confusion, the sub-director having absconded with part of the funds. The director told Joyce that there would no longer be room for two English teachers, and James, who was in a mood of boredom and frustration, baffled in his first efforts to get *Dubliners* published and unable to get on with *Stephen Hero*, jumped at the chance of a change. He answered an advertisement for an English-speaking correspondence-clerk in a Roman bank, and in July he, Nora and their one-year-old baby Giorgio went to Rome. Joyce quickly took against the place—he felt it to be a giant cemetery (it was there that he conceived the story 'The Dead'). He also disliked his fellow-clerks, who seemed, he said, always to have something wrong with their testicles and to want to confide in him about it. He did little actual writing in Rome, though a considerable amount of reading, as well as a great deal of drinking. Nora complained against their way of life more and more bitterly, and to add to their difficulties she became pregnant again. Finally, after eight months or so, and after a final disastrous evening of drinking, when his cronies knocked him down and robbed him, Joyce, with his 'mouth full of decayed teeth and his soul of decayed ambitions', took flight back to Trieste.

This was in March 1907, and there now began a long period in which, apart from occasional journalistic activities, Joyce lived by private tuition, in rivalry with the Berlitz School. Some of the teaching was done in his own flat, but he also visited various pupils in their homes, which was sometimes a considerable undertaking—for example his regular expedition, described by Herbert Gorman, to give lessons to the captain of a boat which came to Trieste every fortnight from Bari:

Joyce would leave his house, walk across the Piazza Giambattista Vico, walk through the tunnel of Montuzza, take an electric tram to the gate of the Free Port, enter and take a horse tram to the Punto Franco, make signals to the ship until a small boat was sent out for him, board the boat and be taken to the ship, climb aboard and have a sailor search for the Captain, look for a quiet spot to give the lesson, give it (the Captain was intensely stupid), then look for a sailor to take him back to the Punto Franco, enter the horse tram and ride to the gate of the Free Port, board the electric tram which would take him to the mouth of the Montuzza tunnel, walk back through it, cross the Piazza Giambattista Vico and so reach his house. For this extraordinary exertion he received payment amounting to thirty pence. (*James Joyce*, New York, 1939, p. 191)

Svevo was one of those whom he visited in this way, and for a time Livia also took lessons. It was agreed that Joyce, the 'gerund-monger' as Svevo once called him, should come out to Servola three times a week, and the two quickly became friends.

The lessons themselves turned out to be characteristically Joycean. Joyce took a high-handed line about grammar and loved improvising fantastic literary exercises. He was perhaps not strictly a very good teacher. (There is a nice story told by Stanislaus of Joyce's being asked by Svevo to explain Shakespeare's line 'And brass eternal slave to mortal rage'. He replied 'I don't know what it means, but I suppose Shakespeare was thinking of German bands'.) Mainly, however, the lessons turned into free discussions, conducted in a mixture of English and Triestine; Joyce loved the Triestine dialect, and the family went on using it at home even in his later years.

One of the favourite topics was Joyce's own writing, and he brought along the manuscripts of his poems and some of the *Dubliners* stories. Late in 1907 he read the Schmitzes 'The Dead', which he had recently completed. After the reading Livia went down into the garden to pluck a bouquet and offered it to him in homage.

Svevo one day admitted to Joyce that he had been a writer himself, and lent him his two books. 'Schmitz has given me two novels of his to read', he told Stanislaus that evening. 'I wonder what kind of thing it is.' At the next lesson he told Svevo that he was an unjustly neglected writer. There were pages in *Senilità*,* he said, which Anatole France could not have improved on, and indeed he could already repeat some from memory. Svevo could not believe his ears. He walked most of the way back to his flat in Piazza Vico with him, talking about his hopes and disappointments as a writer and the ban he had finally imposed on himself. It was the first time he had spoken so frankly of his bitterness.

Joyce took up Svevo's cause energetically, as he usually did in such cases. He made propaganda for Svevo's novels around Trieste, claiming that Svevo was the only contemporary Italian novelist he found at all interesting. (Joyce had a fondness for championing neglected talent in this way, no doubt seeing parallels to his own case; he was later to go to fantastic lengths in promoting the cause of the Irish tenor Sullivan.) He had no success among the Triestines, however, and for a time he himself remained the only exception to the 'unanimity of silence' which Svevo had become resigned to.

All the same, the friendship was a providential one—uniquely so for Svevo, since it was Joyce who eventually got attention for him as a writer, but certainly for Joyce too—indeed it was to be his only close relationship with another writer in the remaining years before the First World War. Svevo was the kind of audience which Joyce always had need of, and which was later provided by Frank Budgen and others. It was always a fairly formal relationship. They remained on surname terms, and after Svevo's death, having refused to provide a preface to the English translation of *Senilità*, Joyce was rather inclined to minimise the friendship, saying that he never crossed the Schmitz threshold except as a paid teacher. He also wrote to Stanislaus, apropos of the preface which Stanislaus had written in his stead: 'I wish it

* The title (*As a Man Grows Older*) of the posthumous English translation by Beryl de Zoete was suggested by Joyce.

were a little clearer than it is that Schmitz was very careful with his money'. In fact, Svevo seems to have been one of Joyce's great financial standbys and was repeatedly making him loans and advances on fees. 'Poor Joyce!' wrote Svevo to Livia in 1911, at the time of the winding-up of Joyce's Irish cinema venture. 'We have got a fine leech on our hands. Now I've got to send him money to Ireland too.' He was also able, through his business connections, to introduce Joyce to likely pupils. Indeed the whole household at Servola was a support to Joyce, and he tended to rush round there at moments of trouble. He once left a dog called Fido in the Schmitzes' care while he went to Ireland; it disappeared, to Svevo's anxiety, but was later found with a litter of puppies. Svevo's father-in-law also lent Joyce money during the war, and employed him for a brief period in 1914 as a correspondence-clerk. The Schmitzes didn't get on so well with Nora. Livia was shocked by Nora's slovenly housekeeping, and Nora in turn, according to Joyce, complained that Livia grew short-sighted when she met her in the street.

As personalities Joyce and Svevo complemented each other in a number of ways—Svevo outwardly the perfect bourgeois, urbane, ironic and pessimistic; and Joyce, young, restless, arrogant, flamboyantly bohemian. For Svevo there was evidently a likeness to his old friendship with Veruda, who had something of Joyce's intransigence and bohemianism. He was content to let Joyce take the dominant role in conversation, though Joyce was by twenty years the younger (he was then twenty-five) and had published nothing but a small volume of poems. He later reflected on an article, 'The Day of the Rabblement', that Joyce had written at eighteen, in which he paraphrased Dante, hinting at himself as the new Dante: 'Elsewhere there are men who are worthy to carry on the tradition of the old master who is dying in Christiania. He has already found his successor in the writer of *Michael Kramer*, and the third minister will not be wanting when his hour comes. Even now that hour may be standing by the door.'

'The conviction of power in that young man, in whom it could only have been latent as yet, leaves one dumbfounded', he wrote. 'If I had read that article in 1901, when it was written, I should have laughed at it. Now it makes me wonder.'

Svevo understood a good deal about Joyce. He noticed the combination in him of moral courage with physical timidity. 'The physical appearance that Joyce presented on his arrival in Trieste has not changed much.'

Slender, agile, tall, you might think him a sportsman if it weren't for the fact that he walks with the carelessness of someone whose limbs aren't of the least importance to him. I believe indeed that his limbs have never had the slightest attention paid to them and have never experienced sport or gymnastics. I should mention that seen at close hand he is not at all like the strenuous fighter his pugnacious works would suggest. Very short-sighted, he wears strong spectacles which magnify his eyes, and that clear blue eye, imposing even without the glasses, stares out with an eternal curiosity and an eternal coldness. I cannot help imagining that this eye would be no less curious and no less cold when fixing a personal adversary. Here again, you see, I am making the mistake of picturing Joyce as physically combative. It must be because I see him so rarely and think of him so often. (*Saggi*, p. 204)

He had his own interpretation of Joyce's pugnaciousness—he thought he was essentially a mother's boy, who did not expect to find hostility in the world and was extravagantly indignant when he encountered it. His attitude towards Joyce was rather protective on the whole. He was distressed by his troubles and always talked feelingly about the hostility and prejudice Joyce had had to face. He felt there was something childlike and helpless about him, and used to tell an anecdote (rather highly-coloured, I think) to illustrate this. One morning Joyce had gone out to the market with Livia to help with the shopping, and when she got back she reported that she had lost him. Svevo promptly organised a search party, and found Joyce at last, in tears, sitting on a sack of potatoes outside a greengrocer's shop. 'I'm lost!' he exclaimed, miserably.

As an exercise Joyce once set Svevo the task of describing himself (Joyce) in English. Svevo did so rather brilliantly:

Mr. James Joyce described by his faithful pupil Ettore Schmitz.

When I see him walking on the streets I always think that he is enjoying leisure a full leisure. Nobody is awaiting him and he does not want to reach an aim or to meet anybody. No! He walks in order to be left to himself. He does also not walk for health. He walks because he is not stopped by anything. I imagine that if he would find his way barred by a high and big wall he would not be shocked at the least. He would change direction and if the new direction would also prove not to be clear he would change it again and walk on his hands shaken only by the natural movement of the whole body, his legs working without any effort to lengthen or to fasten his steps. No! His step is really his and of nobody else and cannot be lengthened or made faster. His whole body in quiet is that of a sportsman. If moved that of a child weakened by the great love of his parents. I know that life has not been a parent of that kind for him. It could have been worst and all the same Mr James Joyce would have kept his appearance of a man who considers things as points breaking the light for his amusement. He wears glasses and really he uses them without interruption from the early (?) morning until late in the night when he wakes up. Perhaps he may see less than it is to suppose from his appearance but he looks like a being who moves in order to see. Surely he cannot fight and does not want to. He is going through life hoping not to meet bad men. I wish him heartily not to meet them. (Quoted by Richard Ellmann in *James Joyce*, New York, 1959, p. 281)

When Joyce, who in 1909 had formed a company with two Triestines to introduce the cinema into Ireland, found that he was to be done out of the £40 he had been expecting as his share, he made bitter complaints. Svevo wrote to him consolingly, in English:

. . . You were so excited over the cinematograph-affair that during the whole travel I remembered your face so startled by such wickedness. And I must add to the remark I already have done that your surprise at being cheated proves that you are a pure literary man. To be cheated proves not yet enough. But to be cheated and to present a great surprise over that and not to consider it as a matter of course is really literary.

It amused Svevo, who was accustomed to the unpuritanical tone of Trieste, that when he made a rather free joke to Joyce, Joyce reproved him gravely. 'I never say that sort of thing, though I write it.' Svevo comments: 'It would appear then that his works are not ones that could be read in his own presence'—a typical Svevian *Witz*.

As for Joyce's feelings about Svevo, it seems possible to hear an echo of them in the relationship between Bloom and Stephen Dedalus. At least, Stanislaus thought so. '. . . it may not be too far-fetched', he wrote, in the introduction to the English translation of *Senilità*, 'to see in the person of Bloom Svevo's maturer, objective, peaceable temper reacting upon the young man's fiery mettle'.

Though in many other ways utterly unlike as writers, they were in one or two important respects rather close. They were both authors beginning as doctrinaire exponents of Naturalism who had discovered a method of going beyond it. Both had developed (and Svevo was to develop even further) a fanatical devotion to objectivity in self-description—though Joyce's self-portrait is so vast and centrifugal, the spokes are so long, that one tends to lose sight of the hub, whilst Svevo was always exclusively interested in the hub itself. It was one of the smaller features which Joyce was attracted to in Svevo's novels, that they named real streets and places, as Joyce did in *Dubliners* (to his cost, as far as finding a publisher went). Both had a superstitious feeling that invention in trivial points like this was an unnecessary, and perhaps dangerous, disloyalty to veracity. It was Svevo, incidentally, who tried to argue Joyce out of his admiration for d'Annunzio. He offered to bet that if they were to open d'Annunzio at random they would come across a phrase that was pretentious and meaningless. Joyce took the bet, and on the page they opened they found the phrase 'il sorriso che pullulava inestinguibile, spandendosi fra i pallidi meandri dei merletti buranesi' ('the smile which pullulated inextinguishably, spreading among the pallid meanders of Burano lace'). Joyce admitted, grudgingly, that Svevo had made his point.

Svevo succeeded in stimulating Joyce's own writing during 1909. Since April of the previous year Joyce had felt discouraged and had been unable to write. He could get no publisher to take any interest in *Dubliners* and having written three chapters of *A Portrait of the Artist* couldn't see his way to go on. In February 1909 he showed these chapters to Svevo and as an English exercise made him write a criticism of them. Svevo's answer was in the form of a letter:

Dear Mr. Joyce,

Really I do not believe of being authorised to tell you the author a resolute opinion about the novel which I could know only partially. I do not only allude to my want of competence but especially to the fact that when you stopped writing you were facing a very important development of Stephen's mind. I have had already a sample of what may be a change of this mind described by your pen. Indeed the development of Stephen's childish religion to a strong religion felt strongly and vigorously or better lived in all its particulars (after his sin) was so important that none other can be more so. I like very much your second and third chapters and I think you made a great mistake doubting whether you would find a reader who could take pleasure at the sermons of the third chapter. I have read them with a very strong feeling and I know in my little town a lot of people who would be certainly struck by the same feeling. Every word of these sermons acquires its artistic significance, by the fact of their effect on poor Stephen's mind. At last the reader has a full knowledge of the education got by Stephen, it could not be fuller even if the two previous chapters had dealt especially with it. I object against the first chapter. I did so when I had read only it but I do so still more decidedly after having known the two others. I think that I have at last also discovered the reason why these two chapters are for me so beautiful while the first one, which surely is of the same construction by the same writer who has surely not changed his ways, written evidently with the same artistic aims, fails to impress me as deeply. I think it deals with events deprived of importance and your rigid method of observation and description does not allow you to enrich a fact which is not rich of itself. You are obliged to write only about strong things. In your skilled hands they may become still stronger. I do not believe you can give the appearance of strength to things which are in themselves feeble, not important. I must say that if you had to write a whole novel with the only aim of description of everyday life without a problem which could affect strongly your own mind (you would not choose such a novel) you would be obliged to leave your method and find artificial colours to lend to the things the life they wanted in themselves.

Excuse me, dear Mr. Joyce, these remarks which prove perhaps only my conceitedness and believe me yours very truly,

Ettore Schmitz

(quoted by Ellmann, *op. cit.*, p. 282)

The letter, though it contains a false judgment on Joyce, one which would look falser when applied to *Ulysses*, touches on a central issue in Joyce's writing. Indeed its main thesis ('I do not believe you can give the appearance of strength to things which are in themselves feeble') is true in a sense: Joyce when he deals with 'feeble' things doesn't attempt to give them the appearance of strength, as for instance Henry James might be said to do. At all events Joyce was pleased by Svevo's support over the matter of including the three sermons verbatim, and the letter roused him. He told Stanislaus he was going to get to work again. In his new mood he also sent off *Dubliners* to a new publisher.

About *Ulysses*, which he had already begun to plan as far back as 1907, Joyce had endless discussions with Svevo. It became one of the major bugbears and finally one of the greatest interests in Svevo's life. He tells how he rang the bell of Joyce's flat in Paris, years after Joyce had left Trieste, feeling that at last he could stand the fullest examination on the book:

. . . on my arrival in Paris I made confidently for the doorbell in Square Robiac. Confidently, though a little timidly too. Though he is so much younger than I, circumstances are such that I approach him with the respect of a junior. But confidently, none the less, for I had kept my promise and had applied myself thoroughly to his great poem, and knew all its windings and pot-holes. I could see my way in it. I now knew every character and loved them all, Stephen, Bloom and Simon, the Englishman with his cinematic dreams, the irate Citizen and above all Bloom's wife. I responded to the book's varied and complex structure. . . . Then apart from this, I had some questions to ask. Maliciously, I wanted to take the author by surprise. . . . For instance, in the famous dialogue between Bloom and Stephen, the element water is studied in all its manifestations; sea, river, lake and pond. It is analysed chemically, physically and geographically. I wanted to know why the author had not seen it in its humble, but all the same important, form of a human tear.

But the surprise turned out to be all on my side. *Ulysses* has ceased to exist for Joyce. He feels that he has done all he knew how to do for it and now it must get on as best it can in the world. . . . (*Saggi*, p. 230-1)

Joyce took charge of the conversation at once at this encounter. He busily began questioning Svevo about a Triestine dialect phrase. Had it ever been translated into Italian? Why not? He (Joyce) had already translated it into English. Svevo reflected sadly that perhaps what was wrong with Italian writers was that they let words be their masters, instead of, as with Joyce, their servants.

Joyce got a great deal of his knowledge of Jewish customs from Svevo when creating Bloom. Svevo once said to Stanislaus: 'Tell me some secrets about Irishmen. You know your brother has been asking so many questions about Jews that I want to get even with him.' As we have seen, Stanislaus thought there were some traits of Svevo himself in Bloom. Granted Joyce's magpie method of writing this is very likely, though of course Bloom is in no sense a portrait of Svevo, and there was another Triestine whom Joyce used to name as a model—apart from the fact that Bloom was in many respects himself. Richard Ellmann puts it very well:

. . . Bloom is more than Joyce. He resembles in some ways Joyce's good friend in Trieste, the business man and writer Ettore Schmitz (Italo Svevo). The difference in age between Svevo and Joyce was roughly the same as that between Bloom and Stephen. . . . Besides, Svevo also had married a Gentile, and changed his name (though only for literary purposes), possessed a good sense of humour and a fair knowledge of Jewish customs. Where Joyce was partial only to cats, Svevo, like Bloom, had a fondness for dogs as well. Where Joyce could not abide the inner organs of animals and fowls, Svevo, like Bloom, loved them. These are small similarities, but Joyce had a spider's eye. (*Op. cit.*, p. 385)

I also suspect that Joyce was borrowing a detail from the Schmitz family when he makes Bloom, like Svevo's father, begin his working life as a peddler of trinkets. One could add that Svevo's father, like Bloom's, was a poor Jew from Hungary and that Svevo himself was a Jew who had received Catholic baptism for reasons of convenience. But the parallels aren't exact, and Ellmann is probably right in thinking that a more important model for this side of Bloom was Teodoro Mayer, the Hungarian-Jewish publisher of the *Piccolo*.

There was one authenticated borrowing from the Schmitzes, in that, according to Joyce, Livia gave her name and her magnificent golden hair to Anna Livia Plurabelle. It was a point Joyce was fond of referring to. He wrote to Svevo on the 20th February 1924 asking for permission to use Livia's hair:

Ask her, however, not to take up arms, either of steel or fire, since the person involved is the Pyrrha of Ireland (or rather of Dublin) whose hair is the river beside which (her name is Anna Liffey) the seventh city of Christianity springs up, the other six being Basovizza,* Clapham Junction, Rena Vecia,† Limehouse, S. Odorico* in the Vale of Tears and San Giacomo in Monte di

* Villages near Trieste.

† An old quarter of Trieste, named after the Roman arena ('arena vecchia').

Pietà.* Reassure your wife with regard to Anna Livia. I have taken no more than her hair from her and even that only on loan, to adorn the rivulet which runs through my city, the Anna Liffey, which would be the longest river in the world if it weren't for the canal which comes from far away to wed the divine Antonio Taumaturgo,† and then changing its mind, goes back the way it came.

Livia agreed, after a little persuading, though she was disgusted when she later heard there were two washerwomen scrubbing dirty linen in the Liffey. In 1928 Svevo gave Joyce a portrait of her by his old friend Veruda, in which she has her hair down. Joyce once remarked to a journalist: 'They say I have immortalised Svevo, but I've also immortalised the tresses of Signora Svevo. These were long and reddish-blond. My sister who used to see them let down told me about them. There is a river near Dublin which passes dye-houses and its waters are reddish, so I've enjoyed comparing these two things in the book I'm writing. A lady in it will have the tresses which are really Signora Svevo's.' He came back to the point in 1939, when he wrote to Livia on New Year's Day to announce the completion of *Finnegans Wake*:

Dear Signora: I have at last finished my book. For three lustra I have been combing and recombing the hair of Anna Livia. It is now time that she appear on the stage. I hope that Berenice will intercede for her little sister so that she may find in this great world, thanks to the gods, 'at least some small Deo Gratias'. . . . (quoted by Ellmann, *op. cit.*, pp. 727-8)

'Deo Gratias' is an allusion to the last paragraph of *As a Man Grows Older*, a passage which Joyce loved and knew by heart.

---

* i.e. 'St. James in the Pawnshop.' There is a street named S. Giacomo in Monte leading off the Piazza Giambattista Vico, where Joyce had rooms.

† An allusion to the Trieste canal, a very short one, terminating in front of the church of S. Antonio Taumaturgo.

6

The War and 'Zeno'

From 1903 onwards till the outbreak of war Svevo's life, divided between Murano, Charlton and Trieste, fell into a rigid bourgeois pattern. He was becoming indispensable to the firm, the more so as there was friction between Olga and Gioachino and the running of the firm fell more and more on Olga. Gioachino, Svevo reports from England in 1908, keeps grumbling that no one ever tells him anything. It's always '*You* do this', '*You* do that'—though in fact, as Svevo points out, he is always the first one to see the mail. Svevo thinks after all perhaps it will be better for him when Olga comes, as then at least he will be bound to hear about everything that's going on and he won't have so much time to brood. When it was decided in 1908 to set up a branch factory in America, it was Olga who went out on her own to see to it. Gioachino was developing a slightly refractory and schoolboyish attitude towards her; Nicola Bravin told the present writer how, one day at Charlton during the war, Olga had to go to the West End for the day, and left instructions as to the cooking temperature for the day's batch of paint. As soon as she was out of the factory, Gioachino gave Bravin a wink and increased the heat, so that they should get finished sooner.

Some time during this period Svevo was given a ten per cent interest in the business, and from now on he was a comparatively wealthy man. He was, in a cautious way, very generous with his money. He helped various other artists as well as Joyce—for instance the sculptor Arturo Rietti and the painter Tullio Silvestri, who, apparently, was even better at borrowing than Joyce, and indeed actually borrowed off Joyce.

Silvestri's technique for selling his pictures was curious: he went to see Ettore Schmitz, carrying a mysterious package; then he said: 'This package contains a coat and shoes for my daughter. I will show you.' Opening the package, he disclosed his latest canvas, which Schmitz had to buy for the sake of his daughter. (Ellmann, *op. cit.*, pp. 393-4)

Svevo also settled an annuity on Veruda's father, who was blind, and during the war, when the premises of the *Piccolo* were burnt down by rioters, he helped support the ex-editors.

He was, generally speaking, quite faithful to his decision to turn his back on writing, certainly on writing for publication, and the only two pieces of writing of real importance which are definitely datable to this period are the play *Un marito*, which belongs to 1903, and the short story *Vino generoso* (*Generous Wine*) which he wrote before 1914 and revised in the 1920s (the play *L'Avventura di Maria* also probably belongs to the period 1910-20). The only literary exercise he continued to allow himself was writing little fables on this or that occasion. This became a favourite habit of his, and his room was always littered with them, scribbled on old scraps of paper or business envelopes. The habit of telling himself he was not a writer became second nature, and when one day a business acquaintance casually asked him 'Is it true you are the author of two novels?' he blushed and said hastily 'No! No! That's my brother Adolfo'. For some reason the man was still curious, and asked Adolfo the same question; according to Svevo, Adolfo was not flattered.

His life with Livia went on very serenely for the most part. His grand passion had cooled down into a solid affection. Livia was busy and contented looking after Letizia and her menagerie of cats, dogs and caged birds. She had a miscarriage in 1909, entailing further visits to Salso, which

Svevo remarked had always been the 'black cat' (i.e. cause of bad luck) in their marriage, but the days of their serious quarrels seems to have been over.

Letizia was very much Livia's child, though a stronger-willed and more intelligent character than her mother. She and Svevo regarded each other rather critically; he was devoted to her in principle, but tended to shout at her when she got across him, and he remained a comparatively remote figure to her during her childhood. He wrote her charming letters, though—for instance the one he sent her when she was ten years old, thanking her for her poems, and making use of the occasion to warn her ironically against art:

Murano, 10 April 1908.

Dearest Letizia,

I have received your dear letter and I thank you very much for it. I can see the signs of such excellent feelings in your rhymes (which are not bad at all for a ten-year-old) that I am really delighted with them. Just for this once I should like to tell you something that may be hard for you to understand. You are the only poet I enjoy; I dislike all the rest of them. So far all will be clear to you; but now I must try to explain why I dislike them, and if possible make you agree when I shout 'Down with all poets'. I once knew two carpenters. One was a cheerful smiling, silent man; he made the most beautiful wardrobes, much admired by everybody, and he worked the whole day long. The other made a living too, for he had found a new profession. Instead of making wardrobes, which was too tedious a business for him, he had set up as a describer of wardrobes, and everyone listened and paid him for it. Indeed he deserved it, as he could describe things excellently, especially *brunolin* [walnut stain], and the yellow of wood, and all the other colours you find in a wardrobe. He could also describe the different shapes and lines in a wardrobe very well—the scrolls and bosses, and curlicues and other ornaments. And so they went on, year after year, the one making wardrobes and the other describing them. As time went by, the one who made wardrobes went on making good and beautiful ones that people liked to put their clothes and linen in. The *brunolin* was still *brunolin* and the wood-colour was still the colour of wood. The other, however—the one who described wardrobes—began to introduce little deviations, to impress his admirers. He described the *brunolin* as if it were the colour of blood, the blood that circulates in animals' bodies, and the colour of wood as if it were the colour of flesh, human flesh, sometimes white and sometimes brown, but always rosy because of the life-giving circulation underneath. Then, seeing this appealed to people, he began to claim he had known live wardrobes. They walked rather slowly, having such short legs, but instead of waiting for things to be put in them, they actually went to fetch them. Houses became very lively affairs with wardrobes running about them.

A rich man, who had been listening to what he was saying, told the carpenter he wanted one of these wardrobes. 'I wouldn't recommend it', said the carpenter. 'I'm afraid you may find my wardrobes also eat the stuff people put in them.' The rich man, who wasn't worried by this, kept on insisting, so the wag told him, 'Go and see my next-door neighbour; he *makes* wardrobes, I only describe them.' You can imagine the sort of face the real carpenter made when he heard someone wanted him to make a live wardrobe. 'I don't know how to make living things', he said. 'And if I did, I wouldn't be making wardrobes.'

I am sure you can see what a stupid creature that describer of live wardrobes was. But it wasn't really his fault, you know. If you go on describing, day in and day out, and all the time you're making nothing, day in and day out, you are bound to end up describing all wrong.

By that I don't mean to abuse your Salgari,* who I am sure has seen everything he describes. I have never read a word of him, and apparently you enjoy reading him. But if you love me, I hope that as well as reading things you will please me by making something. For instance I should like to see you making your own doll's clothes. And then it would be a good idea if you were to borrow one of Bruno's toy-boxes from him to build houses out of—and build one for me. Will you give me that pleasure? My darling little girl, seeing that I ask it of her, will do me that pleasure, I know. And when you have made the house, I will describe it. What

* Emilio Salgari (1863-1911), an immensely popular writer of adventure stories for children.

a pity it is I can't make them. (*Lettere alla moglie*, Trieste, 1963, pp. 260-3)

The one mild difficulty between Svevo and Livia was over Letizia's education. Livia, with Olga's support, had taken pains to bring her up as a Catholic, but Svevo insisted that she should go to an undenominational school, though he agreed that she could go to convent school for a year before her first communion. Livia would have liked her to stay on there, and there was some mild friction before Svevo got his way and they reverted to the original plan. Svevo was extremely hostile towards organised religion, whether Jewish or Christian, regarding it as an outmoded vexation and nuisance. He sighed when he thought how his brother Ottavio's daughter 'Tenci' had been brought up. Ottavio, who had gone to Vienna as a young man and become a successful banker there, had determined Tenci should not be bothered with religion at all. Normally, in Austria, a child at an undenominational school was supposed to be sent for a fixed number of hours every week for instruction in his parents' religion. Ottavio refused to have this in Tenci's case, and though she used to pass top in every other subject, when it came to religion she would tell her teachers she didn't know what it was. When the school remonstrated, Ottavio threattened to send her to Italy to finish her schooling there. 'What a difference between the two brothers', reflected Svevo.

He regarded Christianity as a puerile affair, and never pretended that he had got baptised for any other reason than to please Livia. There is a characteristic passage in a letter of his from Murano in 1901:

Today I went on my own to the piazza San Marco and, feeling bored, I finally went into the church, to hear the sermon. It was extraordinary the effect it made, against that background of magnificence and human genius, to hear such abject platitudes declaimed by a hoarse-voiced actor in a rage. He talked about the Pope and quite disposed me in his favour, merely from thinking 'If it's a choice between you and him, I choose the one I don't know'. No, it's no good: the only part of Christianity which I can do with is you and Titina [Letizia]. (Letter to Livia; Murano, 24 February 1901)

One of his favourite themes in his later writings, no doubt with Livia in mind, was the idea of an atheist being 'converted' by his widow after his death. There is a very fine late fragment, the last words he ever wrote in fact, later published as *La morte* (*Death*), which deals with this theme. An ageing couple, Roberto and Teresa, have just been seeing their grown-up children off after a visit, and Roberto, seeing his wife looking sad and lost after all the excitement, tries to think of something to distract her, and tells her a secret about himself. It is that his whole existence has always been governed by the thought of death. He wants to face death while he is still healthy and clear-headed, and when he is dying, to remember his healthy thoughts about death—nothing is more despicable than the squirmings of an animal under the knife. If he, as an atheist, can die well, it will help her, who is a believer, to do so too. They have a tender last night together, and then he is struck down by a fatal illness. As he lies dying he tries to tell her that the terrifying deathbed symptoms don't matter, but at last the fever is too much for him, and he gives way to his delirious fantasy—the pain is the work of some enemy, an enemy triumphing over him to the sound of bells. It has every right to do so—his whole life has been one long sin, and he deserves every punishment. He mouths the sound of bells: 'Ding, dong, ding, dong'. He dies muttering the ambiguous words: 'I never knew'. The effect on Teresa is exactly what he had been most determined it should not be. It puts her in a state of mortal terror. As a fruit of their long tolerance of each other's beliefs, she finds her own have become sterile, and in panic and remorse she sets to work to persuade herself that Roberto had a death-bed conversion. 'All that remained of Roberto on earth, that is to say in Teresa's heart, she converted. She converted it silently . . .'

His attitude was coloured, of course, by his relation to his own Jewishness. Curiously enough the first words he ever published were on a Jewish topic (Shylock), and referred to another baptised Jew, Heine:

> That renegade Heine, not knowing how else to reconcile his enthusiasm for Shakespeare with the veneration he still felt for the beliefs of his ancestors, tried, and perhaps not unsuccessfully, not only to justify the contents of *The Merchant of Venice* but actually to approve of them. (*Saggi*, p. 11)

G. Debenedetti, one of Svevo's best critics, suggests that Svevo's deliberate rejection of a Jewish destiny for himself is a key to his whole career. He implies, indeed, that his novels are really, at a deeper level, all about the Jewish character, and that he would have been a better novelist if he had been bolder about exploring 'the mystery of his own origins'. I don't find this convincing, though there is no doubt he liked to minimise his Jewish origin in public, if not in private. For instance, the word 'Jewish' never occurs in the *Autobiographic Profile* which he supplied his friend Giulio Cesari with notes for in 1928 and largely rewrote himself. Likewise Livia, who thought baptism cancelled all (though she herself, being only quarter-Jewish, suffered cruelly under the racial laws during the Second World War) makes no mention of his being a Jew in her *Life* of him. Again, there are no important Jewish characters in his novels, and though he makes Guido in *La coscienza di Zeno* (*The Confessions of Zeno*) a reader of Weininger, he is referring not to Weininger's anti-semitism but to his theories about women. There is some deliberate suppression here, though one should probably not read too much into it, as there was very little anti-semitism in Trieste in Svevo's youth and very little pressure from his family to saddle himself with a Jewish destiny. The subject wasn't forced on him as an issue as it was, say, on Kafka. He often joked about being a Jew in private conversation, but not in the tone of someone obsessed by it. One catches his attitude in a reply he made to a friend of his, Sergio Solmi, one drizzling morning in the gardens of Miramare:

We were talking about races and nationalities, a subject he was particularly fond of, and, among other things, about that undernote of Jewish scepticism and despair which some critics think they can trace in his *La coscienza di Zeno*. 'It isn't race which makes a Jew', said Svevo sadly, 'it's life!' (Sergio Solmi, 'Ricordo di Svevo', in *Solaria*, Florence, 1929, no. 3-4, p. 71)

The year or two before the 1914 war was an anxious time for Italian citizens in Trieste. In 1913 the Governor told the civic authorities to dismiss all foreign employees unless they would accept Austrian citizenship, and in March of the following year a gang of slavophile students shot and wounded an Italian student on the premises of the Revoltella Institute, which shut its doors the next day. When war broke out in August 1914, therefore, Italy seemed already on the point of a definite rupture with Austro-Hungary, and the italophile party in Trieste banked heavily on Italy's joining the Allies and invading Trieste. She remained discouragingly neutral, however, though postcards flooded in to the Italians in Trieste announcing 'marriage certain' and 'hopes for speedy recovery'; and the expected Franco-British naval landings also failed to occur. It was said confidently that Italy was waiting for the 20th September, the anniversary of Vittorio Emmanuele's entry into Rome, but this day passed too, and nothing happened.

In the first months of the war Svevo was at Mülheim, near Cologne, arranging for the setting-up of a new Veneziani factory on the premises of a German chemicals firm. He wrote to Livia in a burst of admiration for the Germans: 'Here everyone goes to the front full of enthusiasm and joy' he said (he was writing in German on postcards, on account of the censorship).

I have written nothing about this before, being so egoistic and thinking only about ourselves. The real, unmistakable enthusiasm

I have been witnessing here is indescribable. I have never admired and understood German might so well before. There is no doubt at all. Victory lies here. They have science on their side, and they will do everything that they have to; they think of sacrifice as natural.

He is struck by the extraordinary calm of the German population: 'You would think it was still peace-time, if you didn't read the papers, or see the preparations going on.'

Italian citizens began to stream out of Trieste across the Italian border, being joined by many deserters from the Austrian call-up. The city began to look deserted and dead, as it continued to do for the rest of the war. The harbour was empty of shipping, there were food shortages and unemployment, and the cafés were full of police spies. The Austrians imposed a rigid censorship of the press, so that the only reliable news of the war was from smuggled copies of Italian newspapers. Passes were required to leave the city, and the army, foreseeing the possibility of an evacuation, was hurriedly building defence-work in the hills above Trieste, emptying whole villages in the process.

As Gioachino and Olga were Italian citizens, they decided to take refuge in England while the war lasted, leaving Svevo, who was an Austrian subject, in sole charge in Trieste. The rest of the family dispersed likewise: Livia's sisters Nella and Fausta went to Zürich, whilst her sister Dora and her husband went to Florence. Letizia decided to join her aunt and uncle in Florence so as not to be parted from her fiancé, Antonio Fonda, who planned to volunteer for the Italian army.

At last, after innumerable rumours and false alarms, on the 23rd May the news came that Italy had declared war on the Central Powers. A relative of the Schmitzes (an Italian) arrived half fainting at Servola with the news, having overheard an Austrian officer and his wife discussing it on the tram. She had got into conversation with them, and as the two women talked (so Svevo's account goes) the Italian woman felt guilty. Here was the war she and all her friends had been longing for for so many years, and now that it had come, she hated it. The women looked at each other miserably, while the officer pretended to be nonchalant; as they parted they would have liked to kiss, but didn't dare to.

After a good deal of telephoning, Svevo decided it was safe to drive her home in his carriage, and when they reached the centre of the town, they found a huge mob gathered outside the *Piccolo* offices and the building itself in flames. For the rest of the night gangs of rioters roamed the streets, wrecking and looting Italian shops and cafés and setting fire to the premises of the irredentist organisations. The police looked on without interfering and the fire brigade were too intimidated to use their hoses. At one stage a large crowd gathered in the Piazza San Giovanni while sailors mutilated the statue of Verdi and smeared it with mud. (When the hero of *La coscienza di Zeno* finally arrives back in Trieste, starving, hatless and in his shirt-sleeves, having been overtaken by the war during an early-morning stroll, they ask him 'Have you been helping with the looting?')

Next day order was more or less restored and the Governor announced the rescinding of the civic constitution and the replacement of the Municipal Council by Imperial commissioners. A state of siege was declared on the 29th May (the Italians complained that it had been delayed deliberately so that the mob could do its work) and the last train for Italy left. The city gradually came more or less to a standstill. Half the shops shut their doors, there were all-night queues at the one remaining bakery, the Austrian banks transferred their assets to Vienna, and the trams stopped running, the tramwires having been commandeered. By day the streets were empty, and as evening came crowds gathered on the quayside to listen to the gunfire from Monfalcone. 'Two months after Italy's entry into the war, Trieste has an indescribable look of desolation', write H. and B. Astori in *La passione di Trieste*:

It is as if it had been a battlefield. In the July sun the long paved streets are like the bed of dried-up streams: a few slow passers-by in the morning and evening, in the heat of noonday nobody at all; not a cart or a carriage either. Even the two or three shops that have stayed open in the main streets let down their shutters for a good part of the day. The silence is broken only by the rhythmic footsteps of the patrols, echoing across the empty squares. And the few soldiers remaining are the final dregs left over from the call-up, the fifty-years olds . . . in faded, untidy uniforms, with muskets from the Franco-Prussian war slung from their shoulders by bits of knotted string. (*La passione di Trieste*, Florence, n.d., pp. 116-17)

(One remembers the Austrian soldiers Zeno ran into on the day war broke out, smelling of 'high game' and carrying the ancient bayonet the Triestines nicknamed 'Durlindana'.)

In August Austrian officials turned up at Servola, announcing they were commandeering certain equipment and materials from the factory and demanding to be told the formula of the 'Moravia' paint. Svevo refused to take this lying down, and during the night he got some of his most trusted workmen to wall up the secret ingredients in a hidden room, presenting the Austrians next day with a bogus formula, which they duly experimented with at the naval base at Pola. They eventually realised they had been tricked and in retaliation confiscated most of the contents of the factory, which had to close. Svevo went to Vienna in September to contest the confiscation, and eventually won his case. There were still considerable stocks of paint to dispose of, and he wrote to Livia from Vienna instructing her how to deal with them.

. . . Sell as little paint as you can. . . . The price of the grease should be 3 crowns, with an extra 8 crowns for the barrel, if required. If you sell by the case, ask Russian the price of cases, as this is no time to be giving things away. At all events, I shall want 500 kg. of no. 1 and 1,000 kg. of no. 2 still left for Hungary-Croatia when I get back. . . .

In December he was home in Trieste, and apparently hoping to continue business operations of some kind. Like Zeno in *La coscienza* he was enjoying having a free hand in business for the first time and felt the relief of not being under Olga's reign of terror; though indeed there was not much competition, most financiers and merchants having left for Vienna by this time, leaving only, as Benco remarks,* 'the four business men without any business who were still quoted by the newspapers as "stock exchange circles"'. He wrote to Letizia, via Zürich, on the 10th December 1915:

Dearest daughter,

You are in a great hurry to have me old. It's still only the 10th and you call me 54, which I shan't be till the 19th. I protest; though it's true these war years count double. Thank you so much for your birthday wishes. The best wish would be for this period to be over altogether. Remember how you left home after just a few minutes' discussion. It was like saying goody-bye for the holidays, and in fact it was for a long, grim school-term. I am writing no more fables; reality keeps breaking in on my dreams too much (if that is possible). I am becoming a serious man of affairs. Papa used to say I should reach the age of judgment at 40. He was 14 years out. (I hope you won't share my precocity.) Till a fortnight ago I was playing the violin every day. Then something came up—nothing too serious, just business-affairs which weren't going right and had to be seen to—and I left off the violin too. . . . (*Vita*, pp. 91-2)

As the war continued, however, his business activity came to a standstill, and he and Livia were left alone and idle in their flat, the house now being full of Austrian officers and their wives. Their friends were almost all the other side of the frontier, or interned, like Silvio Benco and Stanislaus Joyce. James Joyce, who had escaped internment through the influence of his pupils Baron Ralli and Count Sordina, was now in Zürich, giving English lessons to a number of Triestine

* In *Gli ultimi anni della dominazione austriaca a Trieste*, Milan, 1919, vol. 2, p. 198.

refugees, including the Bliznakoff daughters and, for a time, Letizia. Letters filtered through via Zürich, and every evening they met their few remaining friends, 'like conspirators' Livia said, at the Caffé Tergesteo, to exchange news and rumours.

Svevo himself was on the government black list, both because of his own irredentist sympathies and because of his connection with Livia's family, which had a long record of anti-Austrian activity. One of Gioachino's brothers, for instance, had been a companion of the famous irredentist martyr Giuglielmo Oberdan (executed in 1882 for a plot against Franz Joseph's life) and it was a family tradition that Olga herself had hidden a bomb for Oberdan. Two other brothers had fought with Garibaldi, and one of Gioachino's cousins, Felice Venezian, had been the leader of the irredentist movement in Trieste and Istria. Svevo was repeatedly summoned to police headquarters for questioning, sometimes in the middle of the night, but according to Livia he survived his interrogations very coolly and with great presence of mind.

How much weight to give to Svevo's own 'irredentism' is not clear. He was certainly a loyal member of the *Independente* group in his youth, and identified himself with them publicly; for instance, in 1895, when a public funeral procession was organised for Enrico Juretig, a chief editor of *L'Independente* who had died in an Austrian prison, he acted as one of the pall-bearers. Undoubtedly, too, the excitement of the armistice and of the 'redemption' of Trieste from Austrian rule had something to do with his return to fiction. On the other hand, his sudden enthusiasm for German militarism in 1914, at a time when Germany was Austro-Hungary's ally (though of course Italy had not yet entered the war) suggests that his anti-Austrianism never went very deep. 'Irredentism', indeed, was very much the convention among the well-off Italian bourgeoisie of Trieste, and its rhetoric and death-defying defiance of Austrian 'tyranny' have a somewhat operatic ring now. (The one full-length history of Trieste in Italian, by Attilio Tamaro, is more or less unreadable for its rhetorical partisanship.) A friend of Svevo's later years writes rather sardonically about the whole irredentist phenomenon: 'There is an impassable gulf between all that politics came to mean for Europeans after 1918 and that empty exaltation, that comfortable and irresponsible rhetoric, which nationalist politics represented for the well-to-do bourgeoisie in the long years of peace in Europe.' Svevo's politics, he imagines, were simply those of his own class and milieu: 'He would have voted Liberal*; he would have given a modest contribution to the *Lega Nazionale*; he would have felt a certain combative fervour in his box at the *Teatro Comunale* during *I Puritani* or Verdi's "Va pensiero sull'ali dorate",† and would have done his best to feel himself oppressed by Austria—that empire which acted to everyone, and especially all Italians, in the most "gentlemanlike" manner!'

To fill his enforced idleness during the later stages of the war, Svevo began to write again, and scribbled various notes towards a book of memoirs, which never finally took shape. A number of these have survived, including the following, dated the 13th June 1917:

An old man is almost bound to be an orderly man. Now I am 56 I have three kinds of spectacles to look after—a great training in tidiness. So I can take up this volume of memoirs with the firm knowledge I shall carry it through to its end. So many things that were important to me have vanished from my mind; it's a great cause of regret to me. How pale they seem now, all those things and those people! They are abstract concepts now, and therefore false ones. I shall end up imagining I too have always been as I am today, though at present I can still remember loves and hatreds I have long stopped feeling. I have the suspicion, though, that changing in what one desires doesn't change anything fundamental.

* He in fact made a point of returning from wherever he happened to be in Europe to cast his vote.

† The chorus of the Hebrews in captivity, in *Nabucco*.

The essential thing is not what, but how, one desires things. But not having taken enough notes in the past, I can't prove it. Certainly, I remember having violent desires and violent detestations, but I don't know whether I lost the things I was attached to out of laziness or because of fate, or whether the things I hated dogged me because I was too feeble or because they were too strong. Napoleon must have had clearer ideas about his own life, even if he didn't start writing it down till his real life was over. Four years ago, before the world war, I took a long journey all over Europe. On my way, I wished all the fields I passed a good harvest and the peasants, in all their different costumes, a good reward for their labour. I felt I had done a great thing by this, and that Napoleon might have envied me. So when war broke out, each new terror and disaster seemed a pointless waste; I had no need of a war to unload my hatreds. (*Vita*, pp. 92-3)

Influenced by his reading of Walter Schucking and A. H. Fried he also began work on a project for universal peace, though he seems to have given it up in disgust.* His main new intellectual interest, however, was Freud.

Svevo was introduced to Freud's writing somewhere about 1908 by Edoardo Weiss, a school-friend of Livia's younger brother Bruno and later a leading figure in the psycho-analytical movement in Italy. Freudian theory soon began to take hold of him, though he found Freud's actual prose-style very disagreeable. He once remarked that, though no one was going to believe it, considering what was said about his own prose, he really preferred writing to be elegant and perspicuous—however one of his friends explained away his prejudice as a Freudian 'resistance'. He never seriously considered being psycho-analysed himself, though he made some desultory experiments in self-analysis. He felt that by this time he had got on good enough terms with his own 'degenerate' temperament. To cure it now would be to cure himself out of existence. However in 1910 his brother-in-law Bruno, who was studying to be a concert pianist, was

* A substantial fragment has survived (*Saggi*, pp. 121-39).

sent to Vienna to be analysed by Freud himself. The treatment did him no good, and he returned two years later, more neurotic than ever, reporting that Freud had pronounced him incurable. This incident gave Svevo a permanent prejudice against the actual practice of psycho-analysis, but as a method of looking at the world the Freudian theory steadily grew on him. Towards the end of the war he and his nephew Aurelio Finzi began a translation of Freud's *On Dreams* and he began to nurse the ambition of introducing Freud into Italian literature. It was this ambition, combined with his excitement at becoming an Italian in 1918 (Italy, as he said, 'coming to him') that finally turned him to fiction again.

The Austrian authorities eventually re-opened the factory, putting an official of their own in charge. He turned out to be a Czech, and almost as anti-Austrian as Svevo himself, and they got on very well together. Indeed many of the officers billeted on the Schmitzes shared their political feelings, though Livia caused Svevo some embarrassment at the time of Caporetto. One day they noticed that there was no longer any sound of gunfire to be heard. It was the first time since the summer of 1915, and Livia, realising it meant the Italians were in full retreat, spent the day in tears. Svevo made apologies for her, saying 'What can you expect? She's an Italian, you know'.

During the autumn of 1917 there were two Austrian battle-battleships, the *Budapest* and the *Wien*, at anchor in Trieste harbour (or rather, the Vallone di Muggia) just by Servola, and at half-past two on the night of the 9th-10th December, a night of violent storm, Svevo and Livia were woken by a terrific explosion. (As they learned later, it was a torpedo, missing its target, the *Budapest*, and hitting the quayside.) A few minutes later, above the storm, they heard the sound of screams from the drowning sailors of the *Wien*, which had been torpedoed and sunk. It was the famous raid of Lieutenant Rizzo, who had taken two tiny 'M.A.S.' torpedo-boats right through the harbour defences to attack the battleships at point-blank range. Forty-six of the *Wien*'s crew were killed or drowned, the rest being rescued by the *Budapest* or swimming ashore. In defiance of black-out regulations Svevo had the garden-lights of the Villa Veneziani switched on, as a landmark for the drowning men, and eventually eighteen frozen and half-naked sailors were carried in alive to the porter's lodge. They were all from the Istrian coast or thereabouts, and in their local dialect they began cursing their officers, who had been out drinking in the town when the attack occurred.

The district of Servola, with the Lloyd shipyards and seaplane and submarine establishments nearby, was one of the main targets for Italian bombing raids during the war, and the Veneziani household often spent the night in the cellar. When Svevo met Rizzo after the war the latter told him he had made detailed plans for a raid on the Lloyd arsenal at Servola. If it had come off, he said—Svevo thought he detected a note of regret—the Villa Veneziani and its factory would have been blown sky-high. 'I shook his hand vigorously', said Svevo, 'as if making a retrospective effort to restrain him.'

By 1918 the city was nearly starving and had shrunk to half its normal size. There was grass growing in the cracks of the pavement and people were experimenting with clothes materials made of nettles and paper. The shock of Caporetto had gone deep, and when Svevo's brother Adolfo, who had been ill with a heart disease, was dying that August at the Villa Veneziani, they pretended that the Italians had recaptured Udine. 'Too late for me', he said sadly. The Austrian authorities were gradually relaxing their control of the city, and as the internees returned they were shocked at its ghastly appearance.

When the future of Trieste came up for discussion in the Austrian parliament, the Socialists advocated its becoming a semi-autonomous 'Hanseatic' town linked to a federated Austria. The Slavs, meanwhile, were claiming it as an integral part of the new 'Kingdom of the Serbs, Croats and Slovenes.'

And as the trend of events seemed to be turning against the Central Powers, the irredentist party decided to make a decisive gesture. During October the deputy Edoardo Gasser invited a group of irredentists, including Svevo, to a series of meetings at his house to make plans for an Italian-nationalist journal, to be called *La Nazione*. This committee rapidly transformed itself into a *Fascio Nazionale*, which, in turn, after negotiations with the Socialists, elected a Committee of Public Safety.

On the 30th October a troop of students began a march through the city, shouting *Viva Italia! Viva Trieste italiana!* and at this signal a full-scale uprising took place. The mob forced its way into the Municipal Buildings, hoisting the tricolour on the roof, and for the rest of the day it flooded the streets in triumph, ransacking the offices of the pro-Austrian associations, setting the bells of the Cathedral ringing, and opening the prisons. The same day the Committee of Public Safety presented itself at the Governor's palace, demanding to be recognized as the new government of Trieste, and after telephoning Vienna the Governor acquiesced. At noon on this day of revolution, Livia relates, Svevo hoisted a tricolour flag, carefully hidden for the occasion, over the Villa Veneziani. The wife of the Austrian Field-Marshal von Cicerich was living at the villa at the time, and when she came out into the garden and saw the enemy flag, she went pale with alarm. Svevo reassured her ironically: 'Don't be afraid, Signora; you will still be safe in bed, even under the tricolour.'

On the following day a deputation was sent by sea to Venice to invite the Italians to take over Trieste, and on the 3rd November, after two days of confusion (during which the Socialists made a last effort to organise a republic, and released convicts got hold of firearms and broke into the Free Port) a flotilla of Italian torpedo-boats and transports arrived in the harbour, and General Petitti di Roreto, the Governor of Venezia Giulia, disembarked before cheering crowds. Striking the ground with his heel, he declared: 'In the name of His Majesty the King of Italy, I take possession of the city of Trieste.'

Immediately after the liberation, Svevo and Livia rushed off to Florence to see Letizia again, finding her just recovering from Spanish 'flu, and having brought her and her fiancé back to Trieste Svevo set off again, with hampers of food, to rescue Ottavio and his family from Vienna. The city was starving and in the middle of a revolution, and they had a gruelling journey home, but Svevo was in immense spirits and kept them giggling and cheerful. Before long Olga and Gioachino and the rest of the family had returned from different parts of Europe and the Villa Veneziani was once again crammed with cousins and aunts and grandchildren.

For the moment Svevo still had plenty of leisure, as it was some time before the Veneziani factory was working at full pressure again, and moreover Letizia's fiancé had joined the firm and begun to take some of the work off his hands. He kept his promise to write for *La Nazione*, which Benco was editing, though his articles turned out in the end to be mostly non-political; they included a skit on the Servola tramway and some impressions of pre-war England.* After a few months of journalism, however, he began to feel an intense desire to write another novel. The liberation had somehow given him back his literary confidence; after years as an outsider, trying unsuccessfully to interest Italian critics in his writing, Italy had now come to him:

It is certainly true that if Italy had not come to me I should never have thought of being able to write my novel four months after the arrival of our troops, as if it were a perfectly natural thing for a man of fifty-eight to do. With the arrogance of all released prisoners, it seemed to me I had suddenly acquired the right of an 'incolato' [resident] for myself and my patois.

* Livia speaks of his writing 'eight short articles and a satire on the Servola tram-service', but only the latter (a sequence of four brief articles) has been identified.

He sketched the outlines of a new novel, *La coscienza di Zeno*, at high speed (Livia says in a fortnight), and worked on it at intervals during the next two years.

Joyce came back to Trieste in October 1919, but he and Svevo saw less of each other than before. Indeed, as his Triestine friends remarked, Joyce was generally less companionable. Trieste depressed him; it was cheerless and no longer the busy port it had been before the war. Stanislaus was surly and made it obvious he didn't welcome having James and his family on his hands again. And much as he tried, Joyce could not persuade Frank Budgen, on whom by now he had become very dependent, to come to Trieste. In Zürich he had also become very intimate with a young Triestine, Edoardo Weiss's brother Ottacaro, who was studying at Zürich University and was a friend of Jung, but just before he left he had a quarrel with him, having convinced himself that Weiss had advised a patroness of his to stop supplies. (He later decided that it was Jung who was at the bottom of it.) Svevo, who was a friend of Weiss, tried to arrange a reconciliation, but failed.

Joyce reclaimed his old post at the Revoltella Institute, which was now in process of becoming a university. The job only entailed an hour's teaching a day, and according to one of his pupils, interviewed in 1954 by Richard Ellmann, he conducted his classes very casually:

He found drills too tedious, so he spent an inordinate amount of time in giving his students the names of foods, insisting 'These words are very important'. He attempted a disquisition upon Gladstone to explain the Gladstone bag, but was thwarted, to his great irritation, by their not knowing who Gladstone was. (Ellmann, *op. cit.*, p. 487)

He abandoned the job in June 1920, asking the Revoltella to give it to Stanislaus instead (which a year later it did), and left Trieste, this time for ever.

Letizia and Antonio Fonda married in 1919 and set up

house in the Villa Veneziani, having their first child Piero the following year. Gioachino died in August of the same year (1920), and the event prompted Svevo to write Livia a letter of farewell to be read after his own death:

Yesterday we buried Gioachino, and it seems important for me now, not to make my own last requests, but to make sure that after my death my lifelong companion, my wife Livia, should have a word of farewell and encouragement from me. I want her to remember, to help her in the nervous agony any death in the family causes her, how invariably sweet and loving she has been to me, and how much I always valued her sweetness and love, and lived on them. I want her to know that I am content with the affection she has given me during my life and would prefer (though I won't insist on it) for there to be no mourning and solemnity after my death. She must live as her feelings promdt her, and I want my death to confirm and enlarge her liberty, which I never willingly encroached on. In short, all I want really to do is to send her a last loving kiss. Goodbye, dear Livia. I entrust her to my son and daughter Antonio and Letizia Fonda. May she find in them all the support, respect and love she deserves: by which I mean, not that I command them thus, but that I believe it is what they will do of their free will. I send them a loving kiss also, hoping that they will never lose the love which brought them together and made Livia and me so happy. I should like my funeral to be simple, quiet, and a *civil* one. I want to be the least trouble possible to my friends and neighbours and for things to be done in the most simple and straightforward way, without ostentation of any kind, even of simplicity.

He ends by asking Livia to look after various dependants whom he has been supporting, such as Veruda's father and his nephew Umbertino Ancona.*

In the summer of 1922 Svevo, Livia, and Letizia and her family rented a villa at Poggioreale in the foothills of the

* Son of Svevo's sister Ortensia. His mother died in 1897, and when his father married again, his stepmother quarrelled with him and had him thrown out of the house. He died in tragic circumstances in 1923.

Carso, just above Trieste, and Svevo now set to work, in a state of intense excitement, to complete the final draft of *Zeno*. He spent the whole day, and occasionally part of the night too, at the typewriter, smoking like a Turk. The book possessed him completely, and he was convinced that he had done something new and important in it.

7

The Miracle of Lazarus

Late in 1923 *La coscienza di Zeno* was published by the firm of Cappelli of Bologna, at Svevo's own expense. It fell more or less dead, as *Senilità* had done a quarter of a century before. Silvio Benco gave it a warm review, as did one or two other local critics, but the Italian press in general ignored it almost completely, though the *Corriere della Sera* eventually gave it a brief notice, saying it was interesting but formless. After the fever of excitement and optimism in which he had written the book, the disappointment hit him badly. He felt he had broken all his old and solemn resolutions only to make a fool of himself again, and at an age when he had no right to be taking such risks (he was now sixty-two). The whole fiasco began to affect his health and seemed to be aggravating a mild heart trouble he had been suffering from. In January, as a gesture of defiance he later said, he sent a copy of the new novel to Joyce, who in fact had already obtained one, asking for advice on how to interest Italian critics. The letter was a turning-point in his fortunes and the first step towards the 'miracle of Lazarus' of his last years.

His relations with Joyce had been desultory since Joyce left Trieste. Six months after he had gone, Svevo had received an appeal from Joyce, in his best fantastic manner, and mostly in the Triestine dialect,* asking him to find someone to rescue the notes of the Ithaca and Penelope episodes of *Ulysses* which he had left behind:

* They corresponded in Italian otherwise.

LIVIA
with the long hair borrowed by Joyce for Anna Livia Plurabelle

(*Above*) LIVIA'S PARENTS
Olga and Gioachino Veneziani

(*Below*) THE VILLA VENEZIANI
and adjacent factory

Boulevard Raspail 5
Parigi VII

Dear Mr. Schmitz,

The Circe episode was finished some time ago, but four typists refused to have anything to do with it. Finally a fifth appeared on the scene, but she works very slowly, so it won't be ready before the end of this month. I am told that it will occupy a hundred and sixty pages, of the usual format. The Eumaeus episode, which is nearly finished, will also be ready near the end of the month.

According to the plan arranged by my lawyer in New York, *Ulysses* will appear over there about the fifteenth of June in a privately-printed edition limited to 1,500 copies, 750 being for Europe. The price will be 12.50 dollars or £6 a copy. I am to receive £1,000 sterling as hush-money! At the same time, however, article upon article is being prepared to lay the foundations of the citadel. I don't know what the result will be, and am not much concerned.

Now for the important matter. I can't leave here myself (as I thought I was going to be able to do before May). Indeed for months and months I haven't got to bed before 2 or 3 in the morning, and am working without a break. I shall soon have exhausted the notes I brought here with me to write these two episodes. There is in Trieste, in my brother-in-law's quarter of the house identified by the street and building number via Sanità 2, and precisely situated on the third floor of the said house, in the bedroom at present occupied by my brother, at the back of the building in question, and overlooking the house of public insecurity,* an oil-cloth folder, bound with an elastic band of the colour of a nun's abdomen, having the approximate dimensions of 95 cm by 70 cm. In the said folder there repose the symbolic signs of the languid glimmerings which have sometimes flashed upon my soul. The gross weight is estimated at 4·78 kilos. Having urgent need of these notes for the due completion of my literary labours entitled *Ulysses* or your bitch of a mother,† I address the respectful request to you, most honoured colleague, that you

* i.e. police station.

† Literally 'tua madre grega': your Greek mother (a Triestine term of abuse).

should inform me whether anyone in your family is proposing to visit Paris in the near future; in which case I should be grateful if the said person would have the exquisite kindness to bring me the manna referred to overleaf.

Thus, dear Signor Schmitz, if there is someone of your family who is travelling this way, he would do me a great favour by bringing me the bundle which is not in the least heavy since, as you will understand, it is full of papers of which I have made fair copies in ink and occasionally in 'bleistiff' when I had no pen. But be careful not to break the rubber band because then the papers will fall into disorder. The best plan would be to take a suitcase which can be locked so that no one can open it. There are many articles of this kind on sale at 'Greinitz Neffen's' just opposite the 'Piccolo' which my brother, the Professor at the 'Berlitz-Cul'*, passes by.

At all events, let me have a few words from you; how are you? The Revoltella have written to me saying that there are boys to examine at five 'fliche'† per person, and then there are the doctors of the revolver‡ as well, and that I should go there to give them an English 'Aufgabe' for 5 'fliche'; but I didn't answer because the whole business seems shady, and besides, the stamp and paper would cost me 3 'fliche' with money what it is, and all they want to advance me is two 'fliche' to pay for the train and food and drink for three days. But what can one expect?

Cordial greetings, and apologies for my exhausted brain. We still have a little fun now and then.

Write to me soon, soon,

James Joyce

(*Vita*, pp. 101-3)

Svevo brought the notes himself in the course of one of his trips to London, which continued after the war, and for the next year or two he only saw Joyce on flying visits of this kind. Moreover he had learned not to expect casual letters from him; like most of Joyce's old friends, the most he

* An obscene pun on 'Berlitz School'.
† Austrian crowns.
‡ Joyce is punning on the word 'rivoltella', i.e. revolver.

generally got was a Christmas card. However, Joyce responded at once to his appeal.

30 January 1924 Victoria Palace Hotel
Rue Blaise Desgoffes
Paris rue de Rennes

Dear Friend,

I went to the station but no train arrived or was even expected at the time you mentioned. I was very sorry about this. When will you be passing through Paris again? Couldn't you spend the night here? Thank you for the novel with the inscription. I have two copies in fact, having already ordered one from Trieste. I am reading it with great pleasure. Why be discouraged? You must know it is by far your best work. As to Italian critics I can't speak. But send copies to Valéry Larbaud, Benjamin Crémieux, T. S. Eliot (Editor Criterion), F. M. Ford. I will speak or write to them about it also. I shall be able to write more when I've finished the book. So far two things interest me. The theme: I should never have thought that smoking could dominate a man like that. Secondly, the treatment of time in the book. You certainly don't lack penetration and I see that the last paragraph of *Senilità*, 'Yes, Angiolina thinks and weeps etc.' has been growing and blossoming in secret . . .

James Joyce

P.S. Send also to Gilbert Seldes, The Dial, New York.

Joyce, who was by now a great expert at literary promotion, was as good as his word. He wrote again in February:

Victoria Palace Hotel,
5, Rue Blaise Desgoffes,
Paris
Rue de Rennes.

Dear Friend,

Send the books without fear. I have already spoken about you to Larbaud and Crémieux. Make use of my name when you write to Seldes and Eliot. Also send a copy to Lauro de Bosis and to Enzo Ferrieri, the director of *Il Convegno*, via S. Spirito 24, Milan.

Your book will certainly be appreciated. Who could not

appreciate the learned Doctor Coprosich (*sanctificetur nomen tuum*) who 'also washed his face'? But with that name you have given him he should have performed quite other *lacacri*! . . .

By April he was able to report that Larbaud had read *Zeno* and admired it greatly; he had promised to write a review of it in the *Nouvelle Revue Française*. Larbaud, the author of *Poésies de A. O. Barnabooth* and *Ce vice impuni, la lecture*, was very much a key-figure on the Parisian literary scene at the time. A rich amateur, with a private library of 50,000 volumes and a famous collection of toy soldiers, he had a passion for travel and for literary discovery. He was, for instance, the first to introduce the French to Ramon Gomez de la Serna, Samuel Butler, Landor and James Joyce. He was also a devotee of Trieste, which he professed to prefer to Venice:

Nothing materialised immediately, and in June, after another gloomy letter from Svevo, Joyce made a further approach to Larbaud:

. . . I had a letter from 'Italo Svevo' this morning. He is in despair about his book. If you could manage a short note on it somewhere or, as you suggested, give some pages of it in the second number of *Commerce* you would do much more for him than my mention of *Les lauriers sont coupés* did for Dujardin.

He also sent reassurances to Svevo, whose reply showed him in a mood to avoid further snubs from the literary world:

Trieste, 10 June 1924.

Dear Friend,

Thank you for your letter of the 6th. . . .

I leave for London tomorrow. Thank Larbaud on my behalf and tell him he can do whatever he likes with my novel, even translate it *in toto* (a good idea?) I don't write to Larbaud myself only because of my past experience, which is that men of letters in general are badly brought up (at least Italian ones are) and never answer letters. Of the three novels I sent to Italy none appears to have reached its destination. It is to my shame still to be worrying about my book; all the more, since I can only do it through you, and you, with your own great triumphs and anxieties (I mean about the operation) have plenty to occupy you already. When you have finished with these overtures to M. Larbaud, let's both leave the novel to its fate.

I've got hold of *Ulysses*. When I get back I will read it chapter by chapter, trying to live in it. Your brother has promised me that after I've worked through each chapter as thoroughly as I can, he will give me some help. Apart from you, I don't think I could have a better assistant . . .

One day in January 1925 Svevo and Livia were at lunch together with Letizia and her children, when he opened a letter with a Paris postmark, and the first words, 'Egregio Signore e Maestro', astonished him considerably. It was from Valéry Larbaud, and it continued:

Since I received and read *La coscienza di Zeno* I have done all I could to make this admirable book known in France. Propaganda by word of mouth only, but efficacious, as you will see.

Last summer the review *Commerce* was founded, directed by our greatest poet, Paul Valéry, by Léon-Paul Fargue, known to the *élite* as one of the best *avant-garde* writers, and by me; and this review immediately sprang to the front rank of French literary reviews. The idea of the publication came from the Princess Bassiano,* wife of Prince Roffredo Caetani, of Rome, and she provides the financial backing and gives us useful advice.

Before the review was founded I had given the Princess *La coscienza di Zeno* to read, and now that we are at work preparing numbers IV and V, she wants to publish some fragments of it—between 10 and 15 pages. The translation question presents no difficulty; among our best *avant-garde* writers there are three or four excellent translators from Italian, and they are quite ready to translate the pages we select. The only thing lacking, therefore, is your own permission and that of the publisher Cappelli.

---

* Marguerite Caetani, née Chapin, Princess of Bassiano (1880-1963), born in New London, Connecticut, friend and patron of numerous Parisian artists and writers and later founder and editor of the periodical *Botteghe Oscure*.

As for myself, I should like to publish a brief study of your work in *Commerce*, republishing it later in an enlarged form in *La Nouvelle Revue Française* or the *Revue Européenne*. However, I don't know your other books, which I searched for without success in Bologna and Florence last summer, and I should be most grateful to you if you would be kind enough to send me them.

Our friend James Joyce, as you will know, has had to undergo another operation on his eyes, but is now well and working again.

I beg you to excuse so many requests, and believe me, egregio Signore e Maestro,

Your devoted admirer,

Valéry Larbaud

(*Vita*, pp. 105-6)

Svevo was dazzled by this turn of events, Livia had never seen him look so radiant, and he lost no time in sending off copies of *Senilità* and *Una vita*. Another letter arrived from Larbaud on the 20th February, announcing further details of the 'Svevo campaign' which Joyce had set in motion.

All Svevo's own literary enthusiasms revived with a rush, and he replied, in French, full of new plans and confidence:

Trieste, 16 March 1925.

This is a good occasion to remind you of my existence. I see you have been named Chevalier de la Légion d'Honneur. I congratulate you sincerely, though I think I know you well enough now to be sure you won't attribute too much importance to official recognition. All the same it is a good opportunity for me to add a letter of mine to the thousands you must be receiving. I hope it won't bore you any more than the rest.

You can imagine how passionately interested I am in all that concerns you. I've also read your controversy with Mr. Boyd,* on

---

* Ernest Boyd attacked Larbaud in his *Ireland's Literary Renaissance* and elsewhere, accusing him of 'colossal ignorance of Anglo-Saxon literature' and of 'touching absurdity' in believing there was such a thing as 'European' literature. Larbaud replied in a letter in the *Nouvelle Revue Française* of 1st January 1925.

the subject of James Joyce. It's quite a new phenomenon to find a French critic teaching an Irish one to appreciate one of his own writers. But new things are happening everwhere, and perhaps most of all in France. Your Sainte-Beuve knew and loved foreign writers, as long as they were decently dead and had the backing of their own countrymen.

I have the unpleasant feeling that I mustn't discuss your own work or I shall be suspected of trying to repay my debt. I know perfectly well I could in fact never repay it, but I don't want to seem to be trying. So not a word about your books.

I am surprised to find how detached from life I am in my old age.

If you knew what an upheaval your two letters have caused in my existence! I have re-read *Senilità* and now see the book, which I had resigned myself to thinking of no value, in the light your judgment throws on it; I've also re-read *Una vita.* James Joyce always said that there was only room for one novel in a man's heart (he hadn't even begun *Ulysses* then) and that when one writes more than one, it is always the same book under different disguises. But in that case my only novel would be *Una vita.* Except that it is so badly written that I ought to re-write it. And I am not sure I shall have either the time or the health for it. Your two letters have come too late. All the same, owing to you, I now have a vivider feeling of my own life and past.

I am doing other reading too. My education is beginning over again. I have obtained Lalou's history of your literature from 1870. You know that we were out of the civilised world in Trieste during the war, and perhaps for that reason the last name that reached me from your country was Anatole France. But in fact I have the impression that people in this country follow your literary production less than they used to.

You may know the Italian literary world better than I do, and I may be wrong; but I know in my youth a book published in Paris was in our hands in a matter of hours. Today, indeed, there are some French books bought and read, but not the best ones. The objection people raise against Proust aren't of a kind to stop his being read. At bottom they are the same objections which might have injured Zola too. But he had the luck to find in Italy a critic as brilliant and influential as Francesco de Sanctis. . . .

In the spring, on their way to London, the Schmitzes spent two days in Paris, and Joyce arranged a dinner at a restaurant for Svevo to meet Larbaud. He also invited Benjamin Crémieux, who had been reading and admiring *Zeno* too. Crémieux was as valuable a recruit for the Svevo campaign as Larbaud himself. He was a great talker and literary law-giver and an immensely prolific critic, appearing regularly in half a dozen different literary periodicals. Like Larbaud, he was an ardent italophile, and had been the first to spread the fame of Pirandello in France. He wrote as a declared cosmopolitan and European, preaching a doctrine of 'humanist realism', and was once attacked by Charles Maurras as a 'destructive Jew'; he ended his life in Buchenwald.

Svevo was in tremendous spirits at the dinner, and next evening the same party met again at the Princess Caetani's villa at Versailles, where he was again lionised and told them about the new story he was beginning, the *Corto viaggio sentimentale* ('Brief Sentimental Journey'). During the same stay in Paris he began a friendship with Marie Anne Commène, Benjamin Crémieux's young wife, a handsome Corsican from the little Greek colony of Cargèse. She was related to the Stéphanopoli de Commène who founded the colony in 1676 and who were themselves descended from the Imperial Byzantine family of Commenus. Later a successful novelist herself, she became one of Svevo's great admirers and his best link with Paris. He said she was the only inhabitant of Paris who had the postal service regularly at her command. During the whole visit he was in an extraordinary state of euphoria and was later ashamed of how much he had played the lion.

In June he was corresponding from London with Larbaud, who was at work translating passages from *Senilità*. No more was said about the *Commerce* project, and when Svevo passed through Paris again he was aggrieved to find the Princess Caetani not at home to him. He wrote to Larbaud from Trieste on the 15th September:

I have had no news from Paris for so long that, as I write to you, the memory of those two unforgettable days I passed there comes back to me quite fresh.

. . . I was in Paris again for a few hours and M. Crémieux greeted me with great kindness.

Then came the rub: I was almost convinced that there was living in Versailles a Princess who had once smiled at me. And indeed it was true there was, but I had been foolish enough to send her my books, and after that she no longer wanted to see me. And from July on the climate grew chillier in general, for I wrote to Crémieux twice but he didn't reply.

I must admit experience teaches me that lack of success has its advantages too. I am living here quite restored to submarine paint and to modesty.

Success (and I had it for an hour or two, as you know) makes those who aren't used to it greedy and petulant. A baby 64 years old can't have such an experience with impunity. So you must come here and see me as I am now. I want to blot out the memory of those days. I wasn't myself. I remember among other things, telling you that I had some things to show you [Svevo presumably meant some of his own writings] which would be sure to please you (how I curse myself now!). And all the same, it is true I *could* show you some extraordinary things: some amazing grottoes, the bare landscape of the Corso, and the sudden break it makes with the fertile land at the point where water gives out, and finally some of the ancient townships of Istria. In fact you could take the presumption in my remark as cunning, as a way of baiting the hook for you. Still, I think simplicity will get me furthest. When are you coming? Let me know, as I want to be absolutely free when you are here, which is not always so easy.

What really had happened in Paris, though Svevo didn't know it, was that Larbaud had had a quarrel with the Princess Caetani, and at the end of the year he also quarrelled with his old friend and co-editor Léon-Paul Fargue and resigned from the board of *Commerce*.

On the 3rd November Svevo was writing to Larbaud again, in much the same vein:

. . . My impatience is really childish and is becoming a serious nuisance to you, who don't deserve it. I would try to defend myself in this way: I am not anxious for fame or glory. Through your efforts I've already had more of those than I could have dreamed of. If I really wanted fame. I could have spread the news of that interview between Cremiéux and Dora Salvi, which came out in a paper* very few people know about. I could even, if I'd had the bad taste to do so, have shown your letters to people; that would have been quite enough.

But it's not that I want. I am curious about myself, and what I want is to know something about myself before I die. I am enclosing my short story, but I have no idea if there is anything in it to interest you about me. I have written many things that I destroyed afterwards, feeling how empty they were. Do with the story whatever you feel. I have nothing else ready. For three years after my novel came out I wrote nothing. Encouraged by my first visit to Paris I began an endless *novella* in London, called *Corto viaggio sentimentale*. I keep thinking about it. But having got back here I haven't touched it again, always wondering as I do whether I ought to go back to scraping my violin. That is how I am made, and perhaps by now I am on the down-grade, and prone to give up more easily. For the moment you and that great lady Mme. Crémieux have put me on my feet again. I shall be good for several months now, and when I feel myself crumbling again I shall cry 'Help!' . . .

However, later that month Joyce was able to write to Svevo that in place of the *Commerce* scheme, a similar project was now being planned by a new periodical, *Le Navire d'Argent*, just launched by Adrienne Monnier. The latter was the famous 'nun of literature' who kept a bookshop in the rue de l'Odéon, a place much frequented by the Parisian *avant-garde* and the scene of the celebrated *conférence* on *Ulysses* in December 1921. Mme. Crémieux wrote on the same day and with similar news, and Svevo, who was still 'living on the sounds that came to him from Paris', replied nostalgically:

. . . That unforgettable salon of yours, only spoilt by the photo-

* *La Sera* of Trieste, 19 March 1925.

graph of Pirandello (to whom I sent my novel as well as a letter four months ago, without his deigning to reply, so that now I can't stand him: it isn't enough to write masterpieces, you must be able to understand *La coscienza*)—that salon, I say, plays a part of the greatest importance in my good fortune (which I already regard as a *fait accompli*) and I shall never forget it. There is not much chance that I shall be passing through Paris again soon, since the firm considers I am too old to take on the Anglo-Saxons. I should be glad of this, if it weren't that it meant I can't thank you in person for all you have done, and wanted to do, for me. You were the only one who never hesitated a moment and who didn't even waste a single word on my supposed linguistic failings. . . .

If the *Navire d'Argent* lives up to its name, I shall be able (perhaps) to break free from all my commitments to submarine paint. In my family (I'm not referring to my wife) they need to see money before they will have any faith in literature. If I could, I might be able to polish up my language a little. Meanwhile the long serpent I wrote to you about (it is called *Corto viaggio sentimentale*) is lying curled up in a drawer. The end of the year is on us, and I spend all my days in the office.

It would be marvellous to come and see you as a real man of letters. To arrive in Paris and find a reception-party at the station! Then to live for a couple of months in that great city, and to get to know it and feel it, away from that crowd of foreigners we usually live among. Not too long ahead though! While I'm writing the sun outside is brilliantly shining. It is cold, but this only makes the air more transparent. So I sometimes think that instead of transporting me to Paris, we had better transport you to Trieste. When will M. Crémieux be free so that he can travel, or write useful things like *La coscienza* . . . ?

In those last few sentences he was hinting at his own premonitions of death, which came to him frequently during the year or two left to him; and perhaps also at the new and more 'transparent' kind of writing he thought old age was helping him to achieve. At all events, whatever the family's doubts about his famous 'senility', he was soon on his way to London again, and was able to stop in Paris to make the acquaintance of Adrienne Monnier.

Meanwhile the young Montale, on a visit to Paris, kept hearing the name 'Svevo' referred to as that of a major figure in contemporary Italian fiction. When he got back to Milan he got hold of the three novels, and was overwhelmed by them, especially *Senilità*, and in the November/December issue of *L'Esame* he published an article hailing Svevo's work as 'the poem of our complex modern madness'. He explained the ignoring of his early work as a symptom of the unhealthy state of Italian letters at the time—devotees of d'Annunzio on the one hand, and on the other 'latter-day purists, bankrupt Manzonians, watered-down "spiritualists" and other such gentry'. This was the first time an Italian periodical had paid Svevo any attention, and the article antagonised many Italian critics. Giulio Caprin, who had reviewed *Zeno* very briefly and dismissively in the *Corriere della Sera* when it came out, now wrote to the Crémieux, rather defensively, justifying his original opinion and repeating his objections to Svevo's style. The 'Svevo case', so much written and argued about later, had begun. Svevo refers to Caprin's letter in one of his own to Marie Anne Commène:

67 Church Lane, S.E.7
26 January 1926.

. . . I am not only grateful, I am overjoyed and everlastingly grateful to M. Crémieux for all he has done for me. And further, I must say Caprin's letter, which has an air of embarrassment about it (don't you think?), is the greatest satisfaction I could have hoped for. Did he manage to get hold of my book? He received five copies two years ago. Am I now supposed to resemble Larbaud? If so, my 'extreme poverty and style and language' must resemble the very acme of French clarity, where every thought is so exactly matched by words that the words themselves seem new. All the same, Caprin hints that the whole enterprise is a great responsibility. Knowing Crémieux, I am certain he will take the responsibility. But will he be wise to? Apparently there are a hundred writers who are going to take it as an affront. My advice to them will be to be patient and wait till they are 64.

Excuse this little outburst.

I promise not to speak about this business again, except to thank M. Crémieux. I find I'm a success again, and I must take care not to make a fool of myself as I did the last time in Paris. A 64-year-old baby is easily spoilt. . . .

Next January a copy of *L'Avenir* arrived at Charlton, announcing that the forthcoming number of *Le Navire d'Argent* was to be devoted to him and heralding him as the 'Italian Proust'. Livia shouted the news to him through the bathroom door, and he rushed out dripping and in high excitement. They decided to go over to Paris for the actual publication, and this took place early in February, the number containing, as planned, an essay on Svevo by Crémieux and translations of passages from *Zeno* and *Senilità* by Larbaud and Crémieux. They spent the days with their new friends, also seeing Joyce, who was still practically blind after a double eye-operation (his seventh). Joyce's *Exiles* was to have its première at the Regent Theatre on the 14th of the same month, and though Joyce wasn't fit to attend it himself, Svevo was back in London and reported on it:

London, 15 February 1926.

Dear Joyce,

I wrote to the address you mentioned, enclosing the note. But they replied, saying I had forgotten to enclose your letter and inviting me to present myself at the box-office with it on the night of the performance. I did so and all was well; I got two magnificent seats and, against the custom of the country, *gratis* too. I owe it to you and so thank you! Not entirely *gratis*, as they confiscated your letter.

All the way through the evening I had the delicious sensation of being present at the unveiling of one of your major works, and one so different from all the rest. I read *Exiles* some years ago in manuscript, in that precious calligraphy which now everybody knows, and which I love but can't read very well if it isn't tracing Italian symbols. Nor in fact did I get every word when I heard it acted, and I am hoping to get hold of the printed text by this evening. It was particularly true of Rowan's last speech, which, I imagine provides the essential clue to his behaviour and which escaped both Livia and me completely, perhaps partly because we were rather far from the stage. Usually in London we sit so near the actors that when we say 'I beg your pardon' the actors, or at least the kinder ones, repeat themselves. I'm impatient to have the book, since on Thursday I am going to try to get in free to the 'Debate on *Exiles*' and would like to have understood the work completely.

Miss Black-Roberts was unforgettable, I thought. It can't be an easy thing to do, to give that character something of the woman of the world, yet make her sincerity ring out like a bell, and without it seeming overdone. Instead of clapping, I blew her a kiss, and I hope as much of it reached her as did of Robert Hand's.

Rupert Harvey gave me a start. I don't know if it was intended, but he moves, sits down, gets up and looks about him just like you. I should like to see him in another part now, to see if it was deliberate. He's certainly a powerful actor. He seems to me like a man who would enjoy taking actions without counting the consequences. He never hesitates about things and whenever he gives explanations for his actions he does it in the quietest possible manner, as if he rather hoped not to be understood. He often succeeded as far as I am concerned, seeing that he always spoke in English.

William Stack, who took the part of Robert Hand at the last moment, was also good.

The audience was magnificent, though of course there had to be one or two boors among them. A man next to me said 'They want to force on us Italian ways'. It's well-known, of course, that Italians are jealous even without being in love.*

A great deal of applause. Loudest after the first and second acts.

I hope to see you in Paris, at least for a moment, on the 25th.

Your most affectionate
Ettore Schmitz

---

* There were others in the audience who found the play's morality strange. A woman sitting next to Harriet Weaver walked out during the dialogue between Richard and Bertha at the end of Act I, exclaiming 'I call this collusion'. Bernard Shaw spoke up for the play at the debate which Svevo mentions.

Have you seen the article by G. Caprin in the *Corriere della Sera* of the 11th of this month? It's a bad look out if there are going to be any more like this. He accuses me of every crime except larceny. Heaven knows what Crémieux and Larbaud are going to think. And even you come into it, respectfully of course, still you come into it too, my poor Joyce!

The article by Caprin which Svevo mentions in his postscript was entitled 'A Proposed Celebrity' and it talked once again about Svevo's 'incredibly poor and confused language'. It accused him also of being so totally analytical as to 'dissolve the whole substance of the narration . . . into an infinite series of isolated moments'. We can be grateful to our friends in France, however, says Caprin, for having drawn our attention to an 'anti-literary curiosity' in Italian literature.

Shortly after this the Schmitzes returned home to Trieste, and on their way they stopped at Milan so that Svevo could take out a subscription to the *Eco della Stampa*, a press-cutting agency. As he came out of the building he was accosted by a group of young writers, led by Montale, who had gathered there to do him honour. He arrived home feeling a famous man.

'The author of this letter is, more or less, a celebrity', he wrote to Mme. Crémieux shortly after his return.

Every newspaper, one way or another, has mentioned my name, in a more or less flattering way. As for actual criticism, there hasn't been any. They say it will come . . . I am still amazed at the way that one great kick of Crémieux's has opened the door of fame for me. I am known everywhere. Even in Trieste they are beginning (just) to be glad to have me among them.

If I told you I was happier before all this, it would be a lie, as I can remember my bad temper and impatience, and how it drove me to pester my friends. What I will say is, I expected to be happier in my present situation than I am. So you see, nothing is ever right in this world. They say it leads to progress. . . . (*Vita*, pp. 131-2)

One of the pleasant parts of being welcomed by Trieste was to find himself a great man in his own circle at the Caffè Garibaldi. This little *cénacle* met nightly and contained most of the better-known writers and artists of the city—one of them, Umberto Saba, being a poet of European reputation. Saba was a Jew and a Freudian and ran an antiquarian bookshop in Trieste, where many of the circle, including Svevo, used to congregate; he was famous for his egotism and his dislike of soap and water. Other members were the writers Silvio Pittoni and Giani Stuparich (who has described the circle in his *Trieste nei miei ricordi*), and the distinguished dialect poet, Virgilio Giotti, as well as the young Roberto Bazlen, a close friend of Svevo's and the first to introduce him (as indeed he was the first to introduce Italy) to the work of Kafka. There were also several artists, such as the painters Tullio Silvestri, Emerico Schiffrer and Vittorio Bolaffio, and the sculptor Ruggiero Rovan. The circle had been in existence for many years (Rovan claimed to have founded it as far back as 1900) and many of the members had lived, or were still living, a hard-up and bohemian existence. Rovan was always penniless and repeatedly having his furniture seized by the bailiffs, Schiffrer worked behind a post-office counter, Giotti worked for some years in a newspaper kiosk, and Silvio Pittoni was said to have spent most of his waking life at the café table. (It was a reflection of the comparative comfort of conditions under Austrian rule that Schiffrer, despite his humble job, managed to own a grand piano and a fine library and to give his son a decent education.)

It is worth trying to fix an impression of Svevo at this period, which was on the whole the happiest and most characteristic one of his life. One or two of his friends have left excellent physical descriptions.

'When I listen to him talking', wrote Stuparich,* 'I can never stop staring at his forehead, which juts forward like the

* *Giuochi di fisionomie*, Milan, 1942, p. 219.

prow of a ship, or at his cranium, which is divided from the forehead by a shallow depression and swells out behind it like the outsize head of some baby, poised precariously on its inadequate neck.' A young English friend, Cyril Ducker, who knew him at Charlton in the 1920s, thought it 'quite the most colossal human head that I have ever seen'.* His face, according to Ducker, 'was not greatly intellectual. In one sense the most easily discernible trait was the twinkle in his eyes full of a sincerity so great as to be well-nigh artless. So solemn at first sight seemed all the great mass of him, so lethargic, so dignified: yet his eyes never ceased to dance such illusions away and cheat him out of the respect due to a serious middle-aged philosopher—for that I imagined him to be. . . .' Leo Ferrero, a friend from the *Esame* circle in Milan, noted a racial contradiction in his features.

His face was a curious paradox; for nature had given him a German physiogonomy, something between Hindenburg and Thomas Mann; two sharply-marked Mephistophelian eyebrows formed a strange Y with his Jewish nose, and his mouth was overhung by grey moustaches; but the eyes were sparkling with Latin mischief and humanity. (*Solaria*, Florence, 1929, no. 3-4, p. 39)

He dressed plainly in a rather English fashion, and Ducker remembers his odd appearance in the English winter, smothered in an overcoat so enormous that it hid everything but his eyes and shoes. He hated jewellery and soon gave up wearing even a wedding-ring, telling Livia that it strangled him. He spoke slowly and socratically—as if, says Nino Frank, a friend of Joyce's who knew him in Paris, 'he were looking all round each word before he spoke it'. His gestures were calm, and he had a slow and rather awkward walk.

What most struck Cyril Ducker was the contrast between his genial and rather commonplace everyday manner, the bland and charming way he handled his mother-in-law for

* *The Stork*, vol. 1, no. 1, March 1930, p. 7.

instance, and the extraordinarily free, sceptical and anarchical turn of his conversation when you got him alone. On strangers he made an impression of a rather massive, cosseted elderly gentleman, with an air of surprised good-nature and ingenuous irony. 'His good-nature', says Nino Frank (he is writing in French), 'his innocent vanity, his gentleness, they frighten you, for you feel they must hide so many *arrière-pensées*, so many *arrière-sentiments* as you might say, all ready to be touched into motion. How complex the mental workings of that man must be, a man whose mind is a mine of recollections, names, reflexes and numbers, though he claims to have no memory at all, and a man who, for all that, is the gayest, and the least like a man of letters, that you can imagine.' He talked a great deal, and, so Stuparich said, sometimes rather naïvely.

> His way of goggling, his simple-minded shouts of amazement, bursting on you like thunderclaps, tend to put me in mind of an overgrown baby. And certainly he retains something of the baby, a baby of genius, even in his sixties. You have only to see him marvelling at the most trivial and commonplace sights and booming his amazement at the mildest discovery. . . .
>
> He is as talkative as a boy showing off before his friends, jumping illogically from subject to subject for the pleasure of hearing himself talk . . . but behind his love of talking there lies something different, the struggle and desire to express; it is the tone that counts, a tone that is never banal or commonplace, always *above* the subject in hand. Nothing of the boy there! (G. Stuparich, *Giuochi di fisionomie*, Milan, 1942, pp. 219-20)

He was, on the other hand, an excellent listener, opening his eyes wide in a good-natured pantomime of sympathy. Whatever company he was in, he always set out to please. He made a constant stream of little jokes or *Witze*, generally at his own expense, and was always ready to clown and talk nonsense to put people at their ease. A friend of his, the editor Leo Ferrero, thought he made too many *Witze* and regarded them as a defence mechanism.

. . . one couldn't say Svevo was a happy man; in the depth of his eyes one could see the light of obsession, an anxiety, a constant *Angst*, which he tried to allay by chatter. (*Solaria*, Florence, 1929, no. 3-4, p. 39)

One could tell from his jokes how much he was preoccupied with death. Saba said that when he took a taxi he always told the driver to drive slowly: 'Remember who you've got in the back'; indeed he talked to Livia about death to such an extent that she had to beg him not to. And very occasionally, and always unpredictably, he would burst into a fit of uncontrollable rage. When Letizia was a child she sometimes had to bear the brunt of his fury, and her mother used to warn her to lie low till it was over.

Svevo's absent-mindedness, according to Livia, was colossal. He was liable to put on two pairs of cuff-links and then complain of a certain heaviness about the forearms. He was perpetually losing his umbrella, though Livia always bought him specially brightly-coloured ones, and once in Paris he came out of the *Crédit Lyonnais* in a fury, complaining that another customer had snatched his umbrella. The man had insisted it was his own and had become so violent that, after some hot words, Svevo had let him go off with it. 'What a shame', said Livia, who wasn't at all surprised, when they got back to their hotel, to find his own umbrella safely waiting for them there. Once, as they were getting off the Venice packet-boat, Livia said to him 'Don't forget the plaid', and he obediently draped himself in the cabin tablecloth. Then there was the time when they went to the chemist's together to collect two boxes of pills. As they were leaving, Livia said 'Bring the medicine with you', and on emptying his pockets when he got home Svevo produced about a couple of dozen assorted pill-boxes and medicine-bottles. When Livia screamed 'What's all that?' he replied innocently 'Didn't you say "bring the medicine"?'

After the first shock he usually managed to take these disasters cheerfully, but once or twice they turned out more serious, as when he took Letizia to the fair and lost her. And there was one incident which gave him sleepless nights for a week. He had left the office with 150 lire in his pocket to make some urgent purchase for the firm and came back some hours later with a large packet of sweets and 160 lire. The mystery was never explained, and for some days afterwards he made himself ill with worry over it.

Everyone agreed that Svevo was naïvely delighted at his sudden rise to fame, 'like an honest shopkeeper who has won a sweepstake' as one friend said, and made a point of not concealing it. 'He took the halo which had been offered him and put it on with his own hands', wrote Stuparich. 'No writer ever so enjoyed his fame, or was so little spoilt or disturbed by it.' As we have seen already, he was perfectly aware of the impression he was making, and liked to burlesque it. When Mme. Crémieux asked him if he had read the article by André Thérive in *L'Opinion*, which called *Zeno* 'an incredible success', he looked at her in mock amazement. 'Thérive's article? But I read it every morning, and making my wife read it too!' A. R. Ferrarin quotes him in his 'Ricordi di Italo Svevo':*

Till a year ago, I was the quietest, the humblest, the least ambitious old man in the world. Now I am suffocated by ambition. I have become greedy for praise. All I live for now is the management of my own glory. I went to Paris, where, after all, there are so many interesting things, and all I could see was Italo Svevo: Italo Svevo among the treasures of the Louvre; Italo Svevo on the stage of the fifty or so Paris theatres; Italo Svevo in the Elysées, and Italo Svevo at Versailles. Italo Svevo everywhere. The *ville lumière*, with all the men and things it contains, seemed to exist merely as a function of my glory.

Success rejuvenated Svevo for the moment, and 1926 was extremely active year for him. First there was the question of a French translation of *Zeno*. Crémieux was insistent that the

* In *Augustea*, Rome, 15 October 1928.

novel should be published in France as soon as possible, and for a time Svevo hoped that he and Mme. Crémieux would do the translation themselves. They were too busy to do so, however, and when a certain Swiss was suggested as a substitute it turned out that he didn't know French very well; Svevo remarked mildly, remembering what the Italian critics said about himself, that he didn't want quite such a faithful translation as that. Finally an excellent young translator named Paul Henri Michel was found, and a contract was signed with Gallimard.

Throughout the summer and autumn Svevo kept up an anxious correspondence with Michel, and by the end of the year the translation was substantially complete—only to Svevo's chagrin Gallimard, supported by Crémieux, insisted on considerable cuts. 'As if there weren't longer novels than mine in French', he complained to a friend. 'I was a bit long-winded, perhaps, but it is a painful business, for someone who *is* long-winded, to be cut off short—the sort of trauma, according to Freud, that is bound to cause repressions.' Otherwise he was delighted with Michel's work and had few criticisms to make, though he asked him to restore the passage about Zeno's violin-playing. 'Valéry Larbaud once singled it out to praise', he told Michel, 'and I treasure the smile he gave me when he did so as the finest part of my success.'

Meanwhile the spectacle of his own reactions to success, and all the feverish impatience and egotism it produced in him, caught hold of his comic imagination, and in October or November of the year he sent Michel a new story of his, *Una burla riuscita* (*The Hoax*) which translated it into fiction. The hero, Mario Samigli, a middle-aged bachelor who wrote a romantic novel in his youth, has settled down in perfect contentment, supported by the vanity of regarding himself as a writer, to earn his living in a humdrum way and to look after his invalid brother. This innocent vanity, however, has annoyed one of his friends named Gaia, a failed poet turned commercial traveller, and the latter decides to play a hoax on Mario. He tells him he has met a publisher's traveller, from the famous house of Westermann in Vienna, who is very anxious to buy the translation rights of his forty-year-old novel. A meeting with this fictitious agent (one of Gaia's friends dressed up) is arranged, and Mario, rendered totally credulous by this appeal to his egotism, swallows the whole performance without question and signs a contract. At once he becomes a torment to himself and to everyone round him. His whole tranquil system of life is destroyed; he can't sleep, he bullies his unoffending brother disgracefully, his whole character goes utterly to pieces. He is only saved by the belated discovery of the hoax—from which, after all, following a favourite pattern in Svevo's stories, he accidentally profits, for having bought the promised 200,000 Austrian crowns 'forward' as a safeguard against a rise in the exchange-rate, he makes a handsome profit when the time comes to pay for them.

The story was based on a real-life incident, for some time during the year a Triestine journalist had called on Crémieux in Paris, anxiously asking for Svevo's address, and had then written to Svevo, making flattering proposals. Svevo had replied eagerly, but could never get another word out of him. He wrote the story, he told Crémieux, to console himself while he waited. However, the offer made by 'Westermann's' seems to have been a favourite fantasy of his, and Livia quotes a fragment of his describing how an American, with a dead-white face and gold teeth, offers him $100,000 for the translation rights of his novel. He hastily closes with the offer, telling himself that if he were to ask for a single dollar more the man might take offence and go off to buy a novel recommended by the *Corriere della Sera.* 'I realise, he remarks, 'why nothing surprising, no unexpected event, has ever happened to me in my life. They were all ready to happen, but I was too good at anticipating them. . . . Clearly, when anything has been imagined in such detail there is no need for it ever to happen.' Michel, rightly, took *Una burla* as Svevo's apology for the way he had been pestering him all summer, though he assured Svevo that Gallimard was no Westermann. Svevo, who could never get Gallimard's to answer his letters, said he wasn't so sure, and from then on always referred to the firm as 'Gallimard-Westermann'.

During the same year 1926, he also wrote *La novella del buon vecchio e della bella fanciulla* (*The Story of the Nice Old Man and the Pretty Girl*), a brilliant return to the theme of *Senilità*, this time with a genuinely senile hero. He also wrote a play, *Con la penna d'oro*, and rewrote *Vino generoso* and the fable *La madre* (*The Mother*), hoping to publish them in *Commerce*. With the help of his son-in-law and another friend he also made extensive verbal alterations to *Senilità*, trying to improve it from the language point of view, and having done so, approached the firm of Treves about the possibility of a second edition. As usual he got no reply for a long time, but eventually they wrote refusing to publish at the moment, as it was a difficult time for them, and saying that, anyway, if they were to republish him at all, they would want to issue a Collected Works. He wrote back angrily, breaking off relations with them, arguing that he was now an old man, that he might not have the time or the health to revise his complete *oeuvre*, and that though people were talking about him now they wouldn't be doing so in two or three years' time. He was more successful with the publishers Morreale, and the second edition of *Senilità* eventually appeared under their imprint in 1927. It contained a preface by Svevo defending the novel's title and paying tribute to Joyce, who had rescued him from oblivion.

This second edition of Senilità was made possible by a generous word of James Joyce, who for me, as not long ago for an elderly French writer (Edouard Dujardin), was able to repeat the miracle of Lazarus. That a writer, whose own work makes such imperious demands on him, should have had the goodness of heart, on a number of occasions, to waste his precious time on behalf of his less fortunate brethren, is such an example of generosity as, in my view, explains his own extraordinary success; for all the other words he has spoken, all those making up his own vast *oeuvre*, are expressions of the same greatness of spirit.

The older-established literary circles in Italy were still not very welcoming to Svevo, but the younger writers and critics began seeking him out, and his morning mail was full of letters from strangers. He wrote to one of his young admirers, the critic Alberto Rossi: 'You guessed right; my success with the reading public has been anything but great. All the same (as you say yourself) every now and then a friend emerges from this crowd of strangers and stretches out his hand to me. That is why, in Italy, I am "the man of many successes". So many of the young, each at his given moment, welcomes me as one of them, that I enjoy it more than a single grand success.'

Between Svevo and his most vocal Italian admirer, Montale, an affectionate friendship had grown up. Montale visited the Schmitzes in Trieste soon after their first meeting in Milan, and he followed up his eulogistic article in *L'Esame* with several more, in which he declared his conversion to *Zeno*, a novel which he had previously found forbidding after *Senilità*. He explained the tactics of his Svevian propaganda:

I have only expressed a part (and perhaps the least part) of my admiration for you in my articles. It was necessary, in addressing an unprepared public and a timid and ignorant body of critics, to go very cautiously, or one might produce exactly the opposite of the effect one intended. (Letter to Svevo; Genoa, 3 March 1926)

The names of the two writers soon became linked in the public mind, and in June 1926 Montale wrote commiserating with Svevo over the recent article (which he believed to be by Orlo Williams) in the *Times Literary Supplement*. This took as its starting-point Montale's article in *Il Quindicinale*, 30 January 1926. *Zeno*, Montale had said, was the contribution of our literature to that group of ostentatiously international books which hymn the smiling and desperate atheism of the latest Ulysses: the 'European man'. Not, be it noted, that we have here cosmopolitan visions, exceptional spirits, or other resources of that kind, but these bourgeois figures of Svevo's are burdened with unconfessed history, they are heirs of thousand-year-old ills and grandeurs, exiles and outcasts of a civilisation which is consuming and swallowing itself up. The 'imbecility' of Svevo's characters, rather than the eternal misery of man, is, therefore, the suitable quality of protagonists in this tempestuous age of ours.

'This defence', the writer remarks severely, 'is not one that need necessarily be accepted; indeed in our view, it needs to be combated. It will certainly be combated in Italy, whose new and forcible political faith, yet to become a genuine inspiration in literature, will certainly not find that positive element on which it prides itself in the grotesque domestic vicissitudes of the gelatinous "European" Zeno Cosini, the autobiographical hero of this book.' He goes on to express what was a fairly common hostile reaction to Svevo at this period:

Italo Svevo has no exceptional talent, a restricted vision and a slipshod style. His hero, either in his complacencies or in his indecencies, has no sublimity, and his recollections of an imaginary invalid's states of mind, far from being an effort, like M. Proust's, to arrange and fix valuable sensations of abnormal intensity, are nothing more than the voluble communications of a confessedly futile and despicable person whose little desires and weaknesses are for him the centre of his interest. . . .

In this interminable *bavardage* nothing is left out, no passage has more importance than another. It is not dramatic, it has no organic form, it presents no profound view of humanity, nor has it the passion of good satire. (*Times Literary Supplement*, 20 May 1926, p. 332)

Montale tried to defend the writer, arguing that if he himself hadn't already read the incomparable *Senilità* before approaching *Zeno* he might have been equally baffled by it.

In the summer of 1927 Montale, who much against his will had had to take a full-time job in a publisher's office, wrote from Florence telling Svevo of a new convert he had made, a certain Drusilla Marangoni (*née* Tanzi), wife of the art critic Matteo Marangoni, and begging him to send her an inscribed copy of the first edition of *Senilità*. 'She is conducting a tireless and quite astounding campaign of Svevian propaganda', wrote Montale. 'You can rarely have aroused such devotion in a reader, male or female.'

Montale also sent Svevo his own poems, *Ossi di sepia* ('Cuttlefish Bones'), but Svevo, who disliked poetry (he said it seemed such a pity only to use a part of the paper when you had paid for the whole of it) never managed to read it. He apologised to Montale, who replied cheerfully: 'Don't trouble to gnaw my "Bones". They would stick in your throat, and so Italy would lose its finest novelist.'

Svevo was often invited to literary circles in Milan, which in the years 1925-30, before Fascism got the upper hand, was enjoying a brief and brilliant period of culture, possessing at least four important literary periodicals—*L'Esame* and *Il Quindicinale*, both run by Enrico Somarè, a weekly called *La Fiera Letteraria*, and the *avant-garde* organ *Il Convegno*, directed by Enzo Ferrieri, which also ran its own literary club and experimental theatre. Svevo frequented the salon of Signora Ferrieri and was also friendly with the Somarè circle. The younger novelists at this time, with their eyes on France and the U.S.A., regarded him as the solitary pioneer of the modern novel in Italy, the one Italian writer they felt they could learn from. 'Italo Svevo was the aged great-uncle of our literature', wrote Ivan Goll, after his death.

As with all elderly uncles, we never knew him well. He was a semi-mythical member of the family, one who lived in a far-away country and had made astounding discoveries there; but our strait-laced parents, when they talked of him, lowered their eyes in disapproval.

One day, however, we discovered he had died a millionaire. . . . And now that the will is being read, all the nephews and nieces of literature are crowding round the bier, hoping for a legacy. They will not be disappointed. . . . (*Solaria*, Florence, 1929, no. 3-4, pp. 43-4)

The 'Svevo case' had made a strong impression in Milan, and Giovanni Comisso, one of the Somarè group, noticed that editors were surprisingly eager to publish his own work, as if they were frightened to repeat the mistake that had been made over Svevo. Being out of touch with literary talk, Svevo found the pace strenuous, and once, after an evening at the *Quindicinale* offices, he remarked 'one comes out of the *Quindicinale* feeling as if one had been at the *Esame*' (i.e. taking an examination).

In fact he was never a good literary talker, or indeed, in the usual sense, an intellectual at all. His naïvety in literary and artistic matters, according to Bazlen, was 'disastrous—no taste, no sense of form, ignorance of every sort of aesthetic problem. No ear, no sense of rhythm, stone-deaf to poetry—practically speaking at the level of the Bourget/Foggazzaro era.' When he talked about books the main impression he left, says Bazlen, was of 'his staggering (seeming) primitiveness—or better, what the Germans call *Ahnungslosigkeit*: not so much unsuspiciousness as lack of the organ for suspecting'.

None the less, in the summer of 1926 Ferrieri invited him to give a public lecture on Joyce on the *Convegno* premises, and he agreed, though he soon wished he hadn't. He wrote to Cyril Ducker (in English) early in the following year:

I want to send you, if not a description of my life, an account of some troubles which befell me in consequence of a certain conceitedness of mine (rather increased in these old bones by senility) quite the opposite of what we try to pretend young people like you are afflicted with. In June last year I stayed for some days in Milan, and was entreated by Doctor F. (the president of a very fashionable literary club) to deliver a lecture on James Joyce. I accepted. Of this author I knew the short stories and his *Portrait of the Artist as a Young Man*. Of *Ulysses* I knew only a very few pages, of which I talked a great deal, in order to make them appear more. I was now obliged to read it, and set to work immediately I got home. It was simply awful. Whole phrases remained for a long time a mystery to me, and the vocabulary did not help me very much. . . . The worst of it was that the reading of the book lasted so long that when I reached the end I had quite forgotten the beginning. . . . Now my lecture is finished, but I fear it will reflect these hardships, and be itself very boring.

However, when he finally delivered it, on the 8th March 1927, it went very well, though he remarked that Ferrieri, by arranging the lecture for five o'clock in the afternoon, had made sure he had an audience entirely of women. During the same year *Il Convegno* published his fable *La madre*, and *La Fiera Letteraria* published *Vino generoso*.

He also paid occasional visits to literary circles in Florence, and was to be seen at the writers' café, the Giubbe Rosse. The younger writers in Florence, mostly associated with the review *Solaria*, which was committed to promoting the 'novel of analysis', admired and lionised Svevo, and during 1927 he met a group of them, including Arturo Loria, Alessandro Bonsanti, and Rafaello Franchi, at the house of Drusilla Marangoni. She had pinned a placard over the door for the occasion, saying 'Svevo Club'. He was often asked to write for *Solaria* and in February 1928 they published *Una burla riuscita* as a special number. After his death they, like *Il Convegno*, published a special number in his homage.

In November 1927 a young Italian in Paris, Valerio Jahier, wrote him a long letter about *Zeno* and what the discovery of it had meant to him, but saying he couldn't agree with the critics who called Svevo the Italian Proust. Svevo was impressed by the letter and sent him a warm reply:

. . . Don't think I mind being set apart from Proust. They were two such different destinies! His was so much more distinguished than mine; there could be no resemblance between a crude man like me and the finest flower of so exquisite a civilisation.

Upon this Jahier wrote again, describing his own neurotic miseries and asking Svevo's advice. 'I am thirty years old', he wrote, 'and I envy the aplomb of boys of fifteen . . . I earn a ridiculously small salary, but if they reduced it tomorrow it would seem the most natural thing in the world to me and I should probably not have the courage to complain.' Should he try psycho-analysis? he asked. Svevo replied that he thought Freud more useful to writers than to sick men, and asked why he didn't first try auto-suggestion, under one of the doctors of the school of Nancy. And anyway, why did he want to be cured?

Do we really want to deprive humanity of the best thing about it. I sometimes believe that my greatest success, the success that has given me peace of mind, is to have reached that conviction. We are a living protest against that ridiculous conception of the Superman, which has been so much drummed into us (particularly us Italians).

He wrote him several letters on the same lines, and on his last visit to Paris, in March 1928, he met Jahier and his wife, but after this the tone of his letters changes, as if he had privately decided that there was not much to be done for him. And in fact some years later Jahier killed himself.

In April 1927 Svevo's one-act play *Terzetto spezzato* ('The Broken Trio'), written long ago, in the 1890s, was staged by the Teatro degli Independenti in Rome, with moderate success. He was still writing plays, and continually tinkering with old ones, always having the feeling that there was something he hadn't quite mastered about playwriting. Among his papers he left a draft of a letter to a famous playwright (presumably Pirandello) asking him for help:

You will hardly have heard of the writer of this letter. Years ago I published a novel which Domenico Oliva and others thought worthy of praise, but apparently critics don't have much influence on the public, because they didn't buy my book. I crept back into my corner, but I assure you I followed the careers of my more successful colleagues with entire sympathy and without the slightest resentment. This is to the credit of my character, but it also (though I only say this to win confidence from someone whose help I need) did credit to my taste. For in order to be successful it is not enough to have good, and even perhaps original, ideas; one must also know how to give them finished and definitive form. I am a poor devil who can only produce half-done things, never anything complete and whole; and never have I felt this so acutely as now, when I appear to have completed a play! You know all too well that, however complex the thought in a play, the actual writing must be clear and lucid. I know it too, only the trouble is, when I try to achieve this lucidity (what a painful business) everything falls to pieces in my hands. I hack and patch and mangle, but can let no light in; the light is split in the prism and is lost. Is it my ear or my hand that is at fault? I don't know, and perhaps I never will know unless you help me.

I won't presume to discuss your work, but clearly the greatest of all your gifts is the one I lack. I asked myself which of our authors would be most disgusted by this weakness of mine, and I thought of you.

The proposal that you should rewrite my play for me is one however, that I shall not make to you—till I know you have accepted it. (*Vita*, pp. 152-3)

If this was to Pirandello, and was sent, Pirandello didn't reply, nor did he respond to other letters from Svevo, though the two eventually got to know each other slightly and Svevo once took him and the actress Marta Abba on a sight-seeing tour round Trieste.

In the winter of 1927 Crémieux, who was secretary of the French P.E.N. Club, organised a dinner in honour of Svevo, the other guests of honour being Isaak Babel, Ilya Ehrenburg and the Roumanian poet Ion Pillat. Jules Romains was in the chair, and Svevo sat beside him, a little bothered at not being able to talk to him about his work, which he had never read. Joyce was there with Nora and talked nostalgically about Triestine sea-food. Ehrenburg later wrote a cynical account of the dinner:

The reception was presided over by Jules Romains, who introduced the guests. On the subject of Svevo he said that he was an Italian and an excellent writer and that one of his books had even been translated into French. About Babel, he said that he was not acquainted with him, but that he would be delighted to be, as one of his works was also being translated into French. As to the Roumanian poet, he said that as well as writing he took part in his country's politics. I don't remember if he prophesied that one of his books would be translated into French. After the speeches everyone turned to their own concerns. The writers began to talk, in the liveliest fashion, with the publishers. The young ladies cast devoted looks at Joyce. . . . The *ratés* and the misanthropes sipped their acorn-coffee. Everything was as it should be, and closely recalled the choice symposia of the aesthetes in M. Maurois' utopian kingdom. It was here that I got to know Italo Svevo. There was a twinkle in his eyes. Despite the ghastly food and the world's applause he was laughing at this select idyll. When I saw that twinkle I realised I had in front of me not an aesthete but a Boeotian in love with life and that in spite of the eulogies of Larbaud here was, not an amateur of rare books, but an authentic living human. He smoked one cigarette after another. . . . (*Solaria*, Florence, 1929, no. 3-4, p. 35)

Since his rise to fame Svevo had been reading more adventurously, and every now and then got excited about some discovery—for instance the novels of Pea, or *The Way of All Flesh* in Larbaud's translation. He was evasive on the subject of Proust, and probably never read him, but he was bowled over by Kafka, and thought of writing about him, though eventually he fought shy of it. He also made propaganda among his Parisian friends on behalf of other Triestine writers. For instance he sent Larbaud a copy of Saba's poems; and when, in 1928, Crémieux published his *Panorama de la littérature italienne*, he wrote to him complaining of his neglect of other Triestine authors. A review of Crémieux's book which he wrote for the *Popolo di Trieste* (20 May 1928) ends on the same note:

Various writers from Venezia Giulia are mentioned, but others, and by no means unimportant ones, are ignored. We should have liked to name them, but it is better to be silent. Such neglect is our fate. The picture of Italian literature in the last half century would not be complete without it.

Like many Triestines, Svevo had not found Italy the kindly mother he had dreamed of her as being—and not merely in regard to his own writing. Trieste had remained a ghost of her pre-war self, commercially speaking, and it became plain that the Italian government had no intention of encouraging her at the expense of Venice. Moreover, as *Italia redenta*, she was a natural breeding-ground for Fascism (some of the pre-war irredentist organisation took a strongly Fascist colour when revived after the liberation), and when patriotic pressure began to be brought on ex-foreign nationals, like Svevo, to adopt Italian names, he found himself snubbed by the authorities. He asked for official permission to call himself 'Svevo', but was told that if he changed his name at all it must be to the dictionary equivalent in Italian. 'I have got two names already, what do I want with a third?' he complained angrily; and he remained 'Schmitz' to the day of his death.

Svevo certainly enjoyed his year or two of fame, such as they were. All the same, when he said that success had ruined his character, he was not altogether joking. The excitement of the first dazzling year left a reaction. Livia noticed that he lost some of his gaiety; there were fewer *Witze*, and having a reputation to lose now he began to find writing more of a labour. And apart from this, his health began to break down rather rapidly during 1927. He was suffering from high blood pressure and heart trouble; he had to give up eating lunch (he was normally a heavy eater) and was having difficulty in sleeping. His premonitions of death came to him

SVEVO AND LIVIA
on their wedding day and in 1899

SVEVO IN OLD AGE

more and more frequently, and he used suddenly to shake his right fist at an invisible enemy, saying: 'I can feel it coming! I can feel it coming!' When Livia asked him what, he replied 'The stroke'.

During the spring of 1928 he became possessed by the idea of a vast new novel, dealing with Zeno Cosini in old age. It was to be called 'The Old Old Man' or 'An Old Man's Confessions'; and at intervals he drafted a number of fragments towards it. He wrote to Crémieux on the 16th May:

. . . after several not-too-good weeks I feel so well again that, on the spur of the moment, I have begun writing another novel, *The Old Old Man*, a continuation of *Zeno*. I have written 20 pages and have enjoyed myself hugely. If I never finish it, it doesn't matter; in the meantime, for once more in my life, I shall have had my laugh.

In a fragment belonging to this period he states the theme of the novel, half-caricaturing it as he goes along:

I will describe the present, and that part of the past which has not vanished for ever, not in order to preserve their memory but to remind myself who I am. . . . How vivid it all is still, and how dead the part I never put down on paper; sometimes, anxiously, I go in search of it, feeling myself mutilated without it, but it won't come back to me. And I know, too, that the part I did write down is not the most important. It only became important because I wrote it down. So now, who am I? Not the one who lived but the one who described. Oh! The only real part of life is meditation. When everyone understands this as I do, they will become writers too, life will become literature. One half of humanity will spend its time reading and studying what the other half has written, and contemplation, freed from the sordid business of living, will be the great business of existence. (*Vita*, p. 149)

He was still going to the office every day, continuing to do so even when they moved to their summer villa at Opcina, and in the time left to him he worked on the new book as he could, with the rhythm of old age, sometimes losing heart for a week or two. In the early summer he was writing to Crémieux again:

I am producing nothing apart from submarine paint. A little while ago, in a good mood, the aged Zeno wrote a preface to his memoirs. Then he didn't have the heart to go on. *Convegno, Fiera Letteraria* and *Solaria* all want an article on Kafka from me. Not being able to decide about it, I have done nothing.

And so my last years or months pass away even more idly than I had expected.

Later that summer, however, he talked enthusiastically about 'The Old Old Man' to Giovanni Comisso and told him that by the end of the year he hoped to devote himself entirely to writing; for the moment he was still to be found in the office every day from 9 to 12 and from 3 to 6—'I am like the ant, I work in the summer and take my rest in winter.' In a letter to Mme Crémieux, the last he ever wrote to her, he tells her that he has drafted various chapters of 'The Old Old Man' but that they will all have to be rewritten. 'There is a false note which keeps creeping in. Is it the fault of old age?'

In the same letter he repeats his continual complaint, that the Crémieux are always promising to come to Trieste and never do.

Don't think you neglected us in Paris. We had everything from you and your husband that we could have expected, and more, as always, than we deserved. We are not strangers now, and we know what your life is like. Indeed I have completed my studies on the dogs of Paris, and have discovered that they resent being stared at: in Paris no one ever has the time to stare at them. For us to see one another properly you will have to come to Trieste. There are so many things there that I am proud of and would like to show you. It's true I also have my engagements (with submarine paint) but in exceptional cases I can be free. And no case could be more exceptional than the arrival of yourself and M. Crémieux. All this horrible summer here I've been in Trieste or Opcina, telling myself that a fragment of Paris (a small one but important) was coming to console me. As the years go by my gratitude to

M. Crémieux (and to you, the one person who encouraged me before that sluggard [i.e. Crémieux] got to work) goes on increasing. I laughed heartily at the *Corriere della Sera* yesterday, seeing Borgese rebuke Crémieux for not saying more about me in his *Panorama*. All he gets is rebukes. And he deserves them. For he won't come to Trieste. He *doesn't* pay me enough attention.

In a few days I am also going into the mountains for a fortnight, to Bormio (Valtellina). But I shall certainly be back after the 10th of September. And I would willingly come back before if I heard that you were here. (*Vita*, pp. 154-5)

He and Livia set out for Bormio, a spa in the Italian Alps where Svevo had already taken a cure the year before, towards the end of August. They took with them Letizia's second child, Paolo, who was then six, and Svevo wrote to Letizia to report on him.

Bormio, 1 September 1928

Dearest Letizia,

Your little man is good company for us. I am a great annoyance to him, but he gets his own back excellently. It's a good thing he won't be with us for more than twelve days as I am not sure I shall be a good influence on him. In the swimming-pool he is an adorable little frog and he is better-behaved than usual there as I think the great pool induces a certain respect in him. He calls me 'the prince of sorrows' because he heard me twice complaining about my health. And when I sigh, 'Poor Schmitz!'* he interrupts me, saying 'Happy Schmitz!' On the whole we get on well enough for him to hesitate a moment when we ask him if he hasn't had enough of his grandparents. There were some children here who were even wickeder than he and actually dared to pinch him. I told him I had sent you a telegram to say we had finally found someone wickeder than he. 'Not wickeder than me!' he said furiously. You should be pleased to hear this. . . .

During their stay at Bormio Svevo was writing continuously, and one day, from the next room, Livia heard him exclaim: 'After all, I can die, can't I? I have known what it is

* A favourite exclamation of Svevo's.

to be happy.' On the day they were to leave for home he was still in the middle of writing when Livia called him to say the car was waiting. The fragment he had been working on was the one later published as *La morte*, in which the old atheist explains his system for preparing for death.

On the 12th September, the second day of their journey, they lunched in Treviso and set out again in the pouring rain. Crossing a bridge at a place called Vecchia Collalta, near Motta di Livenza, the car suddenly skidded on the wet road, and as the chauffeur tried to right it, it went into a zig-zag skid in the other direction and crashed into a tree. When Livia came to she felt a violent pain in her head, Paolo's face was covered with blood, and Svevo was moaning 'My leg, my leg!' She managed to crawl out of the car, and the chaffeuur, who was unhurt, dragged Svevo out and sat him down at the edge of the road in the pouring rain. Passers-by came up, and cars were fetched from Motta to take them all to hospital. When they got there, the doctor, taking one look at Svevo, treated him as the gravest case. His injuries, in fact, were not very serious in themselves; he had some cuts and bruises, and had broken his femur, but the shock had been too much for his heart and it soon became clear that he was dying. The three of them spent the night in the same room, their beds side by side, and in the morning Letizia and her husband arrived with Aurelio Finzi, Svevo's doctor nephew. Svevo, who was already very weak, and had a swollen tongue, so that he could only whisper, saw Letizia in tears. 'Don't cry,' he said. 'Dying is nothing.' (Saba, who, however, was not an eye-witness, reports this as a *Witz*: 'Is this all dying is? Why it's very easy—easier than writing a novel.') One of the nurses asked Livia if she wanted a priest called, but knowing Svevo's views she said it was better not. She noticed that he had overheard, however, and seemed to be clasping his hands together, and she asked him eagerly 'Ettore, do you want to pray?' 'When you've never prayed all the rest of your life,' he whispered, 'it's too late to begin.' Seeing Aurelio smoking a cigarette, he gestured to him to give him one too, and when Aurelio refused, he murmured: 'That really would have been the last cigarette'. At half past two the same day he died.

Svevo's reputation swelled in the years immediately after his death; a flood of articles appeared about him, *Il Convegno* and *Solaria* each published a whole issue in homage to him, and his major novels were translated into various languages. Livia, when she was well again after the accident and a long illness which followed it, made up her mind to devote herself to his posthumous fame. She was soon spending the whole day dealing with letters and callers and negotiating with editors. Leonard Woolf remembers her visiting the Hogarth Press, some time after 1929 when he had published *The Hoax* in Beryl de Zoete's translation: 'She was an impressive sight in my recollection, the black widow whom one saw so often in those days in France and Italy but is gradually becoming extinct.' On the 26th April 1931 a bust of Svevo, by Giovanni Mayer, was erected, at the family's expense, in the Public Garden (near one of Veruda). The speeches at the unveiling proclaimed Svevo as an Italian patriot; and it was noticed that the telegram from Joyce, the real author of the 'miracle of Lazarus', was not read out. In 1942 the Fascists overturned the bust, scrawling over it 'Bronze for the fatherland'.

During the early days of the war, Livia, who was quarter-Jewish, was told she must ratify her racial status with the 'Race Office'. She went to Rome to do so, and spent weeks there trying to register herself as an Aryan—with no result, till it was finally explained to her that what was necessary was a bribe, of fantastic proportion, and in despair she finally declared herself a Jew. By doing so she put herself in serious danger; and in August 1943, she fled from Trieste and took refuge at Arcade in Treviso province, taking with her a huge trunk full of Svevo's manuscripts and letters. Letizia and her youngest son Sergio (her two eldest sons had died, both in the same month, March 1943, as prisoners of war in Russia) went into hiding with her; and for the next two years Livia, living in daily terror of the Nazis, worked on her biography of Svevo. The book, which she completed with the help of her friend Lina Galli, came out finally, after innumerable publishers had rejected it, in Trieste in 1950.* Livia lived on until 1957, a serene old lady, surrounded by a whole circle of young protégées, and a prey to begging-letter writers and unscrupulous publishers' agents. Letizia's son, Sergio, returned to Trieste to take part in the uprising of the 1st May 1945 and was killed in the street-fighting, almost under the eyes of his father, who was helping to lead the insurrection. In February of the same year the Villa Veneziani was reduced to rubble by American bombs.

* In the Edizioni dello Zibaldone, an excellent series of Triestine publications, run, almost single-handed, by Anita Pittoni, niece of Svevo's old café-companion Silvio Pittoni.

PART TWO

The Writer

8

'Una vita' and *'Senilità'*

The direction which the 'modern' novel took in going beyond the great achievements of Naturalism was towards totality. It made it its ambition to get everything in, to find a single thing (a single day in Dublin or a single set of memories) which would incapsulate the whole of human experience. The novel in the hands of Proust and Joyce became more objective, exaggerating Naturalist techniques to a further extreme of particularity, and more subjective, digging below the moral and sociological level (the level of 'character-drawing') to the unconscious. And these developments went hand in hand and were part and parcel of each other.

The earlier nineteenth-century novel depended on a set of long-perfected compromises. In the novels of, say, George Eliot or Turgenev there was an unspoken agreement between the reader and author to ignore the fact that, when a scene was being set or a character introduced, half the detail presented would be in reality arbitrary, and therefore in a sense irrelevant. A certain quantity of detail was necessary, and accordingly the novelist specified the colour of the carpet as such-and-such, and equipped a certain minor character with such-and-such idiosyncracies; but both novelist and reader were aware that the colour might have been a different colour or the character have been fitted out with a different costume or foibles. Similarly, it was tacitly understood that the novel reflected time passing, and when the novelist paused in his narrative for a piece of character-drawing or scene-setting, or to give essential information, the number of pages of print devoted to this bore a certain implicit relationship to the flow of time; when he returned to the scene in hand events would have moved on at a given pace. And he had various other conventions, too, for representing time passing —for instance the trick of pretending to revisit the world outside the novel from time to time, before re-introducing the reader to the leading characters as if they were strangers to him.

To the Naturalist and the post-Naturalist novelist these compromises and conventions had come to seem worn out, a sort of impurity in the novel which it was for them to eradicate. The Naturalists demolished the convention of 'scene-setting' by multiplying descriptive detail and raising it to a 'scientific' status. The cry went up against them, when they did so, that they were merely presenting a 'slice of life', that they were being unselective. And when Joyce deliberately went far beyond the Naturalists in prolixity of minute detail, the cry was raised even more loudly. Its absurdity now became obvious. For the most striking thing about the post-Naturalist novel (the novel of Joyce, Proust and the Lawrence of *The Rainbow*) is its extraordinary unity, the way it has shaken off everything arbitrary and inorganic. In Joyce, solid detail, through its mere abundance, has become transparent, a phenomenon of mind rather than of matter. Every kind of material in the new novel was unified in a perceiving consciousness. And this meant that the novel was liberated from its compromises. There need no longer be anything merely instrumental or mechanical in it. If it described, then description would be, for the moment, the *raison d'être* of the novel, not a mere accessory of 'plot' and 'character'. If it was concerned with time, then it would not merely mimic time but investigate it as a subject in its own right. As a consequence of this revolution, the concept of fictional narrative changed and was attenuated. The new novel began to resemble a circle, or series of concentric circles, rather than a curve, to offer itself as a comprehensive statement rather than a plot pursued to its dénouement. And similarly, the way it was to be read was less clearly prescribed. The reader could enter it from a number of different angles and explore it by a variety of routes.

Svevo's three major novels, which together span the period of the rise of the 'modern' novel, illustrate the whole development rather beautifully. From a novel written in the Naturalist manner he moves on to one (*Senilità*) which is covertly, and another (*Zeno*) which is undisguisedly, in the 'modern' style. His novels were attacked as being formless and unselective, whereas what strikes us about them, or at least the two later masterpieces, is their extraordinary coherence, the impression which they give of the whole being contained in every part. In the early days of his fame Svevo was hailed as the 'Italian Proust'. It was rather a stupid description on the whole, but there is one marked resemblance between the two. Like Proust, Svevo trusted the patterns of his own mind and would follow the clue of a given idea wherever it would take him. He created (this is especially true in *Zeno*) by a process of unfolding—almost as if onc starting-point were as good as another. For him any bit of his heroes' behaviour, if looked at steadily enough, turned out to epitomise the whole. G. Debenedetti puts it well when he says:

> When he transports his *petits faits* out of the realm of the possible into that of the actual, it seems as though he feels each one of them to be the unique example, the symptom *par excellence*, that will let him penetrate to the core of the person or thing he is describing. In consequence, the usual foreshortenings, by which one episode takes pride of place over all others, and serves as an organising and clarifying principle for them, have to be performed by the reader rather than the author. In this sense, the novels of Svevo remain malleable in the hands of those who rethink them. (*Saggi critici*, new series, 2nd ed., Milan, Mondadori, 1955, p. 99)

It is safe for his novels to be 'malleable in the hands of those who rethink them', because of the superlative organisation of his mind, a mind possessed at every point by its single central subject. His art was an illustration of his favourite Schopenhauer's dictum:

The thing-in-itself . . . is present entire and undivided in every object of nature and in every living being. Therefore we lose nothing by standing still beside any single individual thing, and true wisdom is not to be gained by measuring out the world, or, what would be more to the purpose, by actually traversing endless space. It is rather to be attained by the thorough investigation of any individual thing, for thus we seek to arrive at a full knowledge and understanding of its true and peculiar nature. (*The World as Will and Idea*, trans. R. B. Haldane and J. Kemp, 1907, vol. 1, p. 168)

Svevo's three major novels are fairly close to each other in subject. They are all equally studies in weakness, a weakness he spent a lifetime studying in his own person, and they represent a steady progress towards optimism. His term for the weakness he studies in himself is 'senility'. In the preface to the second edition of *Senilità* (*As a Man Grows Older*), published twenty-nine years after the first one, he discusses Valéry Larbaud's objection to the title. 'I too,' he writes, 'who now know what real senility is, sometimes smile at having attributed an excess in love to it . . . [But] it seems to me it would be mutilating the book to deprive it of its title, which I feel explains and excuses something about it. The title guided me and I lived it.' Senility, in this metaphorical sense, is an infection of the will, a withdrawal from reality into day-dreaming, an incapacity for taking real decisions combined with the constant illusion of doing so, an inability to plan one's conduct, combined with an equal capacity for beginning imaginary new lives and inaugurating laudable new régimes. The 'senile' character can get no grasp of actuality. He dreams and speculates but can form no firm picture of what to expect from other people; other people's actions constantly take him by surprise, and so do his own.

As exhibited in Svevo's first novel, *Una vita* (*A Life*),

this condition is a disease without redeeming features. Its hero, Alfonso Nitti, is a country boy employed in a city bank (the place is clearly Trieste). His life is divided between the drudgery of the office and grandiose literary day-dreams cultivated at the public library. He gains the entrée to the pretentious and second-rate salon of the bank-director's daughter, Annetta, persuades himself into having an affair with her, and eventually seduces her. He then half-heartedly lets the affair slide while he goes back to his native village to attend his mother's death-bed, and on his return finds that Annetta has accepted another suitor. He could not have contrived his own ruin more thoroughly. He is now an embarrassment to Annetta and her fiancé, and a worse one to his employer, and all through initiating an affair he never knew if he really wanted. But if he did not want *that*, what does he want? The question is unanswerable, and he kills himself.

It helps in reading *Una vita* if you think of it as an ironic commentary on Schopenhauer, in particular on the concluding section of *The World and Will as Idea*, dealing with 'The Assertion and Denial of the Will to Live'. Again and again Alfonso persuades himself that he has achieved philosophic calm, the ideal state of the abnegation of willing (as of one who, as Schopenhauer would say, had 'torn the veil of Maya') only to notice next moment that whatever he wanted he wants just as much as ever. It is only the things he never wanted he finds it easy to give up. He has 'renounced' Annetta (though of course he has actually lost her through his own passivity), so he ought to be glad when Annetta's friends ignore him. In fact it enrages him beyond measure. He makes a further sacrifice, a real one this time. His landlady's daughter (a girl he rather dislikes) being pregnant, and her fiancé proving recalcitrant about marrying her, he pays away a large part of his inheritance to buy her lover back for her. At last a pure act of renunciation, he hopes. He is soon undeceived; he catches himself in the act of squeezing the very maximum of personal satisfaction from it, encouraging the girl and her parents to treat him coldly, so that when they at last realise what he has done for them they will be even more amazed at his generosity. His will is as active as ever. It only fails when for a moment it is offered nothing that it wants, or when he is attempting, as he was with Annetta, to *direct* it in a Napoleonic way—acting, without the proper endowment, the role of Julian Sorel or Rastignac. 'Alfonso', says Svevo, 'was to be the very personification of the Schopenhauerian affirmation of life which is so close to its negation.' Alfonso himself sometimes can't help laughing at his own hopeless, fundamental self-contradictions (this is the seed of Svevo's later comic style). And seeing no way out of them, he kills himself—the most un-Schopenhauerian action of all. For as Schopenhauer affirms, 'Far from being denial of the will, suicide is a phenomenon of strong assertion of will; for the essence of negation lies in this, that the joys of life are shunned, not its sorrows. The suicide wills life, and is only dissatisfied with the conditions under which it has presented itself to him.'

What Svevo is diagnosing in Alfonso, of course, is the *mal du siècle*, which indeed was the reigning idea of the literary period in which he began writing. Mario Praz dates the vogue of the concepts of the *mal du siècle*, of 'decadence', and of the *fin de siècle*, as running from 1880 to the end of the century. 'A universal nausea fills the heart of the Slavs, the Germans and the Latins and displays itself in the first in the shape of nihilism, in the second in the shape of pessimism, in us in the shape of solitary and bizarre neuroses', writes Paul Bourget in his *Essais de psychologie contemporaine* (4th ed., Paris, 1885, pp. 15-16).

The murderous rage of the conspirators of Saint-Petersburg, the writings of Schopenhauer, the incendiarism of the Commune and the savage misanthropy of the novelists of Naturalism . . . reveal the same spirit of negation of life which every day clouds western civilisation more darkly. We are far, no doubt, from the suicide of the planet, the ultimate desire of the theoreticians of misery. But slowly, surely, there develops that belief in the bankruptcy of nature which promises to become the sinister faith of the twentieth century, if science or a barbarian invasion does not rescue a too intellectually self-conscious humanity from the fatigue of its own thinking.

According to the famous populariser of the concept of 'degeneration', Max Nordau, the 'degenerate' type was rapidly increasing in numbers, and the moral insanity which it exhibited, its unbounded egoism and inability to resist sudden impulses, was in fact, though the sufferers were unaware of it, a biological morbidity—something of the same kind as lobeless ears or supernumerary fingers or the stigmata of Lombroso's 'born criminal'. (Nordau thought the Impressionist painters painted as they did because of optical degeneration.) The 'degenerate' type was a racial deviation induced by the unprecedented rate of industrial and social change, and by its very nature a sterile one. By the end of the next century the apparent senility of the world, of which so many thinkers seemed convinced, would have been revealed as an illusion. 'There will be a generation which will know how to find its ease in the midst of a city inhabited by millions, and will be able, with nerves of gigantic vigour, to respond without haste or agitation to the almost innumerable claims of existence' (*Degeneration*, originally published 1895, English translation 1913, p. 541).

In his analysis of the degenerate type Nordau might be describing Svevo's Alfonso word for word:

They are lost if they are alone: for anti-social, inattentive, without judgment or prevision, they are capable of no useful individual effort, and still less of a common labour which demands obedience, discipline, and the regular performance of duty. . . .

But they are still more surely and rapidly lost if, instead of being alone in the world, they have healthy beings living beside them. For in that case they have to fight in the struggle for existence, and there is no leisure for them to perish in a slow decay by their own incapacity for work. The normal man, with his clear mind, logical thought, sound judgment and strong will, sees, where the degenerate only gropes; he plans and acts where the latter dozes and dreams; he drives him without effort from all the places where the life-springs of Nature bubble up, and, in possession of all the good things of this earth, he leaves to the impotent degenerate at most the shelter of the hospital, lunatic asylum, and prison, in contemptuous pity. (*Ibid.*, pp. 540-1)

He also hits off Alfonso's method of compensating for his frustrations by illusory philosophical pretensions:

The degenerate who shuns action, and is without will-power, has no suspicion that his incapacity for action is a consequence of his inherited deficiency of brain. He deceives himself into believing that he despises action from free determination, and takes pleasure in inactivity; and, in order to justify himself in his own eyes, he constructs a philosophy of renunciation and of contempt for the world and men, asserts that he has convinced himself of the excellence of Quietism. . . . The degenerate and insane are the predestined disciples of Schopenhauer and Hartmann, and need only acquire a knowledge of Buddhism to become converts to it. (*Ibid.*, pp. 20-21)

Una vita, then, treats the *fin-de-siècle* malady as a malady pure and simple, and in writing it Svevo attempted, whilst adhering rigidly to the Naturalist formula, to be more comprehensive than Zola. The novel is half a dozen things at once, the study of a milieu and a profession, an *éducation sentimentale*, a tragedy of 'urbanisation' and a case-history, in the manner of Stendhal, of the bourgeois Napoleon-cult. It is an unconscious attempt to go beyond Zola, and it fails in its aim because it only fulfils one of the two conditions of the modern novel; it is centrifugal without having a centre. Svevo has not yet found the 'single thing' which is the corollary of the attempt to attain totality.

In *Senilità*, published six years later, he has unmistakably found it. Montale, as we have seen, originally felt that it was Svevo's best novel, and many critics have followed him in this. Writing of it in *L'Esame* in 1925, he spoke of it as a novel *vieux style* and argued that this comparatively old-fashioned fictional form was the one which really suited Svevo, and that his attempt, in *Zeno*, to write a novel in the new 'totalist' manner was really against the grain. He later changed his mind about *Zeno*, and his earlier view certainly seems a mistaken one, the mistake lying in regarding *Senilità* as an old-style novel. It certainly looks it at first sight, but the more one studies it the more modernist, and the more like *Zeno*, it comes to look.

By the time of *Senilità* Svevo had found the focus he wanted, a 'single thing' which he went on exploring throughout the rest of his writing. This 'single thing' was the Unconscious, in its aspect of unconscious motivation. Stendhal and Dostoevsky had already gone a long way in studying the fantastic or catastrophic irruptions of the unconscious on to the scene of human behaviour. What Svevo did was to isolate unconscious motivation as an everyday phenomenon, not as a special case but as a general one. He managed, by dint of introspection, to obtain free access to that territory of mental behaviour where everything changes its name, where motives are never what they appear to be, where the human actor, in order to affect the world, re-arranges it to his own convenience, where the Ego and the Id fight a constant struggle to outwit each other and the only law is the law of bad faith.

Emilio Brentani, the hero of the new novel, has, like Alfonso in *Una vita*, all the lineaments of the 'senile' soul. At the (symbolical) age of thirty-five he is still living with his spinster sister Amalia, doing an undistinguished job in an insurance office, and still mildly basking in the reputation bestowed by a novel much praised and promptly forgotten by his fellow-townsmen. With innumerable doubts, and what seems to him infinite caution, he has, at the opening of the book, just embarked on an affair with a working-class mistress. A career of the wildest distraction awaits him. The gap between his picture of things and the reality is absolute. His actions are always ludicrously at an angle to his intentions, his feelings move of their own inertia into their opposites or into something quite unexpected; he seems to have the deliberate wish to make every mistake and suffer every delusion. The contradictions of his sadism and his masochism mean that nothing will play its proper role for him—the fact that he has once made his mistress give a cry of unhappiness comes to represent the whole of his love for her; if he goes to meet her full of philosophy and resignation, he ends up throwing stones at her in the street. His self-absorption and divorce from reality are so complete, that he never even remotely comprehends his mistress, and by his neglect drives his sister to a horrifying death. The upshot of the novel, however, is that for all the havoc he suffers and causes, he is really perfectly secure; he possesses a serene, unassailable instinct of self-preservation which makes the painful facts into something bearable to him, even in the end rather satisfactory.

Years afterwards he looked back with a kind of enchanted wonder on that period, which had been the most important and the most luminous in his life. He lived on it like an old man on the memories of his youth. Angiolina underwent a strange metamorphosis in the writer's idle imagination. She preserved all her own beauty, but acquired as well all the qualities of Amalia, who died a second time in her. She grew sad and dispirited, her eye acquired an intellectual clarity. He saw her before him as on an altar, the personification of thought and suffering, and he never ceased loving her, if admiration and desire are love. She stood for all that was noble in his thought and vision during that period of his life. (*As a Man Grows Older*, trans. Beryl de Zoete, standard ed., p. 219)

Between this novel and its predecessor, in fact, there has occurred a decisive shift of viewpoint. Svevo has discovered the fruitful destiny reserved by impartial Nature for the 'senile' soul. Alfonso Nitti is a study in maladjustment. For the hero of *Senilità*, adjustment is already in full swing. By the time we meet him, circumstances have allowed Emilio, as they did not allow Alfonso, to perform an essential step for the Svevian hero. He has supplied his own deficiencies by attaching himself to the 'healthy'—here in the shape of his friend Balli, the sculptor. He is doing what all the later avatars of the Svevian hero do, forming a little universe, in which the 'healthy' sun provides a fixed centre to the gyrations of his 'senile' earth.

There is, once again, a strongly Schopenhauerian note in the conception of Emilio.* Once he has begun his affair with Angiolina, freedom—the possibility of reasoned action—disappears for him completely, for to be free to act, and equally to refrain from acting, on the world, you have to be able to imagine it truly, and the observer in Emilio is irremediably corrupt. His feelings, like any other natural event, have their consequences, but since one of these consequences is to alter his picture of the world, they get him no nearer effective action. In a new world, new decisions are demanded, so he is back where he began.

Emilio represents, in the form of a human temperament, merely a signal example of what is true of the rest of the universe. If he lives among illusions, and is always recreating the world according to his own fears and desires, well, the world and the universe are anyhow only a realm of illusion and shadows, mere temporary objectifications of the thing-in-itself, that blind, restless and ever-unsatisfied 'unconscious will' which lives on itself, because there is nothing else apart from it.

Svevo has chosen a 'decadent' and supremely ineffectual

* René Dollot points out, in an article in the *Mercure de France* (1954, p. 483) that the 'great pity for himself' with which Emilio finally sends himself to sleep at the end of Chapter 8 is an echo of Schopenhauer: 'Weeping is sympathy with our own selves, or sympathy directed back on its source' (*The World as Will and Idea*, trans. R. B. Haldane and J. Kemp, 1907, vol. 1, p. 486).

hero, not as an exception to the general law of human existence but rather as a striking example of it. The endless chain-reaction between Emilio's reason and feelings and their secret gravitation towards pleasure are, in essence, a model of existence itself.

The form of *Senilità* is dictated by its subject-matter and is more original than it appears at first sight. The thing contemporary critics objected to was that it was formless and pedestrian, that Svevo went on, laboriously and unpoetically, analysing everything that there happened to be in the consciousness of his insignificant hero. The same things were said about Joyce, and they reveal a failure to understand the methods of the 'modern' novel. The point is that Svevo's heroes are themselves in every detail of their lives; for them the same dramas and paradoxes repeat themselves everyday, it is only for us that their lives have a structure and a dénouement. Far from being unselective, *Senilità* has a quite extraordinary unity and concentration.

Svevo has remained faithful to the laborious Naturalist minuteness of *Una vita*, but instead of applying it distractingly to a dozen different things he focuses it on one. The flood of ideas moves in a channel instead of spreading outwards into the sand; his immensely fertile imagination has got into step with the progress of the story, so that each new twist of Emilio's consciousness becomes, not a pause for analysis, but a step forward in the narrative. The narrative, to a greater extent than appears at first sight, takes place in Emilio's consciousness; and the peculiarity of this particular narrative is that, while seeming to get somewhere, it never does. After all the fantastic gyrations of Emilio's feelings he is the same, or more or less the same, at the end of the novel as he was at the beginning. He has learned nothing and forgotten a good deal. His incapacity for influencing events has its compensation in his capacity for converting events into what he would like them to be.

The novel, therefore, though there is plenty of action in it, has a solid, unchanging centre. It is not really, though it appears to be, tending forward. In his continuous analysis of Emilio's thought-processes Svevo was trying to seize, as it was the ambition of the 'modern' novelist to seize, the actual unchanging substance of life. He interrupts the flux of Emilio's consciousness at one point, when the self-absorbed Emilio suddenly finds himself in the middle of someone else's tragedy (his sister dying in *delirium tremens*), then in a last wonderful page or two he goes back to it.

The point of the action tends to lie not so much in the effect the leading characters have on each other as what analogies, contrasts and connections we perceive between them. Emilio himself is always noticing analogies: how Amalia's manner with Balli resembles his own with Angiolina, what a similarity there was between his ways of parting from his sister and from his mistress—the one couldn't hear his farewell words, and to the other he couldn't say them. One of the leading motifs of the book, indeed, is the spectacle of useless intellect. Emilio *sees* a great deal, but it is almost never any use to him to do so. (This was a favourite theme for Svevo, whose own life was, in a way, an illustration of it. He was a busy clerk or business man all his life, living in the thick of a commonplace bourgeois existence, and the extraordinary intelligence which he applied to this existence flourished, more or less unsuspected by others, and in a sense useless to himself, at a millimetre's remove from common life, kept inviolate as it were by its own uselessness. When he talked about art he often made a point of its uselessness, as for instance in the fable of the two carpenters, the one who made wardrobes and the one who described them.)

Emilio does, indeed, occasionally succeed in putting the analogies he is always noticing to some use. One of the few advantages he has over Angiolina is her inability to realise that, from the way she talks about other men, he can, by analogy, form a good idea of how he himself is likely to get treated. For the reader, meanwhile, there are other analogies invisible to Emilio, for instance the central analogy between Emilio and Amalia—two dreamers, a day-dreamer and a nocturnal one, a comic and a tragic one, side by side—or again the fact that, for all Balli's disinterestedness, it is his selfishness (his instinctive delight in dominating people) that contributes to Amalia's tragedy quite as much as Emilio's selfish neglect of her. And the contrasts, of course, are equally fundamental. Balli and Angiolina are the representatives of health, Emilio and Amalia of sickness; Balli and Angiolina the embodiments of sunlight as against the shadowy existences of Emilio and his sister ('Too much light!' mutters Emilio as he walks with Angiolina in the street, seeing all the men catching her eye. 'Let's walk in the shade.') And at the heart of the novel there is the ironic and tragic contrast between Emilio, living out a shadow-play of violence and passion, and the unsuspected (and in Amalia's case catastrophic) realities surrounding him.

The role of Balli in the novel is a complex one. As well as being a foil to Emilio, he represents the two sides to Svevo's own art, the pure 'modern' artist and the classical moralist. He symbolises the disinterested artist, absorbed and moved by the general spectacle of life; and it pleases Emilio to see Balli, to whom it never occurred to love Amalia as a woman, suddenly fascinated by her on her deathbed, as an artistic spectacle. 'It was clear . . . Amalia was dying loved by Balli with the noblest love of which he was capable.' On the other hand, though it is a point of pride to Balli, as an artist, never to pass judgment on his friends, but merely to study and understand their workings, we judge Emilio in the light of Balli's attitudes.

There are two striking little passages, in a different key from the rest of the novel, in which we see Balli standing outside the story as spectator and touchstone. In the first he is walking alone in the street, in a bad temper, cursing the carnival that has just begun:

'Oh, if only I had a dog here to take a piece out of their calves!' thought Balli to himself, as two pierrettes with naked legs went by. That carnival with its shoddy magnificence aroused his moral indignation; later on, no doubt, much later, he would be taking part in it himself, revelling in the finery and bright colours, and altogether forgetting his indignation. But for the moment he was conscious of assisting at the prelude to a tragi-comedy. The whirlpool was beginning to form which would swallow up the factory-hand, the sempstress, the poor bourgeois, and withdraw them for a moment from the dreary round of common life only to fling them out again into greater suffering. Some would return bruised and ruined to take up their old burden and find it heavier than before; there were some who would never find their way out at all [literally: 'never again reach Lent']. (Standard ed., p. 76)

The novel was originally to have been called 'Il carnevale di Emilio' ('Emilio's Carnival'), and the passage, which I suspect was written early on, is evidently allegorical—one of those who 'never again will reach Lent' being Amalia. In the second passage, Emilio comes on Balli, again in the street, following the municipal dog-slaughterer's van.

He was no doubt genuinely affected, but he admitted that he indulged in the emotion because it increased his artistic sensibility. He did not pay much attention to Emilio's words, for his ears were deafened by the howling of the dogs, the most melancholy sound in creation, especially when provoked by the sudden and unexpected pain of something drawn tightly round the neck: 'The fear of death is in them already,' said Balli, 'and an immense and powerless indignation as well'. (*Ibid.*, p. 126)

This time it is Emilio who draws the analogy, recalling poor Amalia's surprised, indignant fury when he hinted she was in love with Balli: 'He remembered, with some bitterness, that in Amalia's outburst, too, there had been the sound of surprise and an immense and powerless indignation'.

Svevo's sober and laborious manner in the novel is an essential part of the whole effect. By not highlighting his ironies he leaves the reader to look for them in every sentence, and if he looks he finds them. The style is a thicket of ironies, the densest possible texture of ironical contrasts and analogies and perceived connections. You can hear his little conversational *Witze* in it and realise how far their roots go down and what a dense body of thought they spring from. His style is packed with thought, of the kind proper to a novelist, springing spontaneously out of the matter in hand. The mind at work, far from being plodding, is intensely quick, searching and alive; and moreover all of a piece—the lightest of his jokes, lurking in a phrase or a parenthesis, connect up with his profoundest insights.

Senilità is one of the solidest masterpieces of nineteenth-century fiction. What weaknesses it has, and they are not very important, come towards the end, with the business of Amalia's death from ether-drinking. The scene is perfectly conceived, and of course quite essential to the pattern of the novel, but his actual handling of Amalia's death-agonies is what a dozen other novelists could have done as well. And there is something else not quite right about this section. It is, of course, typical of Emilio both to feel genuine pity for Amalia and to try to exploit it to his own advantage—to wallow in his sorrow as a means of relieving his sense of guilt. And his tergiversations during Amalia's last hours—the way that even under the first shock of finding Amalia semi-naked and raving on her bed, he has time, as he rushes for help, to forget her for Angiolina—show Svevo at his best. But one has the impression that in some curious way Svevo himself is following Emilio's example. By prolonging the agony of Amalia's death-bed (though it is not nearly as drawn-out as the one in *Una vita*) he is trying, in a covert fashion, to put in the conventional decent feeling that his hero is so lacking in. It is quite unnecessary, of course, for we are never in a moment's doubt about Svevo's criticism of Emilio; apart from anything else it is pointed to by the mere presence of Balli.

The weakness, if it is one, is of very minor importance. And one is left wondering why this profoundly original book should have been so ignored. There were several reasons, as I have already suggested, but the most obvious one had to do with his style—or rather, and this is the point, not so much his style as his language. Svevo's style, as I have said, was all part of his originality. It was crucial to what he was doing that the thought-processes of Emilio should be analysed in the most prosaic, laborious, pedestrian and anti-literary manner, without any of the charms and verbal subtleties of 'artist' prose. It was part of the convention of his writing that he should not write *de haut en bas* or put himself, by graces of style, in a superior relationship to his subject. And this, in Italian writing at the time, was a great innovation. It was the age of d'Annunzio, a period when the plastic and musical qualities of prose, the cult of the *belle page*, counted for everything, and Svevo's graceless prose style, with its dogged concentration on meaning and substance, appeared a monstrosity. Elio Vittorini, discussing him thirty years later, saw it as part of his greatness, but also as what prejudiced his contemporaries against him.

Among a nation of repeaters-by-rote like Italy it is always wiser to begin with some old-fashioned motif. A little exordium in the 'Milanese' or Tuscan style . . . would perhaps have saved the Svevo of *Una vita* and *Senilità*, as it more or less saved the Verga of *I Malavoglia*. . . . But he . . . from the very first page of *Una vita*, instinctively pursued a single purpose, the purpose that was to dominate his whole work, i.e. to write seriously. In the face of a will to write so absolute, so creative in its every word, as essential and vital in every molecule as God's own clay, there is no place for elegances, graceful assumptions of negligence, all the qualities that make writing a superior game. (*Diario in pubblico*, Milan, 1957, pp. 16-17)

So far, then, the prejudice against Svevo was a failure to recognise something new, and something which was, in fact, vital to the future of the novel in Italy. The Italian novelists of Svevo's time always inclined to disassociate themselves tacitly from novel-writing. 'Italy had great single novels', remarks Debenedetti; 'what it lacked was a taste for the novel as such.' It needed a writer like Svevo, uninterested in and probably incapable of, the musical refinements that Italian writers of the 1880s and 1890s aimed at in their prose, to stake a claim for the novel in its own right.

When we turn from the style to language, however, there was a real case against Svevo. His language is a very curious phenomenon. He didn't write in dialect,* though dialect constructions turn up here and there. His was a very different case from that of Verga, who employed dialect cadences within a very simple but elegant Italian. What Svevo wrote was a kind of 'business' Italian, almost an esperanto—a bastard and graceless language totally without poetry or resonance. That he should have done so was certainly in part a result of writing a language he didn't normally speak or think in, a point which Zeno makes about himself: 'The doctor has too much faith in those wretched confessions of mine. He doesn't know what it means to us, who speak in dialect though we don't write it, to write in Italian. A written confession is always a lying one.' But one has the impression the thing went deeper than this, and that Svevo was constitutionally insensitive to the formal qualities of prose, as he was to all poetry. (Though this can't be wholly true, for there are passages, for instance the celebrated close to *Senilità*, which are subtly and beautifully cadenced. And Benco records that he once, as a gesture to his critics, produced a model page of *Trecento* prose.) Certainly he sometimes wrote sentences of extraordinary clumsiness, a sort of laboriousness and roundaboutness which reveals not so much carelessness as a genuine incapacity for handling syntax. Moreover he often made definite mistakes in grammar and used impossible archaisms (rather as Thomas Hardy did), and he constantly committed elementary howlers, such as using the wrong preposition before an infinitive—something more possible in Italian, which is still a more fluid language than French or

* He once wrote a little dialect play for his nephews and nieces to welcome Olga back from America.

English and in which for example there is no reason, as far as sense goes, for using 'di' rather than 'da'.

When Svevo, with the help of his son-in-law, set to work in 1926 to correct *Senilità* for the second edition, he did so without much conviction. He made a great many alterations but very much in an *ad hoc* manner. G. Devoto, who has analysed them in some detail, senses the mood behind them as one of 'resignation, lack of conviction and, in fact, insincerity'. Of course, many of the alterations were to the good, but others made things neither better nor worse, and some were positively harmful, as when he substituted a formally correct phrase for something that, in the original, was dramatically meaningful. When he wrote that Emilio 'felt a great satisfaction at being able to tell Balli he had *had* that woman', the 'had' suggests Emilio himself talking, as the substitution 'possessed' fails to do. The corrections, in fact, were done too late, and in the wrong spirit, to be of much value.

9

'La coscienza di Zeno'

When, twenty-five years or so later, Svevo returned to novel-writing in *La coscienza di Zeno* (*The Confessions of Zeno*) he was still the author of *Senilità*, but with larger ambition, and with his weaknesses, apart from his merely linguistic ones, overcome. One does not have to read far in *Zeno* to know that there can be no question of the sort of slightly shamefaced manoeuvre with the reader that I have described in *Senilità*. The whole tone of the book is supremely shameless. In a way it is an old man's book. It is colder, more black and white than *Senilità*. Some of the colour and feeling have gone out of things, and have been replaced by a dazzling, invincible clarity. It is a book, though a very long one, which you can feel was written in a continuous state of elation and sense of discovery.

The outer plot of the novel portrays, or pretends to portray, a Freudian 'resistance' to psycho-analysis. The hero, a rich married man, living on the income of a family business which, by his dead father's express desire, he is allowed no hand in running, decides to fill his idleness with a course of psycho-analysis. As a preliminary to analysis, his doctor suggests he should try writing down his memories, and this he proceeds to do. He describes, in turn, his attempts to give up smoking, his father's death and death-bed curse, his marriage to Augusta Malfenti (how he proposed to each of the three Malfenti sisters on the same evening and was accepted by the one he didn't want), his infidelity (and how it fortified his marriage), and finally his business partnership, and the way in which, to his surprise, it earned him the reputation of a model son-in-law and successful man of business.

The analysis itself, when it finally gets under way, is a fiasco, or so Zeno considers. Dr. S. keeps encouraging him to revive childhood memories, and he obeys, only soon he can't tell if he is remembering them or inventing them. The doctor explains to him that his smoking does him no harm, or wouldn't if he didn't want to believe it did—he is using it to punish himself for wanting to kill his father. Zeno goes home and smokes like a Turk for twenty-four hours, bringing on acute bronchitis; he doesn't know a moment's happiness till he has managed to reinstate smoking as a vice, and can resume his system of 'last cigarettes'. He finally decides to break off the analysis, but hasn't the courage to tell Dr. S., and so is unable to reclaim his manuscript memoirs; and the thwarted doctor, when he finally discovers he is to get no more fees, takes his revenge by publishing the memoirs (i.e. *La coscienza di Zeno*) himself.

In this farcical travesty of the analyst-patient relationship Svevo is, of course, partly on Zeno's side and partly on the doctor's, tacitly implying the truth of Dr. S.'s diagnoses and at the same time mocking his pretensions to 'cure' Zeno. There is a beautiful irony about the last pages of the novel. Zeno suddenly finds he is cured, cured by business! In the confusion of wartime Trieste he hits on the secret of success as a business man—he simply buys things, not just this or that commodity, but anything that is offered him. (True, he begins rather recklessly, by making a corner in incense, on the theory —which in fact he knows to be nonsense—that it can be sold as a substitute for resin. The speculation succeeds beyond all expectations, and he recoups ten times over.) Launched at last into the health-giving human struggle, and succeeding in it, he becomes, as it were by definition, a healthy man. Of course he still has a number of strange aches and pains, but in face of his 'great health' they can be discounted. Pain, love and life itself can hardly be regarded as a disease, just because they hurt.

I am not so naïve as to blame the doctor for regarding life itself as a manifestation of disease. Life is a little like disease, with its crises and periods of quiescence, its daily improvements and setbacks. But unlike other diseases life is always mortal. It admits of no cure. It would be like trying to stop up the holes in our body, thinking them to be wounds. We should die of suffocation almost before we were cured. (*The Confessions of Zeno*, trans. Beryl de Zoete, standard ed., pp. 446-7)

(This whole equation between buying and the acceptance of life is typical Svevo, a joke with another joke inside it—for in his relationship with his mistress, which has occupied so many pages of his 'confessions', what has Zeno been doing but buying her? And there is another passing joke in the incense: having become a praiseworthy and effective citizen at last, what is there to stop Zeno from acquiring religion?) Then in the last lines of the final chapter, a chapter full of transitions, the irony more or less disappears, and Svevo speaks in his own voice:

Every effort to procure health is in vain. Health can only belong to the beasts, whose sole idea of progress lies in their own bodies. When the swallow realized that emigration was the only possible life for her, she enlarged the muscles that worked her wings, and which became by degrees the most important part of her body. . . .

But spectacled man invents implements outside his body, and if there was any health or nobility in the inventor there is none in the user . . . a machine creates disease because it denies what has been the law of creation throughout the ages. The law of the strongest disappeared, and we have abandoned natural selection. We need something more than psychoanalysis to help us.

Under the law of the greatest number of machines, disease will prosper and the diseased will grow ever more numerous.

Perhaps some incredible disaster produced by machines will lead us back to health.

When all the poison gases are exhausted, a man, made like all other men of flesh and blood, will in the quiet of his room invent an explosive of such potency that all the explosives in existence will seem like harmless toys beside it. And another man, made in his image and in the image of all the rest, but a little weaker than them, will steal that explosive and crawl to the centre of the earth with it, and place it just where he calculates it would have the maximum effect. There will be a tremendous explosion, but no one will hear it and the earth will return to its nebulous state and go wandering through the sky, free at last from parasites and disease. (*Ibid.*, pp. 447-8)

The novel depends on its two-edged attitude towards Freud and the two-edgedness has not quite gone in the final defence of the rights of disease. Svevo never whole-heartedly accepted or rejected Freud, and in fact read him, as he read most things, in a thoroughly amateur manner. He was certainly deeply fascinated by him, and this is not surprising when you remember Freud's affinity with Schopenhauer. Freud himself often referred to 'the large extent to which psycho-analysis coincides with the philosophy of Schopenhauer'.

Probably very few people can have realised the momentous significance for science and life of the recognition of unconscious mental processes. It was not psycho-analysis, however, which first took this step. There are famous philosophers who may be cited as forerunners—above all the great thinker Schopenhauer, whose unconscious 'Will' is equivalent to the mental instincts of psycho-analysis. It was this same thinker, moreover, who in words of unforgettable impressiveness, admonished mankind of the importance, still so greatly underestimated by it, of its sexual craving. (*A Difficulty in Psycho-Analysis; Complete Psychological Works*, 1953— , vol. 17, pp. 143-4)

And though Svevo was ready to exploit psycho-analysis for comic ends, he seriously believed at the time of writing *Zeno* that he was making a contribution to psycho-analytical literature; he even pictured Freud sending him a grateful telegram, thanking him for introducing psycho-analysis into Italian literature.* The result of this was a rather Zeno-esque calamity. In his depression at the novel's chilly reception, he

* Freud never acknowledged a copy of *Zeno* which Svevo sent him.

thought of his old friend Dr. Weiss, who by now was a personal friend of Freud's, and asked him if he would give him his professional opinion of it. Weiss inquired suspiciously if he were the original of the avaricious Dr. S., but being convinced by Svevo's denials, he promised to read it, and indeed delighted Svevo by promising to review it in a Viennese medical journal. The next time they met, however, Weiss told Svevo that he would have to break his promise, as the novel had nothing whatever to do with psycho-analysis.

Svevo often ruefully mentioned this snub, so much like all the other snubs he had experienced. He said it gave him 'a second disease' (the first being the chronic one of being told he couldn't write Italian). On the whole, however, he accepted the verdict. He still thought there were one or two authentically Freudian inventions in the book, for instance the incident when Zeno, who unwillingly has to attend the funeral of his once hated rival, manages to get into the wrong funeral procession—a neat case of a Freudian error. (In fact he pillaged the incident from a story written before reading Freud and later destroyed.) Otherwise, he fell back on a rather different defence, i.e. that it was in the nature of art to distort ideas.

> We novelists have a habit of playing with philosophic ideas, without really being in a position to expound them. We falsify them, but we also humanise them. The Superman, when he reached Italy, was no longer exactly Nietzsche's Superman. . . . It's a law of destiny that the artist is inspired by philosophers he doesn't understand fully, and the philosophers in turn don't understand the artists they inspire. You know the story of Wagner and Schopenhauer. Wagner sent Schopenhauer his music with protestations of gratitude to the man he regarded as his master. Schopenhauer wrote back saying that in his view the composer who gave the best reflection of his philosophy was Rossini. (*Saggi*, pp. 172-3)

There are some other details in *Zeno* which strike us as genuinely Freudian, for instance the business of Zeno's first experiments in free association. His first attempt ends in sleep. During his second all he achieves is a perfectly meaningless mental picture of a loaded train puffing laboriously up a gradient, and he gives up in disgust, only to discover later that the puffing train represented the major trauma of his life. It was a reminiscence of listening, in an agony, to his dying father, as he lay struggling for breath. Still, Dr. Weiss's snub was a natural and fair one from a serious Freudian in 1923. Svevo was probably quite ignorant of many sides of Freudian theory, and caricatured some of those he did know. Its serious value to him was that it gave him a backing for some of his own most original insights. In analysing Zeno's behaviour in the novel he might well be describing the Ego in its relation with the Id. Zeno's 'good' and 'evil' impulses seem obscurely to be in alliance or at least to have come to a working arrangement, rather as the Freudian Id is in alliance with its apparent enemy the Ego. This is the knowledge that finally comforts Zeno. 'It is perfect freedom to be able to do what you want, on the understanding that you also have to do things you don't want. True slavery is being condemned to abstention: Tantalus and not Hercules.' He is incapable of saying 'no' to his bad impulses, but as long as he gives in to his good ones too, a devious and obscure mechanism seems, in practice, to harmonise their ends.

Likewise a favourite theme of Svevo's work is the protean character of the 'pleasure-principle'. Things are always turning into something else in his novels. His characters, by logical trains of reasoning, secretly guided by the pleasure-principle, end up doing exactly the opposite of what they set out to, or something totally irrelevant to it. Similarly, their emotions keep metamorphosing into others that suit them better. Emilio, in *Senilità*, can't sleep for the thought that he has been neglecting his sister Amalia for his mistress Angiolina and that though he has driven away the man (Balli), whom Amalia has secretly fallen in love with, for her own good, he has also done it out of his own jealousy of Balli in respect to Angiolina. (*Senilità* is full of algebraic equations of this kind.) As he lies tossing on his bed he hears poor Amalia talking in her sleep, and his thoughts take a different turn—what harm would it have been to let Amalia go on with her innocent dreams of Balli? He begins applying this sentiment to his own case vis-à-vis Angiolina, and self-pity soon sends him comfortably to sleep.

Again, had there not been Freud to encourage him, we might not have had one of Svevo's most original things, his handling of psychosomatic disease. It is one of the perennial themes of the novel, the way Zeno's body becomes a living museum of his worst humiliations and moral crimes. There is, for instance, the wonderful little scene in which Zeno, during the terrible five days in which he is forbidden the Malfenti household, runs into an old friend in a café. The friend has recently become a cripple, and Zeno, who loves discussing other people's illnesses, throws himself eagerly into the subject of rheumatism, learning to his amazement that to make one step the body employs no less than fifty-four muscles. When he gets up to go he has contracted a permanent limp himself. The limp becomes a comparatively harmless habit, overlaid by the much more agonising cramps and disorders he contracts in his fatal duel with Guido, but, like all such afflictions, once it is there, it is there for ever. It is an embodiment of the moral order, following its own obscure purposes, always ready at its own chosen time to intervene and punish him.

Equally Freudian is Svevo's conception of the Unconscious. It is worth noting that the title *La coscienza di Zeno* is a kind of joke at the expense both of Freud and of the hero. The word *coscienza* means both 'conscience' and 'consciousness', an ambiguity which runs through the novel; but Svevo is also implying by the title that, though the novel is an account of a psycho-analysis, he needs go no further than Zeno's *conscious* mind to find all the irrationality he wants. In fact, however, as we can see from one or two of his other writings, Svevo had a vivid image of the Unconscious, and in two curious posthumous fragments he seems to be talking directly about the Unconscious mind and its relations with the conscious one. 'I was sleeping quietly', says the Sleeper, in one of the fragments:

You woke me up with all that activity of yours. But as we are both so feeble now (the Sleeper says, weeping) we can co-operate at last. A good thing too. It was sheer tragedy before. I bullied you by night and you bullied me by day. It was worse for me, for day is longer than night. Now there is no more bullying on either side. Sometimes neither of us understands things very well (the Sleeper says, sadly). Well, that's how it has to be. It's not because we are old, but because we were once young. It is nothing to cry about. It is time to sleep peacefully, instead. (*Saggi*, pp. 324-5)

The same speaker, for some reason now called 'Enrico', seems to be speaking in the other fragment:

You understand nothing at all—and not because you are old, but because you were once young.

That's the trouble. Having been young . . .

Siamese twins. Horrible! Just the two of us! If there were three of us, we could form alliances. As it is, you bully me by day and I bully you by night.

How unjust it is. Day is so much longer than night. And to think that you dare complain. You can speak but you understand nothing; I know everything and can't talk. I shout right into your ear and you don't hear me. Now that we are both so feeble we shall get on better. Your senses are getting dulled. You see, you smell, you hear less now. That means you will hear me better.

And all the more so as I can't shout now.

What a tragedy. (*Saggi*, p. 312)

It is plainly the Unconscious which is speaking in both passages, the part of the mind which knows the truth but can only communicate it through the garbled and grammar-less language of dreams.

The idea of the partnership of the dreamer and the waker is treated at length in *Una burla riuscita*. Mario Samigli, basking in the non-existent glory of his forty-year-old novel, is reconciled to life by his idleness, which prevents him from attempting another novel, but also prevents him from finally renouncing the dream of doing so. His life glides gently and serenely on. He looks tenderly after his invalid brother, and any belated chagrin he may feel about his lost ambitions he gives vent to in little animal fables. By day he seems the happiest of men. But by night things are otherwise, and his bedroom rings with deep groans and strange protesting cries. His brother listens anxiously to them, but Mario never remembers his dreams, and, 'rising refreshed from a deep sleep', never doubts that his night has been as serene as his working day.

It is clear to us that Mario's day, as well as his night, is only a dream; they are two dreams, side by side, like Siamese twins. Only in old age (senility was close to art in Svevo's mind) can the two begin to communicate, and only then in the briefest snatches. For more than this to happen, one would have had never to have been anything but old.

Svevo cherished this notion of two dreamers side by side. It is there already in *Senilità*—Emilio in his bedroom, endlessly day-dreaming, and Amalia in hers next door, murmuring and re-enacting honeymoons in her sleep the whole night long. Both Emilio and Mario are in a sense sleep-walkers in their daily life. Indeed the undertone of all Svevo's work is sleep. His heroes are happily or tragically sleeping as they go about, like Emilio walking in silence beside his mistress who is 'ennobled by his uninterrupted dream'. Youth represents dreaming, and senility (in this context representing art) a sort of partial waking before dawn.

In *Zeno*, the development of the 'senile' hero of *Una vita* and *Senilità* is completed, and he gradually emerges as, for good or evil, the representative of humanity itself. The novel, as Svevo wrote to Valerio Jahier, was a deliberate counterblast to the cult of the Superman, a conscious blow against everything represented by d'Annunzio. Zeno has taken the system of Emilio Brentani to its logical conclusion. He attaches himself, as far as possible, to the healthy—the healthy as defined by himself, that is to say those not sharing his particular 'senile' characteristics. And once having incarnated in these others the qualities he doesn't possess himself, the 'senile' hero can be comfortable, his universe is complete and rounded. He can apply himself with full attention to his own orbit, which for all its regularity perpetually takes him by surprise. He can wake up every day like a new-born child, as if quite unaware that the day will have any resemblance to its predecessors. He no longer nourishes any resentment against the healthy for being healthy, but has a permanent occupation in observing how *his* methods very often work out (though certainly to his own surprise) as well as or better than theirs.

The underlying plot of the three central chapters of *Zeno* is the gradual reversal of the positions of the sick and 'senile' man (Zeno) and the 'healthy' man (Zeno's rival Guido Speier). Guido's first appearance in Zeno's life is disastrous. Young, good-looking, talented, he immediately wins the heart of the beautiful Ada Malfenti, whom Zeno is wooing. On their first evening together in the Malfenti household he routs Zeno utterly. He proves to be an expert violinist—and Zeno is an execrable amateur one. Zeno is in despair, and makes himself futilely offensive. He hints that Guido's playing is showy and vulgar, and is ignominiously shouted down. And as if this phallic victory with his violin weren't enough, Guido wins a second triumph. He does a caricature of Zeno, transfixed by his own umbrella, which everyone finds deliciously funny. Zeno feels a sudden agonising shooting pain in his forearm and hip, and these pains are to stay with him, perpetually commemorating this evening, for the rest of his life. (It is a crucial evening for him altogether, for it is the one on which he proposes to each of the three Malfenti girls in turn and is accepted by the one he doesn't want, and the evening in which, later on, he nearly murders Guido.)

The rest of Zeno's long relationship with Guido is a progressive recouping of his defeat, as Guido is gradually dethroned from his symbolically 'healthy' role and his pathetic inefficacy is revealed. The two set up in business. They are equally and wildly incompetent as business men, but Guido's incompetence is of a more fatal kind. His health and talents prove absolutely no use to him, in fact they are a hindrance, since they prevent him till too late from doubting himself and seeing his own absurdity. And Zeno, who gets quite fond of Guido and forms one of his little 'universes' with him and Guido's mistress Carmen, finds to his surprise that his own defeatist acceptance of inadequacy preserves him where Guido is destroyed. It is an inoculation against disaster which makes him, in the Darwinian sense, the fitter to survive. And after Guido has finally ruined himself on the stock exchange and has, characteristically, managed actually to die of a suicide not intended to be genuine, Zeno continues speculating with what is left of the firm's money and is highly successful, earning great kudos as the saviour of Guido's good name. Nature has decided, in their partnership, to favour the 'senile' against the healthy.

The strategies of Svevo's irony are so elaborate in this apologia for disease that it is important not to mistake his tone. Debenedetti gets it wrong, I think, when he suggests that the tone is self-hatred. He argues that the true though unstated key to Svevo's work is the Jewish character, and he links Svevo with the notorious Jewish anti-semitic philosopher Otto Weininger. In his *Sex and Character* Weininger makes a long comparison between the Jew and the woman, both of whom, he claims, represent all that is weak, despicable and sterile in human nature.

I think that the idea of Judaism consists in this want of reality, this absence of any fundamental relation to the thing-in-and-for-itself. He stands, so to speak, outside reality, without ever entering it. He can never make himself one with anything—never enter into real relationships. He is a zealot without zeal, he has no share in the unlimited, the unconditioned. (*Sex and Character*, authorised translation, 1906, pp. 323-4)

By Judaism, he explains, he means neither a race, a people nor a creed (though the Nazis later exploited Weininger in their racial propaganda). He regards Judaism as a tendency of mind, 'a psychological constitution which is a possibility for all mankind, but which becomes actual in the most conspicuous fashion only amongst the Jews'. Whoever detests the Jewish disposition, he says, detests it first of all in himself:

that he should persecute it in others is merely his endeavour to separate himself in this way from Jewishness; he strives to shake it off and to localise it in his fellow-creatures, and so for a moment to dream himself free of it. Hatred, like love, is a projected phenomenon; that person alone is hated who reminds one unpleasantly of oneself. (*Op. cit.*, p. 304)

And the effort of diagnosing 'Judaism' in oneself is the best path to self-understanding in general. 'Self-hatred is the best foundation for self-examination. All self-examination is a phenomenon typical of the self-hater.'

Svevo's typical hero, argues Debenedetti, is really Weininger's Jew, just as Balli in *Senilità* is his 'Aryan', and the inspiration of Svevo's writing is a Jewish antisemitism very close in some ways to Weininger's:

With an implacability, a taste for vengeance, recalling the passionate ferocity of the semitic anti-semite, he mercilessly harries his hero and leads him to defeat, yet at the same time he accompanies him with an intense fellow-feeling, a defensive sympathy like that of racial solidarity. (G. Debenedetti, *Saggi Critici*, new series, 2nd ed., Milan, 1955, p. 86)

There is no doubt that Weininger's portrait of the Jew, as I have quoted it, is in many ways a lifelike description of Emilio and Zeno. On the other hand, what the comparison brings out, surely, is how completely contrary in tendency are Svevo's work and Weininger's. Weininger's book, for all its real brilliance, strikes us (as it struck Freud) as the work of an extremely sick man (Weininger in fact committed suicide a year or two after writing it). And for all Svevo's paradoxes about disease, what his work most suggests is not sickness but health. His gaiety is real, his pessimism is entirely sane, he is not pretending when he claims to have learned to love himself. If Weininger believed that 'self-hatred is the best foundation for self-examination', Svevo really held, on the contrary, that the best foundation for understanding yourself was self-love. 'You have not yet acquired an essential quality, to love yourself', he wrote (in English) to C. S. Ducker near the end of his life:

Only after you have done so others follow your example. In order to acquire this love of themselves women look in a looking-glass. The writer must do the same, and write every evening the history of his day. It is the only way to get a great sincerity—the most important quality, I guess. For the first time since the creation of the world it is you that writes.

Once again, Svevo's apologia for the 'senile' hero is lent a kind of support by Schopenhauer. Zeno is as far as the 'healthy' soul could ever be from attaining the ideal Schopenhauerian condition, when 'only knowledge remains, the will has vanished'. On the other hand he has the comfort that he is also no *further* from attaining it. And his own life provides such a particularly neat demonstration of the Schopenhauerian view of existence that, as far as his philosophical education goes, he has an advantage over the healthy man. For who so regularly as the 'senile' man is made aware of the Will as the *Ding-an-sich*, the very world itself as we experience it, or of the workings of his own will as something he has as little control over as he has over those of Nature?

There is a joke here, not at Schopenhauer's but at his own expense, and it is one which much of Svevo's humour springs out of. For consider the best-known passage in Svevo,

Zeno's dissertation on smoking, which forms the beginning of *Zeno*. As early as his student days Zeno decided to give up the habit. His system, like Svevo's own, was to choose a significant date for his last cigarette, for instance one with some kind of numerical symmetry (later on he has especially high hopes of the 9th day of the 9th month of 1899), or again one which marked some notable event. His diaries and the fly-leaves of his books are soon full of last cigarettes. ('Today, 2 February 1886, I pass from the study of law to that of chemistry. Last cigarette! ! ! !') He has to have the walls of his room redecorated to cover up the frieze of dates he has inscribed on them, each one in rather bolder lettering than the last—he tried oil-paint at one stage.

The point of the whole passage is that last cigarettes taste better than any other. An ideal world would be one in which all cigarettes were last ones, though indeed the act of nominating some cigarettes as 'last' ones improves the flavour of the others too.

I am sure a cigarette has a more poignant flavour when it is the last. The others have their own special taste too, peculiar to them, but it is less poignant. The last has an aroma all its own, bestowed by a sense of victory over oneself and the sure hope of health and strength in the immediate future. The others are important too, as an assertion of one's own freedom, and when one lights them one still has a vision of that future of health and beauty, though it has moved a little further off. (Standard ed., p. 36)

Zeno's unconscious mind has found the secret of making any transaction with his conscience produce a balance of pleasure. It is as though the Freudian Id had been able to cheat the Ego, or as if the pleasure-principle had invented a novel means of outwitting the reality-principle. Not that (to pursue the Freudian terminology) the Super-Ego has ceased to function. As we have seen, it punishes Zeno by inflicting the most painful cramps and other psychosomatic disorders on him; and it also has more subtle methods of working. For Zeno's aspirations towards good conduct are not in vain; it is simply that they bear fruit in unexpected ways. Zeno, unable to be faithful to his wife in practice, compensates by over-fidelity in theory. He plagues the life out of his mistress Carla with praises of his wife's beauty and angelic nature. The result is that Carla finally asks if she can see her. Zeno agrees, privately deciding, out of prudence and vanity, to pass off his beautiful sister-in-law as his wife—for when Carla sees what a paragon he is sacrificing on her account she will prize him more highly as a lover. His little scheme misfires disastrously. Carla comes back from her encounter with Ada (she has watched her pass in the street, and has picked up her umbrella for her) enraptured by her beauty. So sad, so noble a woman! She must have discovered Zeno's infidelity; Carla could see the grief written on her face. He must go back to her. She (Carla) will never again be the cause of sorrow to such a matchless creature. Zeno is cornered; he can hardly take back all his eulogies of Augusta, now, much as he would like to. The tears spring to his eyes at the injustice of it (that Ada, who had treated him so badly already, should now have done him this further injury); Carla takes the tears as a sign of contrition, and bids him the tenderest of farewells.

Thus, in the life of the Svevian hero, the moral order still operates, only it resorts to indirect methods. And if the hero himself wants to obey its dictates he has to do likewise. He cannot master the will, which it becomes all too painfully evident is not *his* will but (in Schopenhauerian terms) the one universal Will working through him. His own life is a perpetual reminder of Schopenhauer's words:

> The intellect can only cast as much light as it can beforehand on the motives that may bear on a future decision. It can't really assist the choice. . . . It awaits the real decision just as passively and with the same intense curiosity as if it were that of a foreign will. (*The World as Will and Idea,* trans. R. B. Haldane and J. Kemp, 1907, vol. 1, p. 376)

On the other hand he can sometimes outmanoeuvre the will.

After that fatal evening at the Malfentis, Guido, the prime cause of all Zeno's calamities, insists on walking home with him. It is a beautiful moonlit night and on the way Guido stretches out boyishly on a low wall with a thirty-foot drop below him. Zeno feels an almost irresistible impulse to push him over, but manages to stop himself by a most original device. He realises that the temptation arises from his being *above* the reclining Guido, so he has the inspiration to kneel down (so far indeed that his head is almost touching the ground) groaning 'The pain! The pain!', as if attacked again by his cramps. By such oblique means can the Will sometimes be cheated.

One should notice, by the way, how appropriate a background the business world (and Trieste in particular, as a city wholly given up to business) is to Svevo's exposition of the 'senile' mentality. Of course, in one sense it represents the very kind of activity to which the 'senile' hero is least adapted. For Zeno, as for Svevo himself, it stood for all that his father had represented. Zeno's father died with his arm upraised, to all appearance cursing him; and he felt he lay for the rest of his life under this imaginary curse, an irreversible judgment on his talents for business and practical life.

On the other hand, the sickness from which the Svevian hero suffers, the total subjectivity and divorce from external reality, is the quintessence of the bourgeois disease, as seen in Marxist terms. Opposites meet; and spiritually Zeno is, if not a born capitalist, at least a born expression of the capitalist ethos. His temperament is indeed in some ways ideally suited to business. In his commercial dealings he is sublimely incurious about the commodities he buys and sells. They are offered to him and he buys them. But on the whole he has as little grasp of them, and as little curiosity about them, in themselves, as he has of the real character of his current mistress—though like his mistresses, they have an awkward habit of behaving unpredictably. His relation to the things he deals in is purely functional. They, like his mistresses, have no existence except in relation to himself. The anonymity of the Bourse is thus ideally adapted to his turn of mind. It is himself pitted against the unfathomable cosmos; and the various magical practices he is accustomed to applying to his private existence (like the numerology he relies on to aid his anti-smoking resolutions) seem quite in place here too. During his triumphant speculations after Guido's death Zeno spends the most exhausting fifty hours of his life, attempting to influence the market by the pure power of thought. It seems to him that no one has ever worked so hard.

What makes Italo Svevo a major author is the generality and universality of his handling of disease. It should be remembered that the last two decades of the nineteenth century, with their preoccupation with the *mal du siècle*, marked a genuine historic crisis, one out of which psycho-analysis was born. The conviction that something was sick in the whole European society was as authentic as it was ill-defined and superstitious. It was Svevo's importance that he saw the dangers of any such conviction of disease. He perceived that it led either to a tragic and self-applauding embracing of disease—the enrolling of oneself in an élite of damned souls and 'superfluous men' or to the invoking of some violent brand of religious or racial revivalism (Bourget's 'barbarian invasion') as a medicine for the 'declining' West. His own lifework as a writer (and it was especially the task of a comic writer) was to show that if the *mal du siècle* were studied with genuine detachment it revealed itself neither as something to be proud of, as a distinguishing possession, nor ashamed of, as a symptom of degeneracy, but as something familiar and indistinguishable from life itself. It was restored to the order of nature.

How much, in *Zeno*, Svevo was attempting a universal and philosophical description of neurosis can be seen from another aspect of the hero. Zeno has a habit of over- or under-shooting the mark. He either falls in love, fetishistically, with a part of a woman—her boot or glove—or with four sisters at the same time. His timing and emphasis are wrong in life, as they are in his 'paralytic' violin-playing; his eyes are never exactly on the target, so that, for instance, half of his behaviour towards Augusta is really intended for Ada's benefit. He cannot cope with wholes, and in describing his wife to his mistress Carla he instinctively amalgamates Augusta's character with Ada's beauty, creating a chimera which comes disastrously to life. One should notice, by the way, the symbolism of the names in *La coscienza di Zeno*. The Malfenti sisters, whom Zeno woos, are called Ada, Alberta and Augusta, and there is also a younger sister Anna. Zeno, who was always attracted to the qualities he didn't possess, fell in love, even before he met them, with these four bearers of a name at the other end of the alphabet from his; they made him feel 'like someone taking a wife in a distant country'. The name 'Zeno' is, I imagine, also meant to remind us of the paradoxes of the Stoic philosopher Zeno, for instance the one about the archer: that it is impossible to conceive how the arrow ever actually leaves the bow, because at any given moment it has either been loosed or not yet been loosed. Zeno frequently experienced a similar bafflement before the spectacle of action.

Though his writing is mostly about disease, Svevo was an extremely sane writer, almost a Voltairean one as far as his tone goes (and the sanity lies in the tone). One sees a reason why he should have been attracted to the author of *Ulysses*. For both Joyce and he not only celebrated the bourgeois as hero, they cheerfully identified themselves with him. They were the first to do this—for if Flaubert, as he said, identified himself with Emma Bovary, he certainly didn't do so cheerfully, he did it out of detestation of the bourgeois in himself. It had its compensations for Svevo that he was never, at least until the very end of his life, allowed to live the professional writer's life. It meant he was able to study writer's vanity, which he was intensely subject to, from a position of genuine detachment (think of the delicious exposition of it in *Una burla riuscita*). He was sincerely convinced, and not merely out of pique, of the harmfulness of pretentiousness. He disliked all exaggeration. He respected balance, even the ludicrous balance that the heroes of *Senilità* and *Zeno* attain, and regarded disease itself as a supreme case of exaggeration. When Ada in *Zeno* falls ill with Basedow's disease, Svevo describes the process in terms of loss of balance. The pretty pink of her cheekbones becomes a flush, her round cheeks becomes goitrous, her attitudes and emotions are all in extremes.

It was part of Svevo's war on exaggeration to see life in terms of animal parallels. When, in the last paragraphs of *Zeno*, he talks of the dangers of getting too far from the animals, he is saying something which is implicit in all his writings. Animals are a constant point of reference in his work, and it is worth digressing a moment from *Zeno* to illustrate this. There is, for instance, the marvellous little scene in *Corto viaggio sentimentale* (*Short Sentimental Journey*) in which two elderly gentlemen get into conversation in the train. (The reference to Sterne in the title is clearly intentional, and Svevo found something very congenial in Sterne's device of counterpointing the *minutiae* of an actual journey with a sentimental journey in the mind—with comic consequences when their trajectories collide.) Signor Aghios has been studying his reflection in the glass of the advertisement behind his fellow-traveller's head. 'Irredeemably old', he thinks to himself. 'Forehead too high; moustache too straggling': his nephew recently told him that moustaches were the prerogative of burrowing animals. 'Do I look like an animal?' he asks himself. His expression scowls back at him obediently. 'Now there is what one can call a really intimate relationship', thinks Signor Aghios, 'a man and his reflection'; and he applies himself happily to further experiments. His fellow-passenger nervously gets out his handkerchief. 'I think I must have some typewriter ink on my face', he says, blushing. Signor Aghios explains he was looking at his own reflection. 'I have a queer look as a traveller', he remarks. 'No, there isn't a trace of dirt on your face.' (There is.) The other returns the compliment: 'I don't know why you say you have a queer look. I wouldn't have said so. I wouldn't at all.' They fall silent, embarrassed. The first words they have exchanged, reflects Signor Aghios, have all been about parts of the body. To go on in this way would be too much like dogs.

Svevo was particularly fond of dogs, and one of the gayest of his posthumous writings, *Argo e il suo padrone* (*Argo and his Master*), relates how a man tries to teach his dog to talk. The dog is embarrassed at first, and politely looks away when his master gets down on his knees for the daily lesson. However the latter perseveres, and though Argo never learns to speak Italian, his master succeeds in learning dog-language. And the generous and admirable character which emerges from Argo's soliloquy (he dies from neurasthenia soon after the experiments) shows clearly why dogs have fallen behind in the evolutionary race. For Argo always thinks the best of his master. One day the maid announces visitors, and Argo's master promptly gives him a kick. Very proper, thinks Argo: how else would I know he is in a bad mood? But one of the afflictions humans seem to suffer from, as Argo has often noticed, is instability in their feelings. Not two minutes later his master is bowing, opening his mouth and half-shutting his eyes, as people with no tails do to show when they are pleased. Argo bounces up to his master, delighted to see him so happy again, and gets an even nastier kick. He retires to a distance to consider the situation. It must be some wretched misunderstanding. There is his master, smiling and tail-wagging, obviously in the greatest high spirits. Nothing Argo hates more than bad feeling between the two of them, and he decides to make one more overture; he slinks cautiously up and attempts to lick his master's face. His master punches him savagely. At last they leave, and their visit has been such a misery to Argo that he can't resist sending them off with a bark or two. Now he is really in for it, he tells himself, and crawls up to his master dragging his stomach on the ground, so that when he is hit he won't have so far to fall. To his astonishment, however, his master falls on him and hugs and hugs him. 'No one will believe this story', says Argo. 'None the less, it occurred exactly as I have told it.'

Argo admires the simplicity of humans. Dogs' lives are much more complex. When a man meets another, they shake hands quite unsuspiciously; when a dog meets another dog it is all more elaborate. He points his toothed end at the toothless end of the other dog, and if the latter is a good fellow he surrenders his toothless end to him before taking his turn. But it always is a delicate moment. A hostile smell can come from somewhere, and then there is no time for questions as to *whose* smell. Smells speak clearly and have to be listened to; and blood, when it starts flowing, speaks with an even clearer voice.

Composing animal fables was one of Svevo's lifelong habits. His room was always littered with them, and he became even more addicted to them during his exile from serious writing. A few have been published separately,* and a number more appear incidentally in the novels. They play a leading part in *Una burla riuscita*, in which the hero copes with every moral crisis by writing such fables; 'poor little dried mummies', the narrator calls them. (In his youth he chose elephants and tigers to write about, but as time goes on he restricts himself more and more to animals he knows, like the sparrows outside his window.) The moral of these fables often tends to be that of *Argo e il suo padrone*, namely that animals can never hope to plumb the black-heartedness of men. In one of them the ghost of a bullock is singing the praises of his old master, the farmer, who for years fed and cosseted him and in fact proved himself a devoted friend—

---

* *Saggi*, pp. 265-279.

and then one day (a most extraordinary tragedy) this friend went mad and murdered him.

His use of animals as a term of comparison was part and parcel of a concern with Darwinism, another important term of reference for him, though his Darwin was mostly second-hand, and he produced his own version of Darwin in which man is contrasted with the animals, having somehow escaped from the beneficent struggle for survival. He has refused to evolve any further physically, choosing to use tools instead, gaining an advantage over the other animals by remaining perpetually uncommitted and incomplete. Man's history is a record of crime and betrayal. Finding himself, in his early days, hopelessly defenceless and at the mercy of the four-footed and the four-handed, he opted for slavery, giving up his freedom to the kindly Mammoth, who soon grew fond of him and acted as his shield. Every now and then the friendly monster would accidentally put his foot on a man, but otherwise his service was light, and Man could have lived very contentedly with him.

> If man had not had a restless mind he would still be the peaceful servant of the Mammoth and our earth would have been spared many miseries, the magificent virgin forests would still be intact, the home of proud, healthy, independent beasts. But man engineered his first revolution without a notion of its terrible consequences. And so he went on. When he is tired or bad-tempered he lets himself break contracts, forget benefits, and hate what yesterday he loved. He destroys, kills, betrays. (*Saggi*, p. 109)

In Svevo's novels and fables those who obey the wholesome law of tooth and claw, the law of the animals, are in a state of grace. And aggression is as protean in form as the pleasure-principle. The most innocent show their teeth if they are attacked; even his invalids are full of innocent cunning. Mario's brother in *Una burla riuscita*, the mildest and simplest of men, defends his ill-health with great resourcefulness. It is essential to him to be read to sleep at night, and Mario's reading serves the purpose admirably, except that every now and then, just when the tranquil sentences of Fogazzaro or de Sanctis have sent him gently drifting off to sleep, Mario interrupts himself to pass cutting literary criticisms. Giulio, of course, anxiously agrees with them, but it means waking up to do so. However, he has an inspiration; he asks Mario to read *his own* novel to him, and the disagreeable criticisms promptly cease. One day, however, Giulio's cunning deserts him, and he tacitly admits that he never listens to the words when Mario reads—why should he, he knows them by heart anyway; they do him all the more good for that reason. Mario, taken off his guard by this deadly blow to his writer's vanity, turns on poor Giulio in fury, crushing him with a diatribe against those who, to protract their miserable existence, turn the noblest fruits of human endeavour into patent medicines. 'Literature, being attacked, fought back, wounding illness cruelly.'

Svevo's permissiveness towards his weak-willed, self-deluding, hopelessly backsliding heroes went with a doctrine of evolutionary stoicism. If Nature decided to choose you as a victim, you had no right to complain. These are the sentiments of Zeno (whose name is that of the father of Stoicism) when his partner Guido, faced with the consequences of his own bungling, asks him for sympathy:

I had no consolation to offer him. . . . The law of nature does not confer the right to be happy, on the contrary it condemns us to pain and suffering. Wherever the feast is spread parasites will flock to it from all parts, and if there are not enough of them they hasten to breed more. Soon there is only sufficient for the barest need, and very soon all is devoured, for nature does not calculate, she only makes experiments. When there is no more left the number of consumers must dwindle, by a process of pain and death, and thus the balance is restored for a moment. What is the use of complaining? Yet all do complain. Those who have had no share at all of the prey die arraigning the injustice of nature; those who have had their share feel that it ought to have been bigger still. Why don't they live and die in silence? On the other hand it is pleasant to see the joy of someone who has succeeded in securing a good share of the booty, and flaunts himself in the sun, amidst the plaudits of the crowd. The only cry I should allow is the cry of triumph. (*The Confessions of Zeno*, trans. Beryl de Zoete, standard ed., pp. 380-1)

This was always Svevo's tone about Nature. She was an insane experimenter, to whom living beings only existed as material for her experiments:

Mother Nature created pleasure to guarantee reproduction. That obtained, if she allows the capacity for pleasure to go on existing, she only does so out of absentmindedness, just as certain insects go on wearing their mating colours after the mating season is over. Running a firm of that size, you can't attend to every detail. (Title-story in *Corto viaggio*, p. 96)

Nature is deaf to all appeals, not out of indifference, but from her obsession with her own projects—which in fact she takes great pains to hide from inquisitive eyes (this is nearer Schopenhauer than Darwin). 'Mother Nature is a maniac', says the elderly hero of *Il mio ozio* (*This Indolence of Mine*):

She has the reproduction-mania. She keeps an organism alive as long as it has any hope of reproducing. Then she murders it, and she does it in as many different ways as possible, on account of her other mania—that for being mysterious. She wouldn't like to show her hand by always resorting to the same disease to destroy old men—a disease which would make our death seem a rational process, a little cancer always in the same place. (*Corto viaggio*, p. 367)

A good deal of Svevo's humour arises from the play between these two conceptions, the beneficent struggle for survival and the terrifying absent-mindedness of Nature: sometimes explicitly so, as when Signor Aghios in *Corto viaggio sentimentale* holds forth eloquently to a chance travelling companion about the implacable experimentalist Nature, while the latter is studying how to rob his wallet.

One of Mario's fables in *Una burla riuscita* is about the sparrows who starved in thousands in wartime Trieste. He asks them 'Are you in despair?', and they reply, 'No; only there are less of us'.—'Fables are for amusement', says the narrator, 'because the reader is amused. He laughs at that brute of a bird, who completely forgets the despair he has been living side by side with, not having been affected by it himself. Having laughed, he thinks of the impassive face worn by Nature while making her experiments, and then he shudders.'

To return to *La coscienza di Zeno*. One of the striking features of *Senilità* was the way in which the whole structure of the novel was built up out of comparisons. In *Zeno* he took this method even farther. As a novelist, Svevo's mind worked all the time by leaps of analogy; they became the fibre of his writing. In *Zeno* and all his later work an idea only has to be introduced on one page for you to know it will turn up again a few paragraphs or pages later in some quite new application. The themes recur and propagate before your eyes. You feel the dowsing-rod jerking this way and that at the scent of hidden connections. And the way things mirror one another, and unexpectedly lead to one another, in his work represents a belief in the unity of all experience.

Many of the paradoxes of *Zeno* are paradoxes of comparison, illness being compared with health, different kinds of illness with each other, and so on. Augusta's health is a true one, Guido's health is a sham; Zeno's imaginary illness is contrasted with Ada's actual one. He analyses Ada's disease itself (she is suffering from *Morbus Basedowii*, i.e. Graves's disease) in terms of correspondences and connections. It is disease imitating health. When Augusta and Zeno are seeing her off on the train to a sanatorium she smiles radiantly at the flowers they give her. 'Poor Ada, with her eyes opened too wide by happiness, looked like a young bride', reflects Zeno. 'Her disease could imitate all the emotions.' In Chapter 6 of

Zeno there is a wonderfully funny description of people comparing their diseases. Zeno's old friend Copler has come back to Trieste, suffering from a serious illness from which he mistakenly believes he is recovering. He manages to turn every conversation round to illness, a subject Zeno also is very fond of. Zeno admits to being an imaginary invalid, and this infuriates Copler.

> *Malade imaginaire*? Well, I prefer to be a real one. In the first place a *malade imaginaire* is ridiculous and pitiable; and then nothing can cure him, whereas in the case of a real invalid like me there is always some drug that can be found to meet the case. (*The Confessions of Zeno*, trans. Beryl de Zoete, standard ed., p. 189)

Zeno feels worsted, for if Copler can defend his illness so forcefully, it must be Copler who is the really healthy man. Augusta comes to Zeno's rescue, however, saying that he can't really be ill or he wouldn't enjoy life in the way he does. She strokes Zeno's hand, making Copler envious (*he* needs a nurse like Augusta), so the score is evened. They go on with their discussion next day, each still trying to score off the other, till Copler (who wants everyone to be an invalid) proves to his own satisfaction that he and Zeno are on a level, an imaginary invalid is a real invalid too; it is simply that the real invalid's nerves are not quite active enough and the imaginary invalid's are too active. Zeno, however, privately makes a comforting observation: Copler, who has given up his own business for health reasons, has begun to occupy his time with other peoples' affairs. He finds philanthropy an absorbing pastime, but since it is a sacred rule to him only to spend interest, never capital, he has to confine his activities to whip-rounds and appeals. Zeno reflects that if he had been in Copler's shoes, with no family and no great expectation of life, he would have spent his capital on his hobby too; Copler can't do this, because Copler is an 'imaginary healthy man'.

It is one of Zeno's discoveries that health is a matter of comparison. It is by comparing himself, to his own disadvantage, with his rival Guido that he first contracts his psychosomatic pains, and it is by comparing himself with him again, to his own advantage, when Guido has proved a hopeless failure and bungler and has even managed to commit suicide by mistake, that he begins to experience health again. 'Health is only a matter of comparisons. I compared myself with poor Guido and soared, up, up into the air with my victory in the same struggle he had succumbed in. Everything around me spoke of health and strength; even the countryside, with its fresh spring grass. At that moment my whole being was one hymn of health, perpetual health, my own and that of Nature.'

Zeno represents the subject-matter of *Senilità* handled more adventurously, more searchingly and with a more deliberate quest after novelty. Without having read Proust, and with only a very partial knowledge of Ulysses—having, in fact, been out of touch with any literary fashion later than Zola or Bourget—Svevo discovered for himself the new 'totalist' conception of fiction, and wrote the first 'modern' novel in Italian. It was to represent the totality of a man's existence, the whole 'Consciousness of Zeno'. And one of its original features, as Joyce pointed out, was its use of time. By using a travesty of psycho-analysis as his framework, Svevo allowed himself to put things in the order he wanted. Zeno begins to talk about the problem which has most preoccupied him (his smoking) and then about the most significant event in his life (his father's death). And the rest of the novel is an amplification of these two opening themes. His love affair with Carla is a prolonged repetition of his smoking; he renounces her daily, as he renounces cigarettes, and as with cigarettes he employs good resolutions, not so much in order to keep them, as to extract the maximum pleasure from his present lapse. The whole chapter lies under the sign of the 'last cigarette'. Indeed, the day before he actually seduces Carla he writes in his dictionary, against the letter C, the words 'last infidelity'.

Similarly, the scene when Zeno, resisting his temptation to murder Guido, falls to his knees groaning in simulated agony, is a comic repetition of the most poignant part of the chapter 'Death of my Father'. It echoes, in an absurd way, the time when he was begging the doctor to let his father die in his coma (to 'murder' him, in fact) rather than allow him to come back to consciousness and madness. He pleaded with the doctor then, using his tears to mask his hostility, much as he is doing now with Guido:

I knew why I was moaning; it was because I had wanted to kill him, and partly, perhaps, because I had not the courage to do so. The pain and my groans excused everything. It seemed to me that I was crying out that it was not my fault if I hadn't been able to do it. It was entirely the fault of my illness and this pain of mine. (*Ibid.*, p. 166)

Again, Zeno's last words about Ada, with which the whole central section of the novel closes, take up the ones he had once used about his father, after the latter had died apparently cursing him. 'So she was leaving me, and never again should I have the chance to prove my innocence.'

The core of the book, the three long middle chapters, do form a chronological narrative, but not much more obtrusively so than *À la recherche du temps perdu*. The narrative doesn't attempt, like that of a nineteenth-century novel, to convey the passing of time. It plays about with the time-scale, focusing minutely here or high-handedly overleaping transitions there. It is concerned with exploring time rather than mimicking it, and with contrasting different kinds of time—the periods when every second brings violent change, and the periods when everything seems set for ever in the same pattern. The form of the central chapter, like that of *Senilità*, is circular. The two chapters 'History of a Business Partnership' and 'Wife and Mistress' subtly balance each other. Zeno's situation in 'History of a Business Partnership' is, in important ways, exactly the opposite of what it was in 'Wife and

Mistress'. In the earlier chapter he is hating and fearing Guido, in the later he despises him and wishes him well; in the earlier he is vainly in love with Ada, in the later he is irrationally terrified that, owing to her illness, she may decide to respond to the passion which no longer exists. (It would be, he reflects with his usual gift for comparison, like the copper sulphate which Guido ordered from England, and then forgot about, and which ruined him when he finally had to take delivery of it.) Zeno and Guido even repeat their memorable nocturnal walk, and Guido stretches out again on the same parapet; and this time, instead of wanting to murder him, Zeno resolves to be his saviour.

The two short keynote chapters, 'Smoking' and 'Death of my Father', as well as stating the book's themes, are also a statement of the two extremes of Svevo's tone. An entirely new element had come into his style by the time of *Zeno*, the element of grotesque farce or tall story, as in the extravaganza of Zeno in the sanatorium. And he deliberately juxtaposes this chapter with the intensely moving and harrowing one of his father's death. The central chapters lie somewhere between these extremes of tone, and then the book modulates into its original style of wild farce in the last chapter. The pace accelerates and becomes staccato as we return from the endless dream of Zeno's inner life to his antics in the face of present circumstances—Zeno ignominiously rebelling against the hated Dr. S., Zeno panicking when he begins to think the doctor may have cured him of his erotomania after all and hurriedly resorting to experiments to reassure himself. Transition huddles on transition. Zeno is overtaken by the war, while out on an early morning walk, his thought centred happily on his breakfast coffee. War separates him from his coffee and, for an indefinite period, from his family; and symbolically cut off, like this, from pleasure and from moral sanctions, he improbably realises his capacities as a man of business. This modulation back into the style of a farcical novel frames and distances the profounder comedy of the central chapters and adds a further 'Chinese box' effect to the book.

Both in form and content Zeno is an advance on *Senilità*. It is nearer the ideal of the 'modern' novel, a living web of connections, an inclusive form in which everything opens out into everything else. The play of mind is even more quick and darting; and it is in *Zeno*, above all, that Svevo gives the impression of having access to things in one's own mind, private manias and compulsions, which one had never expected to see brought to light. Who else could have written that passage about Ada's ugliness? Zeno, having been rejected by the beautiful Ada, has married her squinting sister Augusta; and Ada, who married his rival Guido, contracts Basedow's disease and loses all her beauty. Augusta, none the less, is still jealous of her sister, and when Zeno offers Guido money, Ada's excessive gratitude arouses her suspicions. To prove his innocence, Zeno has the 'inspiration' to puff out his cheeks and open his eyes wide to make himself look like Ada. 'So Ada is in love with me?' he asks. Augusta laughs, shamefacedly, but has to admit he has imitated poor Ada's face very well. Zeno knows it too, for when imitating Ada he actually had the sensation of kissing her. And later, when he is on his own, he tries the face out again, 'with a mingled feeling of excitement and disgust'. And then, casually and typically, Svevo comes back to the theme in the next paragraph. Zeno has to go to Ada's house to discuss the offered money. 'I had to fulfil my duty', he says, 'painful though the prospect was of seeing Ada's face still more distorted in her efforts to express gratitude.' There is a sort of inventiveness and freedom, a perfect originality, in this, that goes beyond anything in *Senilità*. Indeed the novel is altogether a larger achievement than *Senilità*, wider in its sweep, more intricate in its ironies, and with that permanent colour of novelty about it which places it with the great masterpieces of the 'modern' novel.

10

Last Writings, and Plays

In his last three years, when the belated recognition of *Zeno* had given him courage to write again, Svevo had one obvious subject to hand—old age. Having written so much about it in its metaphorical sense, he was now faced with it in a literal one. He fell on the subject with enthusiasm: 'In such a stupid life as mine has been', he wrote, 'I can't understand how so serious a thing as old age can have happened to me.' And his last writings are, for the most part, a prolonged inquiry into the phenomenon of ageing. His major documents on old age are *La novella del buon vecchio e della bella fanciulla* (*The Story of the Nice Old Man and the Pretty Girl*), a play called *Rigenerazione* ('Regeneration') and the various fragments of a sequel to *Zeno*, which he thought of calling 'The Old Old Man' or 'An Old Man's Confessions'; and the subject also plays a considerable part in *Corto viaggio sentimentale*.

If old age was 'a serious thing' his approach to it was, of course, the comic one. He addressed himself to it in his favourite pose of ironic, wide-eyed discovery—the attitude of *Senilità*: 'How surprising, after all, life went on being!' He saw himself, half-seriously, as an experimental scientist studying a new field of biology in his own body and mind. Old age strikes him as, among other things, a grammatical problem. He is living in a 'mixed' tense, still vacillating between the present and the past, though now without a future. It is the fate of Man to live in mixed tenses, though there are pure ones in his grammar—they seem designed less for humans than for the animals, who when not in a state of fear live joyously in a crystalline present. The present he is living in is not a true present—since it leads to no other present, it stands outside time; we have no 'ultimate' tense in grammar. And of course the new state of affairs is simpler. He no longer suffers all the old absurd remorse, the terrifying fears for the future. How could he be frightened of the future? He is living it now.

Yet for an old man (yes, I am an old man; it is the first time I have admitted it, the first fruits of my new-found serenity) this mutilation, by which life loses what it never really had—the future—though it may make life simpler, it also makes it so meaningless we might be tempted to spend our brief present tearing the few hairs that remain on our deformed skull. ('Il Vecchione' in *Opere*, ed. B. Maier, 1954, p. 1026)

If he writes, instead of tearing his hair, he does so to lengthen his brief present as much as possible, and to find out what the present is—how it can turn into such a different thing as the past. For 'it may be truc, as the philosophers say, that time does not exist, but the receptacles which hold it exist, and they are almost hermetically sealed. Only a few drops filter through from the one to the other.' The whole subject calls for study and experiment; Zeno as a man experiments with monkey-glands, and Zeno as a writer will experiment in memory and art.

In shape *La novella del buon vecchio e della bella fanciulla* is broadly similar to the Carla section of *Zeno*; and it uses the same idea, which Svevo often came back to, of the lover quieting his conscience by giving his love-affair an 'educational' turn. The hero, widowed and senile, combines each visit of his mistress with an improving lecture. And he also has another convenient pretext, equally quieting to the conscience, that a love-affair is important to his health—the story is a triangle drama between himself, his mistress and his medicine-bottles. When his state of health makes love-making too dangerous an exertion, he manages to transfer his pleasure entirely from the girl to the lecturing. Finally, when he has managed to eliminate the girl's image from his mind altogether, the original pleasure re-incarnates itself as literary ambition—he begins a work 'On the Relations between Old Age and Youth', proving from history and logic the importance to the world of healthy old men. The work itself keeps unaccountably changing in its tendency, as his love-affair has done. Old men's sins, he decides, count double as compared with young men's; yes, but if young men's sins count for little, when does the education of old men begin? (He marks it as a question for further study.) As he goes on writing, his resentment against young men grows. It must be their fault if old men are immoral. 'With whom is morality supposed to begin?' he writes in large letters.

Falteringly, he scribbles on, then sits for days staring at the heap of pages, and at last carefully wraps them in a cover, writing on it laboriously several times over, 'Nothing!'—'They found him stiff and cold, with the pen still in his mouth through which his last breath had passed.'

In 'Il mio ozio', one of the 'Old Old Man' fragments, and rather more genial than the bitter *novella* of *The Nice Old Man*, the aged Zeno likewise takes a mistress for hygienic reasons—only, as he discovers, the trouble about a woman is that you can't adjust the dose. His idea in taking her is to cheat Nature, who, he feels, is all ready to knock him on the head as soon as it is proved he can help her no more in the business of procreation. It is his last affair, and when Felicita finally turns him out he decides to give up the hope of being desired by women, and to go on cheating Nature merely by desiring them. Looking at women's legs in the streets is a medicine he can take in strictly measured doses.

As *La coscienza di Zeno* begins with Zeno undertaking a course of psycho-analysis, so, at the start of the new novel, Zeno, bored with his life after his forcible retirement from business and tired of being treated as a helpless dotard, submits to a rejuvenation operation. Physically speaking, it is a fiasco, its only effect being to give him boils. Psychologically speaking, however, the operation—or rather the experience of pinning such hope upon it—works a temporary miracle; looking forward to youth is a kind of youth in itself. For a few weeks he emerges from the shadows into the foreground of life again. It is like reliving his adolescence, and is so uncomfortable that he takes to his pen in refuge.

As Zeno re-dedicates himself to writing, a whole series of new prospects opens up before his sanguine eyes. Writing, for one thing, will be a return to action. What with all the virtues he practises, and the ones other people attribute to him, and with all the affections and duties he seems to have accumulated, he might as well be dead for all the freedom he has. Perhaps writing will give him back his initiative. If he has to be virtuous, he would like to be dramatically virtuous, virtuous in *his* way, and writing may provide the opportunity.

And then, when he re-reads his own ten-year-old confessions (i.e. *La coscienza di Zeno*), he sees what he can do with them, *now*, that he couldn't do before. For a strange phenomenon has taken place in the ten years; he has forgotten everything of the past except what he happens to have written down. Or if he hasn't entirely forgotten it, the only way of recalling it is to re-read *Zeno* and fill in the gaps. He finds he is studying his past as if it were someone else's. It gives him a sense of loss and at the same time a precious new freedom. He perceives a whole new function in writing, the endless sifting out and purifying of one's own past life, an occupation with obvious advantages over mere living. Perhaps this is how everyone should spend their time—half of humanity re-writing its own past and the other half reading what they write.

And if one part of human kind rebels and refuses to read the other half's effusions, so much the better. Everyone will read himself instead; and people's lives will have a chance to repeat, to correct, to crystallise themselves, whether or no they become clearer in the process. For good or evil, they won't go on being as they are now, flat and insignificant, buried as soon as born, with all their days melting into each other, piling up indistinguishably into years and decades. ('Le confessioni del vegliardo' in *Corto Viaggio*, p. 288)

And what is the past? he asks himself. He remembers a recent experience, when he and Augusta, on a trip to the country beyond Udine, got out of the car, and by climbing a little hill nearby came suddenly into full view of another landscape, the foothills and blue peaks of the Carnic Alps. They had stood silent in surprise, and for minutes on end Zeno had amused himself noting how the noise of a blacksmith's hammer, from the valley below them, only reached him when the man's arm was already raised for the next stroke. A few days or weeks later the whole scene had changed in his memory: the sound and the blow coincided as they should and the landscape had rearranged itself according to the rules of composition. When had it happened? He had failed to note the time the process took, and he projects a series of experiments on the same lines, to determine the boundary between the present and the past. 'And so', he says, 'I will end my life, like my dead father, notebook in hand.'

The rest of the fragments, dealing with the present half of Zeno's existence, are in the style of *Zeno*. Zeno, as usual, begins by studying what is nearest to hand—his family, and the new set of relationships he has acquired since writing his confessions: his ill-fated efforts to get on with his son and daughter and his new-found alliances with his doctor nephew and his little grandson Umbertino. As he goes on talking, with the old unremitting analysis, enclosing irony within irony, there is the same interplay and recession between Zeno as actor and Zeno as recorder and between what Zeno himself notices and what we do. Zeno, relegated to the shadows of life, finds existence there just as thick with calamities. He is haunted, as before, by historic parallels and unexpected analogies. He repeats, and (too late) observes himself repeating, the master-patterns of his existence. His *idée fixe* in dealing with his children is to avoid the disasters that his father caused to himself. It is as fatal an *idée fixe* as any other, and produces what it is meant to avert. His elaborate plan to conciliate his son Alfio, by buying one of his dreadful pictures and carefully refraining from a single *Witz* at its expense, ends catastrophically. At the very worst moment (at a crowded dinner-table), and with the very maximum injury to Alfio, he finally makes the *Witze* he has been suppressing—he had felt like laughing; it was a healthy exercise, the one violent exercise allowed to old men. Even Alfio's pale incredulous face doesn't stop him. 'I felt innocent. I wanted to laugh, and for that any subject was good enough.'

In these fragments, 'The Old Old Man', 'An Old Man's Confessions', 'Umbertino', 'This Indolence of Mine' and 'A Contract', Svevo is making a great deal out of little (as he does again, strikingly, in *Corto viaggio sentimentale* in which he spins a hundred pages and more out of the most casual accidents and conversations of a railway journey). What the underlying direction of the different scraps was going to be one can't guess, but in themselves they are often as rich and exciting as anything in *Zeno*; his writing was never more darting and alive. And one feels that the book, if age had not slowed down and death interrupted the writing of it, might have been another masterpiece.

In the last year of his life Svevo also wrote a comedy about old age. It was called *Rigenerazione* ('Regeneration'), and it strikes me as the best of his plays. Svevo, as we know, wrote plays throughout his life, one or two even when he had officially given up writing, but he never, except in *Rigenerazione* and one or two short things (*Terzetto spezzato* and *Inferiorità*) completely mastered the form. The earliest plays, from the 1880s, are mostly light-weight vaudeville-like one-acters, totally artificial in their characterisation though sometimes containing quite amusing central ideas. There is, for instance, *La verità* ('Truth'), in which a professional liar manages, with superlative resourcefulness, to explain to his wife how, quite innocently, he happened to be in bed with her dressmaker in the middle of the afternoon. Or again *Una commedia inedita* ('An Unpublished Play')—Svevo's own title—in which a wife, on the verge of being unfaithful to her husband with a playwright, is tactless enough to give her opinion of his latest play. A later *jeu d'esprit*, *Terzetto spezzato* ('The Broken Trio'), belonging to 1890 or thereabouts, is altogether wittier and more original and has been performed with some success. It is about a business man who has recently lost his wife and invites an old friend of the family (in actual fact, the wife's lover) to take part in raising her ghost. The wife, when she materialises, finds that nothing has changed: the lover soon works up a quarrel, and the husband, after his first awe at her re-appearance, turns very snappish when she won't exploit her opportunities to give him advance market-information. She dematerialises, having had enough of both of them; but as she has carelessly let out that any ill-feeling on her account between mortals will be held against her in Heaven, the husband and lover realise they now have the upper hand. They have only to stage a quarrel to get her back at any time. As the curtain falls, they are busily preparing to spar.

The best of his one-acters, however, is *Inferiorità*, written about 1920 or 1921. It is a sort of commentary on one of his diary entries:

> To bully someone when he hasn't the right or the courage to retaliate means falsifying your relationship with him forever. Never again will he be sincere with you. He has been classed once and for all as your inferior, and ever afterwards will hate and despise you. (*Saggi*, p. 330)

The play is about a practical joke with tragic consequences. Count Alberighi and a companion have decided to play a hoax on their friend Alfredo, who has been brandishing his wallet about, full of money, and scoffing (arrogantly, they think) at the idea of anyone robbing him. They offer a bribe to Alfredo's manservant Giovanni, to terrorise his master and take his money off him at the point of a pistol, and Giovanni, having stood out for a bribe large enough for him to retire on, agrees. Alfredo arrives on the scene, and Giovanni goes through his performance (overheard by the Count and his friend, who are hiding in a closet), but he loses his nerve when his master faints with terror. Whereupon Alfredo, coming to his senses again, turns on Giovanni and bullies him mercilessly. He goes too far, and Giovanni, turning on him again, this time really murders him. With the Count and the Baron battering on the door to be let out, Giovanni quietly puts on his master's hat and coat and escapes; as he goes, he kisses his master's hand, murmuring 'I wanted to be rid of you, and now you will be with me forever'. It is a brilliant little piece, a powerful demonstration of the realities behind practical joking. What's in the air when Alberighi and his friend the Baron arrive in the flat is bullying. Alberighi is burning to bully someone a little; his tipsy friend catches the itch, and so does Giovanni, after they have bullied him on his sore point, money; so, likewise, does Alfredo himself, when he has got over his fright. The play is a study in contagion, worked out with all Svevo's acute perception of consequences, and for once, as a dramatist, Svevo is economical—his quick reversals really surprise and his ironies are truly dramatic.

In his middle years Svevo wrote two three-acters, *Un marito* ('A Husband') and *L'Avventura di Maria* ('Maria's Adventure'), the first in 1903 and the second some time after 1910 (he was constantly tinkering with his plays, so the dates are rather indefinite). *L'Avventura di Maria* is a philosophic triangle-drama about a woman violinist who returns to (presumably) Trieste to stay with an old school-friend, and in pique at her friend's self-satisfied domesticity, and also at the fiasco of her own concert (the Triestines try to be kind, but can't help comparing her with their favourite 'Janson', the master of the cadenza), decides to run off with her friend's husband. The play is a decided failure. There is some nice satire on Philistine Trieste in it, but it is static and diffuse and vacillates awkwardly between comedy and farce.

Un marito, which Svevo set particular store by, is more Ibsenesque and deals with an obsession with the past. The hero Federico, some years before the play opens, has killed his wife after finding her unfaithful. The court acquitted him, but he is still obsessed by what he has done—he who as a young man preached a complete 'modern' tolerance in sexual morals. He has married again, but the marriage is haunted by the past, indeed the only person Federico has any real feeling for is his dead wife Clara's mother, who has sworn to be revenged on him. When this latter tries to break up his marriage, by showing him letters to prove that his new wife, Bice, has also taken a lover, he desperately begs Bice to give him proof of her innocence—not because he cares on her account, but as an answer to Clara's mother. For if Bice *were* guilty, and yet he did not kill her as he killed Clara, he would be admitting the wrongness of the first murder. His wife does all she can to combat his perverse cult of Clara's mother, and finding this useless, decides to take part in it too. The past has won; and as the final curtain falls the two are going hand in hand to the bedside of the avenging old woman. Federico reflects that, with any luck, she may mistake Bice for Clara.

It is a preposterous play, and a very bad imitation of Ibsen, though it deals with themes that meant a lot to Svevo. And it is fairly plain what is wrong with it. Federico, whom everyone treats nervously, in case he takes it into his head to commit another wife-murder, and who is secretly rather delighted at this impressive role, is essentially a comic character; indeed he is just the sort of comic conception that Svevo handled marvellously in his novels. In various places one can feel Svevo letting the play deviate into farce and then pulling it back, and the result, as far as the tone is concerned, is a muddle.

There is no objection of this kind to *Con la penna d'oro*

('With a Pen of Gold'), an unfinished four-act comedy belonging to 1926 or thereabouts. It is close to the novels in tone and contains some splendid material and scenes. It is a play about dependence. The main characters are two female cousins—one rich, the other poor and resenting her patronage—and their elderly Aunt Teresina, who is shuttlecocked between them. The aunt, who has been a domestic tyrant all her youth and middle-age, has decided, now that she is a cripple and thrown on others' charity, to master the art of sycophancy. Svevo's unique tone—profound, humane and utterly immune to sentimentality or platitude—comes out at its best here. Aunt Teresina is not, as would have been the theatrical cliché, triumphantly successful in her manoeuvres from her wheeled chair, nor pathetically unsuccessful. She is merely someone, like ourselves, fighting a minute-to-minute battle for self-assertion against odds. And here we come up against a basic difficulty facing Svevo as a playwright. It was part of his whole conception of the world that people never really change or get cured of their particular folly or humour; at most, like Aunt Teresina, they merely exhibit the same drives in a different context. To take another example, the incorrigibly patronising niece Alberta, in the same play, is still, as the final curtain falls, finding new ways of being patronising; whereas in a comedy of the Molière type she would have been cured or chastened in some way. Svevo's whole view of life was static and, in that sense, pessimistic, and his novels, as I have mentioned, tend to take the form of vicious circles. Believing as he did that all action was illusory, it always gave him trouble to provide the action required in a traditional play. To succeed in drama, in any original way, he needed to find a static and circular form like that of his novels. And he achieved this, to some extent, only in the last of his plays, *Rigenerazione*.

The play is his most ruthless handling of the farce of old age. It is a bitter play, but an immensely gay one also, and his comic imagination finds its freedom in it for the first time. It is very close to 'The Old, Old Man' and deals with the same characters, though sometimes under other names: an old man, Giovanni, his wife Anna, their daughter Emma, her suitor Biggioni, Giovanni's mischievous nephew Guido, the maid Rita, etc. It is a comedy of humours: all Giovanni thinks of is his age, Anna is entirely preoccupied with her pet birds and cats, Emma brings every conversation round to her dead husband Valentino, whilst Biggioni can never forget the fact, which gives him such secret satisfaction, that his best friend Valentino is dead and stinking; Guido, again, thinks only of money, and Rita of avoiding work. The action of the play is purely farcical, and indeed the whole point of the action is that nothing really happens; the events are all ludicrous anti-climaxes, and the only significant events take place in the old man's dreams.

At the opening of the play, Giovanni is in a bad temper with the world. Everyone is bullying him for being senile and absent-minded and suggesting, kindly but firmly, it is time he stopped taking Emma's child for walks. (The last time he took him, he came back without him, convinced he had let him be run over.) His nephew (who has a financial interest in the proposal) suggests he should have a rejuvenation operation, and after a wildly funny scene in which Giovanni haggles about the price (one of his arguments is that as Guido holds out the prospect of a twenty-per-cent rejuvenation, the longer he postpones the operation the more he will get for his money), and earnestly insists that no harm shall be done to his morals, he agrees. Enter Giovanni, rejuvenated, in a smart silk dressing-gown. He struts about experimentally and gives his knee a painful knock. Another elderly gentleman, interested in the same operation, begs to be allowed to inspect him, tactfully inquiring as to the effect on his virility. Giovanni refuses to understand him, but he privately arranges an experiment on just this matter, with the maid Rita as subject. It is not a success, however. After getting Rita drunk, he finally manages to kiss her, but at this point both of them fall asleep, and when the two are found together, snoring, Anna is all solicitude, and goes and fetches rugs. Giovanni, as he sleeps, dreams of murdering Anna.

Next day the position is still the same; neither of the injured parties, Anna or Rita's fiancé, shows trace of decent jealousy; indeed Anna, to Giovanni's fury, asks if he enjoys Rita's company—for if so, she will arrange for her to be free whenever he wants. Humiliation succeeds humiliation, no one will believe in Giovanni's new-found virility, and in the end he gives up the struggle to be young and reverts to harmless, contemptible decrepitude.

The play ends with another dream-sequence—Giovanni is hoeing a stony field, having been led there by Rita. He asks if he can wait a little till the rain has softened the earth, but she tells him they have chosen him specially for the job, he being so young and vigorous now. He tells her to stand farther off, but to sing to him. Anna appears, and he reproaches her bitterly. What were they doing getting married as they did, all those years ago, he in a dress-suit and she all in white? What did they mean eating and drinking so much at that wedding-breakfast, as if they meant to eat and drink like that all their lives? Did they stay together because of it? Well, a year or two perhaps; and then they fell apart for ever. And then he had his operation, and saw what their life had become: a world in chaos, a spectacle of horror, a world where kisses count for nothing any longer. For example, he kissed Rita . . .

ANNA: Yes, as a father kisses a daughter.

GIOVANNI (*furious*): As a father kisses someone else's daughter. There's a difference! . . . And then you told me I could have her whenever I liked.

ANNA: I was only trying to be nice.

GIOVANNI: Thank you, but you overdid it. You gave me more than I asked for. You got the proportions wrong.

ANNA: You shouldn't complain. I thought I was making life pleasanter for you.

GIOVANNI: Make it pleasanter? You've made it a hell for me, treating me in that way, treating my operation in that way.

ANNA: Your operation? What did you expect? A miracle, after three weeks?

GIOVANNI: You didn't have faith. And it means that now I haven't either—I want no more to do with women.

ANNA: Not even with me? Won't you give me a kiss?

GIOVANNI: A kiss? No, absolutely not! I love you. I never wanted to kill you. I love you, I say. For your sake I will love all the animals too, the sparrows, the cats and the dogs. And I will work for you. In your name I will keep and feed mankind. That is the task of us old men, us young old men, us old young men.

There is something strange, teasing and haunting about this whole last dream-sequence. It is, in some not very definable way, a new note, the voice of Svevo as a truly old man. It makes as good a last word as any for the writer who, at the age of thirty, wrote a novel called 'Senility'.

APPENDIX

The Tribe: a translation of *La tribù*

The tribe had found somewhere to settle. In the middle of the desert it had found a broad stretch of cultivable land, rich in water, green fields and trees; and unconsciously, without anyone actually proposing it, the tribe, instead of making one of its brief sojourns there, had taken root in this Paradise; it had become wedded to the soil, and thc thought of moving on again did not occur to it. Apparently it had reached that superior stage of evolution which makes nomad existence impossible, and it was now resting from the march of history. The tents gradually changed into houses; every member of the tribe became a property-owner.

Years went by. Ali, a born warrior, and restless in the new mode of life, saddled his horse and galloped all over what he insisted on calling 'the Camp', shouting 'I'm leaving. Follow me!'

'And who will bring our beloved land with us?' they asked him.

Only then did they all realise that they had become wedded for ever to that plot of earth; and Ali had to go alone.

2

Old Hussein had been called upon to settle a dispute which had arisen between the owners of two adjoining estates. It was a very complicated case. One of the two claimed that the other owed him part of his harvest, since, by mistake, he had ploughed and sowed part of the other's land. The mistake was the other's fault, since he hadn't marked the boundaries of his estate properly.

Hussein, having thought about the matter for a long time, said: 'I will consult the laws of the tribe.'

Next day, however, in the council of elders, he had to admit that the law said nothing about this case. It was the first time a farmer had asked for justice, for there had not been any farmers up to now.

The elders went into the market-place and summoned the whole tribe.

'We don't know the just answer in this case. If someone can tell it to us, let him speak freely.' There was no response. No one in the tribe could solve the difficult problem.

3

Then Hussein spoke:

'My brothers! Our tribe is rich in everything but laws. To come as near as I can, in this present instance, to the justice of which I am ignorant, I rule that the harvest which gave rise to this lawsuit should be divided in equal parts between the contestants. And in order that in the future our judges shall be able to avoid even the small injustice we have done today, let the tribe send one of its members to study how peoples who have lived for many years in a settled community arrange these things. They will certainly have laws to regulate the rights of those who labour and those who own.'

Everyone agreed. It was clear to them that the tribe had to create its own system of justice.

Hussein added these further generous words to the disputants: 'One of you two has been cheated of the exact justice which the tribe owed you. So be it. One day, perhaps, you and your lawsuit will be gratefully remembered by posterity.'

4

Achmed set out on his journey. The elders had elected him, by unanimous vote, to be the tribe's emissary. He was still a very young man, but an immensely active and wise one for his years. The prophets (there were still some prophets in the tribe) said he was destined to increase the prosperity and glory of his race; and the elders, out of respect for the prophets, did what they could to see the prophecy came true.

Achmed set out. Remembering the importance of the mission entrusted to him, as soon as he was alone on the road he repeated to himself the vow he had just made to the elders: 'My country, I will bring you justice!'

Having arrived in Europe, he studied for many years; so earnestly did he study, it was said of him: 'Achmed studies like a whole tribe.'

5

When, after this long absence, he returned to his native country, he noticed, even before he had dismounted and as he was still riding through the little city's streets, that things had changed a great deal in the tribe. He was not surprised by this. It was all too natural that it should have happened. Economic law did not lose its force even in the middle of the desert; and the neat little houses which had originally replaced the tents had disappeared, giving place to sumptuous mansions and squalid hovels. Half-naked men were to be seen in the streets, side by side with men in garments of rich material.

Achmed straightened himself in his saddle to peer into the distance. No! There were no factory-chimneys yet.

'I've come at the right time; I can introduce them myself,' thought Achmed.

The elders met to receive Achmed's report.

But the first assembly took the form of a lesson in practical justice given by Achmed to his fellow-countrymen. He had found his goods and property in others' hands. Perhaps they had sent him away, he suggested, so as to be able to rob him at their leisure?

The elders admitted the justice of his complaint and

decided to give Achmed as much gold as he would have been able to derive from the sale of his land.

This wasn't enough for Achmed, however.

'And what about all the time I have sacrificed for the good of the tribe? Had it not been for that, I should have increased my patrimony tenfold by now; I should be the owner of much more land, I should own not one house but several, if I had not been away when you were legalising private property. I demand that my compensation should be increased by the *interest on my interest*, according to a system which I will explain to you.'

The elders indicated their assent.

6

But the decrepit Hussein rose to his feet and gave a quite different opinion:

'We already know about your system—to our cost. You must know, Achmed, that the tribe is not what it was when you left it. I am afraid your journey may have been in vain, for by now we have more laws than we need. We couldn't wait for you to come back in order to compile them, and we attended to what we thought the most urgent needs, following what we considered self-evident truths. We thought the laws would lead us to happiness, and instead, the tribe of heroes which you left has become a conglomeration of miserable serfs and over-powerful lords. Oh happy Ali, who would not stay here to cultivate this treacherous soil! I tell you, I cannot sleep at night for remorse at advising the tribe to leave the nomad life. I decided I would only wait for your return to end this wretched state of things. If you can tell us of a people which, having abandoned the nomad existence, has been happier than ourselves, then I will see you get your *interest on your interest*. Otherwise you get nothing; and we—at least I hope so—will return to the nomad life.'

Achmed asked for a day to think about this. The affair was too important to decide on the spur of the moment. The interest on the interest of his capital ought to amount to a handsome sum.

7

He read the tribal laws and found there, in embryo, everything you can find in the most perfect modern states. Here and there, of course, he could see things he could improve or make more complete. He felt a strong temptation to show off his own learning by drafting new laws of a kind the tribe had never heard of, its economy still being too rudimentary for it to have needed them. But he wasn't a fool, and he didn't mean to make himself a laughing-stock.

Old Hussein instilled a great respect in him. Once the most heroic and magnanimous of the tribe, he was now the most clear-thinking and shrewd of them. The tribal laws, which were certainly his work, were simple and clear. Having been devised to settle disputes under the legislator's very eyes, they were logical and consistent. His acute and far-seeing mind had discerned the likenesses, and at the same time the differences, between different cases.

Thus, Achmed decided he had better not lie to save his own money. He must tell the truth; and the truth—or at least what he believed to be the truth—wouldn't please Hussein.

He passed a sleepless night, but towards morning an idea dawned on him: 'Perhaps after all,' he said to himself, 'I shall be able to save my money and build my factory with it.'

8

Next day, before the assembled elders, he began by declaring that the history of the tribe was merely the history of humanity itself. In the beginning, while it was still nomadic, the tribe constituted a single individual fighting for its existence; now, with the coming of progress, every member of the tribe had to fight on his own account. The stronger conquered and enslaved the weaker. And it was good that this should be so. Hussein showed himself unworthy of his position when he wept over the fate of the defeated. Every self-respecting citizen would find himself a victor in the struggle, and the whole race would become stronger and fitter to vie with other races in the economic war. 'The path you are on is the right one, and no other path is open to you,' he told the elders. 'Your laws are not perfect, and I would like to help you to complete them—but not to change them. Hussein would be wasting his time trying to lead you back to the nomad life; no one would follow him.'

9

'I bring you something else as well!' said the cunning Achmed. 'I bring you hope. There will be conflict in the tribe for centuries to come. We have seen only the beginning of the struggle; it will become fiercer and fiercer. One part of your fellow-men will be condemned, through no fault of their own, to pass half their day in unhealthy surroundings, to do work that endangers their health, their intelligence and their soul. They will become animals, despised and despicable. Not for them the songs of your poets and the brilliant debates of your philosophers. They will be denied all but the most puerile culture and will not even be allowed to dress and eat like men. The present unhappiness of your poor, who are condemned to labour on the soil, is felicity and riches compared with the fate in the store for their descendants. And only then will the tribe reach the zenith of its destiny. Only then—that is to say, after centuries—will a new era dawn. Man, inspired by the spectacle of so much misery, will conceive a new order of things. The disinherited, united by the very factories that have been their plague, will combine together and, full of hope once more, will watch and prepare for the new times coming. And when these times have come, there will be bread, happiness and work for everyone.'

'And can you tell us in detail what these new times will be like, and what sort of laws there will be?' asked Hussein anxiously.

10

'I have travelled very widely', replied Achmed, 'yet I have never found a country which has reached that high state of organisation. All I can tell you is this: in that far-off future the land will belong to the tribe, and all able-bodied men will have to labour on it. The fruits of their labour will belong to all alike. There will still be struggle, because where there is life there must be conflict, but it will not be a struggle for one's daily bread. That will be ours by right, as the air is today. The victor in the struggle will enjoy only the satisfaction of having served the tribe.'

'And we should have to wait all that time to attain such a state of happiness?' exclaimed Hussein in a voice of thunder. 'You have earned your interest on your interest', he added, turning to Achmed. 'Understand me—*our* tribe means to begin at the end.'

Achmed congratulated himself on his cleverness and took the money. He counted it, and decided it was enough to build the factory he had dreamed of—the factory he was going to build in the very midst of the tribe that had paid him in the belief they had escaped such things.

11

A European, sick of the unhappiness in his own country, knocked one day on Hussein's door and asked to be allowed to join the happy tribe.

'Impossible!' said Hussein. 'We have found by experience that our society won't do for Europeans.'

The European, nettled by this, replied: 'Wasn't it we who invented your laws for you?'

'You invented them, yes, but you don't understand them or know how to live by them. We even had to get rid of an Arab, a certain Achmed, who had the misfortune to be educated by you.'

Trieste, October 1897 — ITALO SVEVO

SELECT BIBLIOGRAPHY

WORKS

The most important posthumous editions of Svevo's writings are as follows:

Opere, ed. Bruno Maier (Milan, Dall'Oglio, 1954).

Corto viaggio sentimentale e altri racconti inediti, ed. Umbro Apollonio (Milan, Mondadori, 1949).

Saggi e pagine sparse, ed. Umbro Apollonio (Milan, Mondadori, 1954).

Commedie, ed. Umbro Apollonio (Milan, Mondadori, 1960).

Diario per la fidanzata, ed. Bruno Maier and Anita Pittoni (Trieste, Edizioni dello Zibaldone, 1962).

Corrispondenza con gli amici di Francia (Milan, 'All'insegna del pesce d'oro', 1953).

Lettere alla moglie, ed. Anita Pittoni (Trieste, Edizioni dello Zibaldone, 1963).

TRANSLATIONS

The following English translations in book form have appeared:

The Hoax, trans. with an Introduction by Beryl de Zoete (Hogarth Press, 1929; New York, Harcourt, Brace, 1930).

The Confessions of Zeno, trans. Beryl de Zoete (Putnam, 1930; New York, Knopf, 1930).

The Confessions of Zeno, trans. Beryl de Zoete, with an Essay on Svevo by Renato Poggioli (Putnam, 1948; New York, New Directions, 1950).

The Confessions of Zeno, trans. Beryl de Zoete, with a Note on Svevo by Edouard Roditi (Secker & Warburg, 1962; Penguin Books, 1964).

The Nice Old Man and the Pretty Girl and other Stories, trans. L. Collison-Morley (Hogarth Press, 1930).

As a Man Grows Older, trans. Beryl de Zoete, with an Introduction by Stanislaus Joyce (Putnam, 1932).

As a Man Grows Older, trans. Beryl de Zoete, with an Introduction by Stanislaus Joyce and an Essay on Svevo by E. Roditi (New York, New Directions, 1949).

As a Man Grows Older, trans. Beryl de Zoete (Secker & Warburg, 1962; Penguin Books, 1965).

A Life, trans. Archibald Colquhoun (Secker & Warburg, 1963).

James Joyce, trans. Stanislaus Joyce (Milan, Officine grafiche 'Esperia', 1950).

Short Sentimental Journey and other Stories, various translators, is due from Secker & Warburg in 1966; a further volume of stories and a play is in preparation.

Translations of his major works have also appeared in many other European languages, including French, German, Spanish, Portuguese, Serbo-Croat, Polish and Danish.

BIOGRAPHY

The Life of Svevo by his widow (Livia Veneziani Svevo, *Vita di mio marito*), written in collaboration with Lina Galli, was first published in 1950 (Trieste, Edizioni dello Zibaldone), and a second edition, with important additions, appeared in 1958, edited by Anita Pittoni.

CRITICISM

I have found the following articles and collections of particular value from the critical point of view:

'Omaggio a Italo Svevo' in *Il Convegno*, Milan, 1929, no. 1–2 (contains articles by G. Debenedetti, C. Linati, G. Stuparich and A. Rossi).

'Omaggio a Italo Svevo' in *Solaria*, Florence, 1929, no. 3–4 (contains articles and tributes by G. B. Angioletti, J. Boulanger, M. Brion, J. Chabas, A. Consiglio, B. Crémieux, G. Debenedetti, Ilya Ehrenburg, G. Ferrata, L. Ferrero, R. Franchi, P. Gadda, Ivan Goll, F. Hellens, James Joyce, Valéry Larbaud, C. V. Lodovici, Paul-Henri Michel, Adrienne Monnier, Eugenio Montale, A. Palazzeschi, G. Raimondi, A. Rossi, Umberto Saba, E. Schwenk, Sergio Solmi, Philippe Soupault, G. Stuparich, B. Tecchi, André Thérive, A. van Schendel).

Silvio Benco, Preface to the fourth edition of *La coscienza di Zeno* (Milan, Dall'Oglio, 1947).

G. Debenedetti, *Saggi critici*, new series, 2nd ed. (Milan, Mondadori, 1955), pp. 49–116.

G. Devoto, 'Decenni per Svevo' in *Studi di stilistica* (Florence, Le Monnier, 1950).

Eugenio Montale, 'Omaggio a Italo Svevo' in *L'Esame*, Milan, November-December 1925.

Eugenio Montale, 'Presentazione di Italo Svevo' in *Il Quindicinale*, Milan, 30 January 1926.

Eugenio Montale, Introduction to *The Nice Old Man and the Pretty Girl and other Stories*, trans. L. Collison-Morley (Hogarth Press, 1930).

Renato Poggioli, 'An Essay on Svevo', prefixed to the 1948 edition of *The Confessions of Zeno*.

Alain Robbe-Grillet, *Pour un nouveau roman* (Gallimard, 1963), pp. 97–102.

Edouard Roditi, 'A Note on Svevo', prefixed to the standard edition of *The Confessions of Zeno*.

'A Man Grows Older', front-page article in *Times Literary Supplement*, 30 March 1962.

Elio Vittorini, review of *Una vita* in *Solaria*, Florence, December 1930.

Elio Vittorini, *Diario in pubblico* (Milan, Bompiani, 1957), *passim.*

There is an extensive bibliography of reviews and articles on Svevo in Bruno Maier's collected edition of the works (1954).

INDEX